YOUR DOG NEEDS YOU, AND THAT'S WHAT THIS BOOK IS ALL ABOUT!

From puppyhood to old age, your dog depends on you for everything from food, water, affection and understanding to vital health and hygiene care. *The Good Dog Book* is much more than a simple how-to guide, for it includes information important to your dog's well-being not found in ordinary pet books.

Aside from providing hard-core instruction on canine health, nutrition, and hygiene, this wise and knowledgable book includes unique sections on the relationship between dogs and children and dogs and other dogs . . . dog disasters . . . dog neurosis . . . reducing the fat dog . . . dealing with dognappers . . . Canine Meditation (CM) . . . and more.

If you have not yet acquired a dog, this indispensable guide can be a big help. If you have been living with your tailwagger for a while, it will help you even more. Remember, beside every good dog stands a good human being trying hard—sometimes making mistakes—but always caring, always loving.

The Good Dog Book

Other SIGNET Books to Help You Care for Your Pet

☐ **GOOD DOG, BAD DOG by Mordecai Siegal and Matthew Margolis.** The famous, successful Basic Obedience Course for training your dog at home, without punishment and with love—plus individual training problems of 66 dog breeds. Generously illustrated. (#J7333—$1.95)

☐ **THE DOG YOU CARE FOR: A Manual of Dog Care by Felicia Ames.** An indispensable aid to the dog owner, complete with training manual, first-aid and feeding charts, an individual health record, information about travel and quarantine laws—and much more. Sixty color photographs by Walter Chandoha. (#E7860—$1.75)

☐ **THE CAT YOU CARE FOR: A Manual of Cat Care by Felicia Ames.** A wealth of sound information to help you deal with your pet's every need. Find the answers to all your questions about care and feeding, breeding, health and medication, training, traveling, and old age. Sixty color photographs by Walter Chandoha. (#E7862—$1.75)

☐ **PARTICULARLY CATS by Doris Lessing.** Doris Lessing, whom the **London Times** called ''the best woman novelist we have'', explores all the complexities and mysteries of a cat's character. (#Q4842—95¢)

☐ **THE BIRD YOU CARE FOR: A Manual of Bird Care by Felicia Ames.** No bird lover should be without this manual which teaches you all the facts you need to know in selecting, feeding, training and caring for your new pet in the best possible way. With 32 pages of stunning color photographs. (#E7527—$1.75)

If you wish to order these titles, please see the coupon in the back of this book.

The Good Dog Book
Loving Care

by

Mordecai Siegal

Consulting Veterinarian:
Michael Lincoln Katz, D.V.M.

A SIGNET BOOK
NEW AMERICAN LIBRARY
TIMES MIRROR

Library of Congress Catalog Card Number: 77-2954

SIGNET TRADEMARK REG. U.S. PAT. OFF. AND FOREIGN COUNTRIES
REGISTERED TRADEMARK—MARCA REGISTRADA
HECHO EN CHICAGO, U.S.A.

SIGNET, SIGNET CLASSICS, MENTOR, PLUME AND MERIDIAN BOOKS
are published by The New American Library, Inc.,
1301 Avenue of the Americas, New York, New York 10019

FIRST SIGNET PRINTING, NOVEMBER, 1978

1 2 3 4 5 6 7 8 9

PRINTED IN THE UNITED STATES OF AMERICA

For Vicki,
without whom
neither this book nor this author
would be possible.

Contents

Acknowledgments

The author would like to express his gratitude and admiration for the meticulous and scholarly attention paid to the text by the consulting veterinarian, Michael Lincoln Katz, D.V.M., Ph.D. Dr. Katz practices veterinary medicine at the Hampshire Veterinary Hospital in Amherst, Massachusetts. He has taught physiology at Cornell University and at the University of Massachusetts, and he is currently a research associate in the department of biochemistry, University of Massachusetts at Amherst. Dr. Katz's primary research interest is olfactory-neurochemical interrelationships. Without his articulate guidance, this book would have fallen far short of its intended goals.

A special note of gratitude to Dr. Jim Corbin, professor of Animal Science, University of Illinois at Urbana-Champaign, for providing much of the nutrition information; Robert W. Mellentin, manager, Technical Services, Gaines Professional Marketing Department; Walter Chimel, director, Gaines Dog Research Center; Mark L. Morris, Jr., D.V.M., Ph.D.; Dr. Fitzhugh J. Dodson; Dr. Lee Salk; Sam Kohl, director, New York School of Dog Grooming; Howard Finklestein of the Montville Kennels, New Jersey; Elizabeth Feldman and her "Misty"; Robin, Megan, Rebecca, and Jessica Finklestein; Janet Bookbinder and her "May Ling"; Mark W. Allam, V.M.D., Assistant Vice-President for Health Affairs, University of Pennsylvania; Stephen R. Kellert, Ph.D., researcher, Yale University School of Medicine; Patricia O'Keefe of the Pet Food Institute; Frances Sheridan Goulart; Dale Tarr, D.V.M. and his daughter, Alicia; Paul Wessberg; Stephanie Fausett; Tom Martin; Captain Arthur Haggerty; Roger Caras; Henry Bernacki; Robert Michell; The National Dog Registry, Carmel, New York; Ident-A-Pet, Melville, New York; Hy Shore, Esq.; Marcia Higgins of the William Morris Agency; and Leslie Lone.

1. Dog Chauvinism

Did you ever wonder what a dog does on his day
off? He can't just lie around the house because
that's his job.*

—GEORGE CARLIN

Getting a Dog

Life begins in plexiglas incubators and ends in glossy-black pro-
cessions on superhighways. In between is Big Bird, the corner gui-
tar store, computerized checkout counters, dirty snow, and Quar-
terpounders with cheese. *Little we see in nature is ours*—except a
four-legged woof with wet nose and adoring eyes. The canine connection reminds us what we are and what's left of the real world,
or what's a dog for.

Dogs are like mushrooms. One dewy morning you look down
and there they are. It is an optimistic notion to believe that dogs
are selected by their masters. All too often it is a conspiracy of circumstances that brings dog and family together. The stray at your
door. The pet-shop window. The neighbor's new litter. The one
that followed you home. Christmas. The story on the nightly news
about the shelter closing down. Injured on the highway. Aban-
doned near your summer rental. Or pressured into it by your kids,
wife, husband, roommate, parents, guru, analyst, scream thera-
pist, consciousness-raising group, cardiologist. Save your mar-
riage, take a dog to lunch.

We succumb to these pressures in response to our best instincts.
The helplessness and dependency of a dog appeals to our generos-
ity, sensitivity, and parental feelings as well as our desire to love
and be loved in return.

For many, having a pet is a great hobby full of activity and pleasurable, personal demand. Some dogs are used for personal protection. Some become emotional crutches substituting for children, parents, spouses, or what-have-you. The most common rea-

*Used by permission of Dead Sea Music, Inc.

son for owning a dog is companionship. Dogs do all that. They are the unsung heroes of modern society and deserve only the best. Whatever your reasons, the selection of a pet must be made with intelligence and logic.

Getting a dog is like having a baby. It is not a simple, casual matter. One must prepare. There will be drastic changes in your life once a dog enters the picture, and there are many factors that can help determine what kind of dog to get and where to get him.

If you are going to live with a dog you must be willing to do all that is necessary for the animal's well-being. He will need a place of his own to sleep. He is going to cost money to feed. His medical needs can be expensive. You might have to have him obedience-trained by a professional trainer in order to save your furniture and his future. You cannot leave town without arranging for his care. He must be housebroken. He must be exercised. He needs personal contact and affection every day. He needs grooming. He'll need collars, leashes, bowls, ID tags, licenses, grooming tools, books on training and care, toys, vitamins, and more. Owning a dog is demanding, costly, somewhat of a drain on your personal inner resources, and should not be entered into without a full understanding. What you get in return, of course, is the knowledge that you are alive.

How to Live With and Take Care of Your Dog

Hidden deep in the recesses of our dog owners' hearts is the cast-iron belief that our pet dogs are a combination of Snoopy, Pluto, and Rin Tin Tin. Looking at life through dog-colored glasses is the inevitable behavior of the Lassie School of Dog Ownership. We want to believe that life with our dogs will fall somewhere between *Bonzo Goes to College* and *Old Yeller*. The majestic stance of Lassie with her lanolin luster of rust and white fur, her intelligent glance, sensitive face, and heroic deeds tempered with fun-loving dog antics creates within all of us a misty-eyed conviction that our own dear Queenies and Muffins look and behave the same. And there's nothing wrong with that, either. It is the most harmless form of daydreaming, providing that the realities of owning a dog do not upset us to such a degree that we finally kick him out or shrink from him in utter disappointment. Bear in mind that Lassie is really six dogs. Pluto is an animated cartoon, and Snoopy is a comic-strip character (a supporting player at that). When you own a dog it is not really necessary to fantasize an ideal fiction about physical beauty, home-on-the-range heroics, or sheepdogs eating your daisies. There is hardly a dog alive that doesn't have a stout heart hidden behind a cowardly lion's costume. And funny. They are all clowns when they want to be. Don't we tell our children that beauty is an inner quality possessed by all, and why shouldn't that apply to every tail-wagger that brightens the room long after he's trotted to his corner for a snooze? This is not fantasy; it's real, but its realization demands a human being willing to set the stage for a great decade-and-a-half of friendship, love, and effort.

Your dog needs you, and that's what this book is all about. It is designed to help dog owners recognize and live with those aspects of dog life that cannot be altered but, rather, demand that humans adapt themselves to the realities of their dogs as dictated by nature. You cannot really change your dog without scaring the hell out of him and distorting his true and brilliant self. Even Lassie requires a rectal thermometer reading once in a while, and the people at the movie studios had better know how to do it. One must become acquainted with hard-core information about physical realities such as illness, hygiene, and proper exercise. Dogs have different nutritional requirements than people. Their emotional needs cannot be ignored without sacrificing a precious part of your relationship with them. Even dogs' hearts pump at a different rhythm and pattern than ours. Dogs are not exotic, but they are unique and demand knowledge from their owners if they are to share domestic tranquillity.

The Good Dog Book is a reference for people who love their dogs and want to know how to take care of them and meet the unforeseen armed with information and alternatives. It is not about obedience training or the alteration of canine behavior. These pages are concerned with people and their desire to live with dogs and how to do that successfully. By providing the latest information about dog care we are, to be sure, serving the dog. But it is human beings who are the most benefited through this enrichment of their dog knowledge.

Here is a typical situation. There was once a gourmet hobbyist who loved cooking in the grand manner. He was a young man, married, and living just outside of Chicago in a smart suburb. Our amateur chef and his wife were the adoring dog parents of an eleven-month-old beagle whom they named Pork Chop. Like many novice dog owners, they really didn't know much about dogs and even less about their own breed. They loved their dog and did their best for him.

One Saturday afternoon, the young wife left the house leaving

$275 in cash with her husband to pay for a C.O.D. delivery of custom-made living room draperies. The draperies were to be hung later that day to improve the appearance of the house for a dinner party that night. They were going to entertain the husband's employer and a prospective client who had a great deal of business to give to their firm. To suit the occasion, the ambitious cook was in the midst of creating a Beef Wellington, quite a difficult assignment for any chef. The pâté, the rolled fillet, and the unbaked crust were being spread out when he was handed the large amount of cash. He set it down, kissed his wife good-bye, and continued with his delicate preparations, failing to notice the look of ecstatic yearning on Pork Chop's face as he sat on the kitchen floor, gazing up.

With the cooking ingredients on his hands, the young man carried the cash from the kitchen to the living room where there were floor-to-ceiling bookshelves. He pulled out Volume One of his prized 1911 edition of the *Encyclopaedia Britannica* and stuffed the money somewhere near Aardvark. He returned to the kitchen and his beautiful epicurean delight.

Like Rodin shaping *The Thinker*, he rolled his Beef Wellington, tied it, and spread out the puff pastry. As he was turning on the oven, the doorbell rang. It was the United Parcel Service man expecting $275 in exchange for the new draperies. Like an Alfred Hitchcock victim, he merrily bounded into the living room to retrieve the money. To his horror, he found Volume One of his Britannica chewed to pulpy shreds. The section on Aardvarks was gone and there were only little green corner points where once there had been American currency. At first he giggled and then he almost fainted. Needless to say, the UPS delivery man was unsympathetic and refused to accept a check. The draperies were not delivered. With a cloudy dizziness in his head, our hero returned to his kitchen for an aspirin and a glass of milk only to discover the angelic Pork Chop atop the cutting board digging into the Beef Wellington. The dog was somewhat upset that the awful puff pastry hampered a clear bite at the rolled fillet.

The young gourmet never realized that his dog was a *scent hound.* When he handled the money, he imprinted the odor of beef and liver pâté on it. The money became a hunting challenge for Pork Chop. Because of his incredible olfactory mechanism (sense of smell) the dog easily located the delicious-smelling money and tried to eat the paper as if it were the roast itself. Not finding the money (or the encyclopedia) very filling, he returned to the kitchen to discover his prey off guard and out of its cave or hole or tunnel. Every instinct that the beagle was bred for came into play. He did what nature and selective breeders intended him to do. For centuries beagles have been bred for their ability to find small game, such as rabbits, and to trap and kill them. In addition, the inheritance of all wild canids (dogs and wolves) is to hunt for food in order to survive. Had the dog's instincts been better understood, the draperies would have hung that night and all the guests would have congratulated Pork Chop's master for a brilliant dinner. Being civilized human beings, the young couple decided to find out more about this strange creature that they were living with. Later that evening (sans Beef Wellington) they took Pork Chop out for his toileting walk, hoping that the mighty beagle would make a gesture toward restitution of the money. It never worked out. His assets were void of cash flow.

What *The Good Dog Book* hopes to accomplish is to guide, instruct, and provoke dog owners into a new perspective of dog care: one that promotes an enjoyable relationship between humans and their dogs based on understanding the dog's nature and his needs as a domestic pet. Living with a dog requires loving care. A good dog is one that has been a pal to someone who in return took the time and trouble to do the right things about canine health, nutrition, hygiene, and friendship. Behind every good dog stands a good human being trying hard—making mistakes, to be sure, but always caring, always loving.

How to Select a Dog

Now comes the commercial. You will not be instructed about which breeds are best for apartments, estates, houseboats, mobile homes, or camping tents. There are complete breed books that cover the subject in great detail. Whether you should own a pedigreed aristocrat or a crossbred proletarian is a matter of personal preference and inner statement. You will learn about selecting a well-adjusted puppy, one that has been socialized. The matter of health as it applies to selecting puppies will also be dealt with along with the eternal question of living with a male or female.

All this is offered despite the fact that many of you have already been followed home and emotionally leashed. Books of this genre are often purchased weeks after a puppy has licked your face and the inked roller has zipped across your Mastercharge. In the chapter titled "Puppy Days," a great deal has been written about preparing for a puppy's arrival and the details of the first minutes up to the first year in your home. Preownership information is offered as a way of touching base with those who have not yet been urinated on by their very own sweet puppy. However, you will not be told that a Great Dane is better than a Chihuahua or which is the smartest kennel to shop at. No one really knows the answers to those questions anyway. If you have not yet acquired a dog, *The Good Dog Book* can help you. If you have been living with your dog for a while, *The Good Dog Book* can help you even more.

THE SOCIALIZED DOG

Assuming the puppy you are interested in is older than six weeks, and that he is weaned from breast milk to solid food, there are physical and mental qualities to look for. There are also a few simple tests to make that will help assure that the dog does not have physical or emotional faults.

If you are buying from a kennel ask the operator if the dog has been socialized. Most serious breeders and kennel operators are familiar with this procedure and practice it. The only way to be certain, however, is to remove the dog from the run and see how he responds to you and other humans. A puppy that has been socialized at an early age will have little fear of you (providing you do not make sudden movements or loud noises). It is also helpful to see the dog with its litter mates, if possible. Watch for reticent behavior, timidity, anxiety, shyness, and a general lack of assertion or confidence. These are all negative qualities that do not promise a mentally healthy puppy that will adapt well to human conditions as an adult dog. Physical beauty, even if it approaches perfection, splendid conformation, and good gait are not nearly so important to a pet owner as having a dog with a good temperament, a healthy emotional system, and a keen intelligence. This is the proper order of priorities unless you are planning to show your dog in the ring. This is important to remember if you are purchasing a pet and not a potential American Kennel Club Champion. You are going to live with this animal for approximately fifteen years, and he'd better be a creature that will be as pleasurable to you as you are to him.

COMMERCIAL SOURCES

If the puppy is coming from a pet shop, purchase one that is between weaning and nine weeks of age, and you can then socialize the dog yourself. You can socialize a dog by holding him gently, quietly, and affectionately for several minutes, three times a day. (You may even conduct a five-minute obedience training session for this purpose.) It is extremely important during this critical period of the dog's life. If this is done properly, the dog's ability to adapt to humans, and consequently to human commands and desires, is enhanced greatly. Do not buy a puppy from a pet shop unless you have been assured that the dog has been socialized or unless the dog is no older than nine weeks. Socializing a puppy is realized to its fullest when the process is begun by the original breeder after the third week of life. The socializing process should continue until the twelfth week by the breeder, the pet shop operator, or the new dog owner. Puppies adapt better to other dogs throughout their lives if they have been allowed to stay with their litters up until eight weeks. These are the optimum circumstances for developing a dog's maximum potential as a pet. Even though these conditions are by necessity compromised when you acquire a dog from a pet shop, you may still be able to develop a fine dog by beginning or continuing the socializing procedure anytime before the ninth week.

A HEALTHY DOG

It is difficult to select a perfectly healthy puppy from a large litter or pet-shop window. There are things that may be wrong that can be detected only by a veterinarian. For this reason you must attempt to procure some form of guarantee from the seller in regard to the puppy's health. It is equally important to have the new puppy examined immediately.

Despite the difficulties in determining a healthy puppy, there are still some guidelines that will help you select a healthy dog. Basically, a litter in which *all* the dogs are in good health is the only acceptable situation. If there is one puppy, either in the pet shop or in a breeder's kennel, that is obviously in bad health do not pick any dog from that group. Look for a dog with clear, clean, and alert eyes. Be watchful for unnatural markings or inconsistent coloring in the corneas. A puppy with a distended belly may have some form of worms or suffer other ailments. A healthy puppy is neither oversized nor undersized in relation to the rest of the litter. A fat puppy, a thin puppy, or an oversized one may be unhealthy. Check the dog's ears for signs of mites or infection, especially if the puppy rubs them with his paws. The puppy's eyes and nose must be clean and not runny or watery.

A mentally and physically healthy puppy is unafraid of humans, somewhat assertive, frisky, playful, and curious about you and new sights and sounds. Shake your keychain gently or drop it in the cage. See which puppies will cower and which will try to nip it, which will run away, which will lick it. Avoid problems later by rejecting the overly shy dog, the one that wins your heart by hiding in the corner looking at you with a pathetic expression. A shy or nervous puppy can develop serious behavior problems as an adult, such as biting, bullying, hiding, or running away.

Clean, smooth, unspotted skin indicates absence of infection or fungus. A glossy coat with no patches of fur missing is essential. Missing patches indicate some disorder such as ringworm or mange. Do not take home a puppy that already suffers from diarrhea or bloody stools.

Some puppies are born deaf and do not indicate it unless tested. Slap your hands together behind the puppy's ears and watch for a natural response. If you have any doubt, speak to the seller and agree to return the dog if the veterinarian determines deafness. Do not be afraid to ask these sorts of questions and do not be inhibited about speaking your mind.

Check the puppy's teeth. From four weeks to five months he will have his milk teeth—there are thirty-two of them. Some time after five months, his milk teeth fall out and are replaced with larger, stronger, permanent ones. There are forty-two permanent teeth. A puppy's teeth should be stain-free and set well with no obvious imperfections. They should be white (they yellow with age) and the unspotted portion of the gums a healthy pink, the same as in a child's mouth.

Before taking your puppy home, ask for a written statement of inoculations received with dates and amounts and types. Find out if and when the puppy has been wormed and have included in the written statement that the puppy can be returned if, after a veterinarian's examination, he is not healthy.

MALE OR FEMALE?

When the right dog comes along, it usually doesn't matter whether it's male or female. When looking for a pet one must be open to emotional contact, and that bypasses the questions of gender. But it is true that there are pluses and minuses for males and females, and they should be considered.

Female dogs go through a physical and hormonal change twice a year in order to mate. This is called *estrus*, or *going into heat*. Each period of estrus lasts approximately three weeks. Some people consider it a nuisance while others do not mind. This time requires patience from the dog owner and tender loving care. The female dog in heat must be sequestered from all male dogs unless puppies are desired. Male dogs are more assertive, harder to train, more likely to wander away. Males are larger than females and need more nourishment and exercise. They can be harder to control.

In his book *Man Meets Dog*, Konrad Lorenz says, "A bitch is more faithful than a [male] dog, the intricacies of her mind are finer, richer and more complex than his, her intelligence is generally greater. Strange that in English her name has become a term of abuse." In the wild state, nature has assigned various tasks and functions to each gender of each species. The domestic dog carries these biological and behavioral functions into the human situation, and the pet owner chooses which set of characteristics are the most desirable.

Where To Buy a Dog

ADOPTION AGENCIES

There are several reasons for listing animal adoption agencies (or animal shelters) as the first stop to make when looking for a dog. One is economy. There is probably no better bargain than the cost of a dog or cat at an agency. The price is usually a voluntary contribution plus a neutering fee or some variation of the two. The average cost is $25. If one is lucky and/or persistent, just about any breed, gender, age, size, or color can be obtained. Of course, mongrels and crossbreeds are more readily available, and they are a good bet when looking for a family pet. Maybe the most significant aspect of obtaining a pet from an agency is the fact that in addition to securing a pet you are also saving an animal's life. With few exceptions, most agencies kill those dogs and cats that are not adopted within a limited period of time. Some are turned over to medical research facilities as experimental subjects.

There are virtually hundreds of fine animal welfare organizations to turn to when you are ready to adopt. They are easily found in the Yellow Pages under "Animal Shelters." In Chicago one can turn to the Illinois Citizens Animal Welfare League or the Anti-Cruelty Society. One of the great shelter systems is the Bide-A-Wee Home Association in New York (which does not euthanize a healthy animal under any circumstances). New York City's

ASPCA is also a fine source of pet dogs and cats as is the Los Angeles SPCA and the San Francisco SPCA. Also recommended is San Francisco's Pets Unlimited. Every area in the country has its own adoption agency and can render inexpensive service to those in need of a pet.

BREEDERS

Purchase a copy of *Dog World Magazine, Pure-bred Dogs—American Kennel Gazette, Dogs Magazine,* or *Dog Fancy* and consult the many advertisements for breeders. For those interested in the best dogs, and if price is not a problem, the noncommercial breeder is the ideal source for obtaining a dog. This is especially true if you are searching for show-dog material.

A commercial breeder is one that supplies a mass quantity of puppies to the pet shop and department store trade. Profit is the only motivation. The noncommercial or hobby breeder, on the other hand, strives for breed perfection with the help of scientifically proven methods and derives pleasure and satisfaction from the activity of dog breeding and showing. At these kennels unsound dogs are never allowed to be mated so that genetic faults will not be repeated. With few exceptions, noncommercial breeders are highly knowledgeable, completely ethical, and very selective about to whom they will sell one of their puppies.

PET SHOPS

Probably more puppies are purchased through pet shops than all other sources combined. The pet shop is the final destination for the millions of puppies that are mass produced from the so-called puppy mills. The quality of the dogs and the knowledge of the retailers is spotty and inconsistent. One cannot deny that many fine dogs are purchased at pet shops. But when you consider that the mass breeder does not cull dogs with recessive genes which lead to physical and mental faults, sends the puppies by air in flimsy lettuce crates stacked in icy cold or intensely hot baggage holds, and does not bother to socialize them, good health and mental stability of puppies from this source cannot be expected as a matter of course. Add to this the caging together of dozens of strange puppies from different litters in a pet shop window display—all it takes is one animal getting sick and most of the rest do, too. This is not to say that many pet shops are not clean and conscientiously operated. It simply means that the odds of getting a healthy, adaptable dog of good conformation are not great.

If you already own a dog, it is no longer of any consequence where or how you acquired him. All that is important now is how you take care of him and that you both enjoy the coming decade together. Assuming the dog is still quite young, the next chapter will be useful even if the little dog has begun to take over your home. Puppyhood is a trying, difficult period, but it is also a treasured time to be experienced and enjoyed only once with your new friend. The fun things and the nasty things in time blend into one solid remembrance to be savored once in a while like dried flowers in an old alabaster bowl. Puppyhood is tomorrow's memories.

2. Puppy Days

The Night Before

You might as well get a box of cigars. Pass them around to all your friends and neighbors as your buttons burst off your shirt. Coming home with a new puppy is almost identical to returning home from the hospital with a pink-faced baby. The difference is that you are mother, father, and doting grandparents wrapped into one large survival source for the new arrival. You can think of yourself as a humanoid vending machine to which the puppy will come, press the right button, and receive food, water, affection, or new paper shredding for its box. And this is the correct situation for all concerned.

Dogs, like wolves, are members of the family *Canidae*. These two species have many behavior traits in common, the most striking being that they adhere to a social structure of dominance and subordination. This is the single most significant fact for every dog owner. With this knowledge, it is possible to create a dog/human home environment that is ideally satisfying to everyone concerned.

For the sake of social integrity, a young wolf will instinctively try to be the leader of his pack until a larger, more dominant member of the pack takes charge. Sometimes it is settled without conflict; sometimes a fight or other form of challenge determines who is the leader of the pack. This same principle is at work when you bring home a puppy. He will eventually attempt to run the household unless you—the human—clearly establish yourself as the leader. Once you assume the position of leadership, the young dog accepts it for the rest of his life. This has many ramifications regarding obedience training and ordinary commands.

Regarding the coming puppy as an infant and assuming full responsibility for his physical and emotional well-being should begin as an attitude before the little dog arrives in your home. This will clearly establish you as the leader of his pack and make life very pleasant in times to come.

Many decisions must be made before the puppy actually comes to live with you. Among them is whether or not the dog will live with you inside the house or outdoors in a doghouse or some such arrangement. In either case, a very young puppy cannot be left alone outdoors in cold weather. It is not a good idea even in warm weather. However, if the dog is more than three months old, he can spend his nights in a doghouse or garage. Whichever it is to be, indoors or outdoors, it is best to start from the first day of the puppy's arrival. Consistency is very important to a dog. His place to sleep or rest must remain the same and represent a sanctuary—a refuge—a place to get away from everyone in the house or apartment.

THE OUTDOOR DOG

Without benefit of his mother's warmth, your puppy must not be left in the cold until he is three or four months old. The most damaging inconsistency for a dog is to be kept indoors all day and outdoors all night. This tends to weaken his resistance to cold and hot weather and thus leads to illness.

There are several options for the outdoor dog. The most obvious one is a doghouse. Designs for doghouses are available in many of the handyman-type magazines, from the public relations offices of various dog-food manufacturers; the American Humane Association in Denver, Colorado; and from your public library. Check the various mail-order catalogs and local lumber yards for prefabricated doghouses.

A doghouse should be constructed tightly so that it affords protection from the wind, the rain, severe cold temperatures, and minor drafts. If the structure is double-insulated and on the small side, the dog's own body heat will keep things warm and cozy. It is useful to understand that a doghouse is for sleeping and resting only. It is not meant to be a play area or a dining room. Do not build too large.

According to the American Humane Association pamphlet, "The Care of the Outdoor Dog"*:

> Weatherproof plywood, at least one-half inch thick, is probably the best building material to use (ordinary plywood does not weather well).
> Wooden surfaces should be covered with an exterior varnish or paint *without lead*. Also, because dogs love to chew, wooden seams and edges should be covered with metal, such as steel or aluminum.

*"The Care of the Outdoor Dog." Copyright 1974. Published by The American Humane Society, Denver, Colo. Used by permission.

The color of your dog's house is also an important consideration. Results of a study made by the Ralston Purina Co. at the Purina Dog Care Center showed that a doghouse painted white was 6 to 8 degrees cooler than a black doghouse when the outside temperature was 25 to 30 degrees Fahrenheit. The white doghouse was 15 to 20 degrees cooler when the outside temperature was approximately 90 degrees. Let your dog's comfort, rather than your preferences, guide you in the choice of paint color.

A tight wooden structure makes the best doghouse. When selecting or building a doghouse, be certain that it is elevated several inches off the ground to avoid dampness, insects, and certain types of parasites. The dog will stay warm if the doorway is covered with a small canvas sheet. The sides of the canvas should overlap the doorway edges by at least one inch, and the material must be thick and weatherproof. An A-frame roof is far superior to a flat roof for drainage and temperature consistency. The roof or one side of the house should be hinged or removable so that the house can be thoroughly cleaned frequently. The inside of the house can be covered with linoleum or floor tile with a blanket or mattress on top. Hay or straw makes good dog bedding, too. Indoor-outdoor carpeting is even better. It is important to seal all seams and cracks to avoid drafts. A cold draft is far worse than complete exposure in many instances. Locate the house in a shady area for the summer and move it to a sunny area in the winter. Moving the house also helps prevent parasites. Keep the doorway toward the south, away from northerly winds.

An outdoor dog must be restrained for his own safety. The ideal situation is a chain-link fence that forms a kennel run. A fenced yard will do, and if that is not possible, run a metal cable several yards above the ground from house to tree or tree to tree. Put a ring on the wire which slides back and forth. Then use a chain or wire leash approximately five feet longer than the height of the wire run and attach one end to the ring and the other to the dog's collar. Do not use a choke collar or any training collar for this purpose. Do not use a metal collar. If this arrangement is not possible, secure the dog to the doghouse or other stationary object with a twelve-foot chain with swivel snaps at both ends to avoid tangles. Keep the doghouse away from trees and utility poles to avoid that one-in-a-million chance of a lightning strike.

A dog that lives in a garage or a toolshed is also considered an outdoor dog, and the same considerations apply. He needs a soft bed to sleep on. He must be protected from drafts, dampness, wind, pests, and the consequences of unsanitary conditions. Dogs and puppies are the most adaptive creatures on earth but will become ill during sudden changes of temperature or weather extremes. If the weather changes and the temperature drops drastically, move your dog indoors. The same applies for a blistering heat spell. Keep the dog cool.

The outdoor dog is more vulnerable to dognapping, poisoning, unwanted breeding, dog fights, spoiled food, digging holes, chewing foreign objects, barking at cars and strangers. These things must be dealt with either through the services of a professional dog trainer or with the help of a good obedience-training book. An outdoor dog will also protect you and guard your property and family.

The Indoor Dog

Once a dog has been exposed to human contact during the earliest phase of puppyhood, his desire to become part of the human family is great. Living the life of an indoor dog makes him happier and more responsive to human beings. An indoor dog can be a true companion and friend and make good company for everyone.

The indoor dog also needs the equivalent of a doghouse—a home-within-his-home. Ideally, an indoor doghouse would satisfy this need, but more practically a place to call his own will satisfy any dog. Within every house or apartment is a spot where two walls meet that will represent a lair or a den to a domestic dog. In the wild, your dog would look for protection in a cave, a hollow, or some other shelter so that he could see all movement with no danger to his rear; have a means of escape; be able to sleep or rest without disturbance; feel safe from the elements. The place you make for the dog can easily fulfill these needs.

A puppy's bed should be placed in a darkened, quiet, draft-free location. A large, high-sided crate is good with cedar chips or newspaper shreds for softness, warmth, and sanitation. Cut down one side so that the pup can climb in and out. An old soft blanket or pillow makes a fine addition. It is important to locate the puppy's nest in the same area he will sleep in when he becomes older. Let the dog claim this area for his own territory. Always respect it as such. This should be the one place where no child or adult can intrude, punish, play, or dispossess the dog in any way or for any reason except for cleaning.

During the early phase of puppyhood, a child's playpen will serve handsomely as a combination bed and restraining area for housebreaking and night wandering. Do not locate the dog's bed near a heat pipe or radiator. In recent years it has been learned that humans are more susceptible to colds and winter-related illness due to extreme dryness in the air caused by too much heat. Doctors recommend humidifiers for humans to counteract the effects of overheated quarters, and the same applies to dogs and puppies, providing the spray from a cold-water humidifier is kept at a distance, avoiding direct contact with the animal.

Another aspect of selecting a bedding area for the puppy has to do with sound stress. No one has proven conclusively that a high noise level is injurious to animals. However, the U.S. Department of Agriculture made a sound stress study several years ago on dairy cattle, horses, and swine that were located near air bases. They were also exposed to laboratory-produced sound levels. All the animals at first were frightened. Initially the cattle lowered their milk production but shortly returned to normal. Psychological studies on the effects of sound by members of the American Association for the Advancement of Science indicated that noise produces changes in the nervous, endocrine, and reproductive systems, and may have a relationship to disease.

The effect of noise appears to be most disastrous to fetuses. Loud sound constricts blood vessels. Decreased blood flow in the uterus and placenta might disrupt the exchange of oxygen, carbon dioxide, and nutrients between maternal and fetal tissues. Scientists have theorized, therefore, that noise stress can cause permanent abnormalities before birth. If this is true, we can infer that psychological harm can be done to puppies and older dogs from undue amounts of noise pollution. It is advisable to keep the puppy in a noise-free environment, especially its bedding area.

One last but important comment about the puppy's bed location: it is all but useless unless the area chosen has the added feature of being able to restrict the little dog's movements *when you so choose*. You must be able to confine the dog when you are going to bed or leaving the house. A puppy can get himself into a great deal of trouble and can make your life miserable if given the run of the house unattended. Can you live with scattered and chewed garbage, shredded socks, nibbled pages of your encyclopedia, feces on your carpet, tears in your suede sofa, or the patter of urine-puddled paws across your hardwood floors? Spare the gate and spoil the house.

Please do not place the dog's bed in one area and choose another for confinement. Remember, we are allowing the dog to claim this territory for his own. Locate the puppy's sleeping quarters in a small room that can be closed off by a detachable gate. These gates, designed for toddlers, have a small plastic mesh which is strong and rigid. They are made of two sliding parts that adjust to almost any size doorway and they can be obtained in most houseware stores. They are not permanently mounted to the door jambs and there are no screws or nails involved.

A gate is recommended rather than a closed door for the emotional and psychological benefit of the dog. Anyone who raises tropical fish will tell you that the growth of the fish is usually influenced by the size of the tank it lives in. Psychologically, the same is true of a puppy. If he cannot see his family and the rest of his domicile, if he spends many hours in solitary confinement, if he is isolated and sequestered from the normal activities of the household, his intellectual and emotional growth will be stunted. His desire to relate to and enjoy being with human beings will disappear. An isolated puppy will quickly become antisocial in both human and dog society. He will become a dog fighter, a child biter, an aggressive bully or a dangerous coward (fear biter), who will cringe at the sight of someone but try to bite that person when he or she turns his back. At the very least, a closed-off dog will become very bored, and that boredom soon leads to mischief as well as alienation.

You get the same bad results from chaining a puppy. Isolation creates anxiety. Anxiety leads to frustration which then leads to problematic behavior such as barking, chewing, and aggressiveness.

Confinement does not mean something similar to a padded cell for dangerous mental patients. At certain times a puppy simply must be restricted from getting into trouble when there is no one to supervise his activities or play with him. During these periods of confinement, the puppy must still be able to look into the next room and see, or at least hear, human activity. Even at night he can hear the rest of the family as they sleep. It gives him an emotional and intellectual connection with the rest of his world, and that is very important.

EQUIPMENT AND ACCESSORIES

For the sake of your puppy and your sanity, have the things you'll need for the new member of the family in the house the night before his arrival. Can you see yourself torn between dashing toward the baby dog as he squats on the wall-to-wall carpet and running out to buy a leash and collar so that he can be taken outside? Be good to yourself and get what you need ahead of time.

A Water Bowl. A Food Bowl. These should be nonbreakable, nontoxic, and shaped so they cannot tip over. A ceramic bowl is acceptable providing it is thick and heavy and has not been fired in a kiln with a leadbased glaze. Your puppy can be adversely effected by lead poisoning just as a baby can. When bitten hard, most plastic bowls will splinter into sharp fragments. Cheaper metal bowls will also develop jagged edges when subjected to constant biting by a teething dog. Stainless steel and hard rubberized plastic are suitable bowl materials, as is heavy-gauge aluminum or other hard metal. If your puppy has long, flappy ears such as the hound and spaniel breeds, buy bowls designed for him. They are wide at the bottom and narrow at the top so that his ears cannot splash inside even if he sticks his entire head into the bowl.

Leash and Collar. A puppy requires only the slightest kind of leash restraint. A lightweight leather leash is acceptable, but a nylon puppy leash is better. It is strong but very slender and gentle. You are always better off with a leash that is too long rather than too short. A six-foot puppy leash allows the small dog some room for exploring the sights and sounds of the great outdoors without wandering too far. If the need arises, you can always take up the slack and maintain greater control on a shorter lead.

Light and gentle is the keynote for a puppy collar as well. A puppy is going to outgrow his leash and collar in a short time, so it doesn't pay to spend too much money at first. Small nylon choke collars are often used if a puppy is to begin training at an early age. However, a conventional nylon or soft leather collar for walking purposes is still necessary. This collar comes in rolled leather form for long-haired breeds and flat leather form for short-haired breeds. When placing the collar around the puppy's neck, make sure there is enough room for one finger to slip in and out between the collar and his neck. It must not be too tight nor too loose.

Before you purchase a collar, examine it for small, sharp bits of metal on both sides. The underside of a rivet or other metal protrusion will soon wear the dog's fur away and scratch his skin. Avoid collars with undue amounts of metal surface attached to them.

A word about getting a puppy used to the idea of wearing a

leash and collar. This equipment is used with the conventional methods of dog training and if your dog is to be obedience trained, he must learn to wear these. It is too frightening to simply strap a collar and leash on a puppy and drag him outside. He must be introduced gently to the idea. It will make things easier if you let the dog claim the equipment as his own property. Just before he curls

A dog with hanging ears needs a specially tapered food bowl to avoid dragging them through the gruel or even chewing on them. The bowl should be wide at the bottom and narrow at the top.

up to sleep, place both leash and collar in a corner of his bed. We do not want him to chew on them, but we do want them to rub against his body and become marked with his own scent. Because scent marking is a basic technique that canids use to claim territory, the leash and collar will immediately belong to your puppy. In the morning, do not give the puppy the opportunity to relate to the leash and collar as toys. Take them away.

On the second morning, clasp the collar around the dog's neck just before feeding time. He will be too distracted by his breakfast to notice anything different. If he does not protest by trying to pull the collar off, leave it on for several hours and put it back in his bed that night. Once he has accepted the collar, repeat the same action the next morning but snap on the leash as well. Because the leash is a bit of a burden and a radical departure from his normal routine, let him drag it around for short periods (fifteen minutes at a time). In a few days, the puppy will accept the idea of a leash and collar with no struggle, and he will experience no emotional stress over them.

You are now ready to walk your dog, providing he has had his vaccinations and is old enough to adjust to the weather. Be sure to check the dog's collar for a safe fit every day once he is wearing it regularly. A dog does most of his growing in the first year and may outgrow a collar two or three times in the first five months alone. If his collar is too small, he will choke. *Be careful.*

There is a method of dog training that does not accept the leash as a means of dog control and training. It is called the Dog Master System and was developed by ethologist Dare Miller. Dr. Miller has a Ph.D. in child psychology and has become an authority on dog behavior. He maintains a private practice in Beverly Hills, California, where pet owners come to him for private consultations about behavior-related dog problems. Dr. Miller's training method utilizes sound on a subliminal level to train a dog in most aspects of obedience. Through the use of a small, specially treated metal bracelet used to create high-pitched sound, the dog is trained without the use of a leash.

Dr. Miller maintains that all dogs have a built-in "opposition reflex." He states in his book, *Dog Master System**:

It is that reflex of the dog which causes him to react with opposition in response to any type of physical restraint. It can be seen in "Positive Thigmotoxis," the dog's opposing any phys-

---

**Dog Master System* by Dr. Dare Miller. Copyright 1975. Published by Canine Institute Library, Santa Monica. Used by permission.

ical pressure. Push down and he pushes and thinks up, pull and he pulls away. An owner's unwitting and constant stimulation of this reflex colors the dog's personality with opposition toward his owner.

This statement should serve as a guideline if you are going to use a leash and collar. It is suggested that the leash and collar be used, if at all, with great sensitivity and gentleness. Because most communities have leash laws, you are going to have to use them sooner or later. It is best to take the time and trouble getting the puppy used to them.

Grooming Tools. Every dog needs a brush, no matter how young or old, how large or small, no matter the length of its coat. For a long-haired puppy, a wire slicker brush is best for brushing out the coat. It has short, thick wire teeth set into a foam backing. The teeth must not be too harsh or too soft. This brush must be used only on the dog's coat and not touch his skin. If you hurt the dog, he will quickly learn to hate the grooming process. A long-haired puppy will also require a steel comb with flat teeth and wide spaces between them. The comb's primary function is to test the coat for mats and therefore should be used with slow, deliberate strokes.

As the long-haired dog grows to maturity, he will need a large pin brush which is used for regular brushing. However, if the long-haired dog is a small breed such as a Maltese or Pomeranian, a small pin brush is used. A boar's bristle brush is also recommended for the undercoat of some adult long-haired breeds.

A short-haired dog requires a rubber brush similar to a curry brush used for horses. It has two oval-shaped rows of short, blunt, rubber teeth. It not only grooms the dog's coat, but stimulates his skin as would a massage. You may prefer a short bristle brush for your short-haired dog that has grown to maturity. When using such a brush on a puppy, exercise care and gentleness.

For short-haired hounds, a hound glove is used immediately following brushing with the bristle brush. It smoothes the coat and brings it up to a luster. Short-haired dogs that receive a lanolin coat conditioner need either a chamois cloth, velvet pad, or silk cloth to bring up the luster.

If your dog does not live in the city or if he does not go outside very often, he will have to have his nails clipped as they grow longer. Dogs that walk on the cement sidewalk every day usually wear their nails down naturally. The best all-around nail clipper is the pliers type. There are two other types of clippers. The scissors type

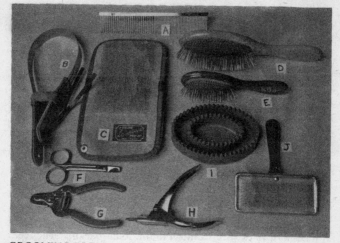

GROOMING TOOLS. (a) Steel comb. (b) Shed'n Blade. (c) Hound glove. (d) Large pin brush. (e) Small pin brush. (f) Scissors-type nail clippers. (g) Pliers-type nail clippers. (h) Guillotine-type nail clippers. (i) Curry brush. (j) Wire slicker brush.

is used for small dogs and the guillotine type is recommended for large breeds.

Many dogs, both long-haired and short-haired, have a tendency to shed their fur several times a year. Some dogs shed their fur in great quantities and quite frequently. To help the situation, you will need a tool called a Shed'n blade. It is simply a jagged-tooth blade, folded into a loop with a leather handle. If your puppy or grown dog is a shedder, you will be glad you purchased this item.

One last implement the novice groomer might purchase is a hand-held warm-air dryer with a brush attachment. Although this appliance is meant to be used by humans for humans, it enables you in one action to brush and dry your dog immediately following his bath. It is extremely useful for long-haired breeds.

Toys

When discussing toys, we must consider the activity known as "play." What is a toy if not an object used to enhance play? The subject of play and the toys used for that purpose is so important that a volume could be written on that one aspect of behavior alone. Mammals are more playful than other animals because of their longer childhood, the period when they are dependent on

Puppy play is a learning process. During such play, one puppy learns to find the most vulnerable spot of the other. It's all good fun at this age.

their parents for survival. Although play serves more than one purpose, the most important one for a dog owner to know about is its learning value. Play is a built-in, self-teaching factor for canids. Play also promotes exercise which in turn creates physical fitness. To play is to pretend or "make believe." When a puppy or kitten plays, it is in the process of learning and then practicing what it has just learned.

When a child sits on the floor and manipulates a toy, one of two things is happening. Some new mental capacity is being developed, such as the ability to measure size and shape, or the child is practicing what he has seen his parents do in adult form, such as hold a telephone and speak into it. When a puppy is on the floor playing he is learning about *prey capture, fighting,* or *escape be-*

Although puppies at play can be a delight to watch, it is a miniaturized version of life in the wild. Submission to a dominant puppy is expressed by turning on the back and offering the throat. Among mature dogs and wolves the confrontation ends at this point.

havior. These are aspects of survival if he were to be on his own in the wild. They are built in and preprogrammed. Nature could never have anticipated domestication and the pet industry. And so, the puppy continues to learn how to survive through his instinct to play despite the fact that he will never even operate a can opener—let alone hunt for game.

Because a puppy is going to go through the learning process brought about through play anyway, by providing the right kind of toys you will be assisting your dog in his natural schooling and saving some of your possessions from destruction.

Some dog toys are dangerous and others may lead to obedience problems later in the dog's life. The puppy should never be given toys that are small enough to swallow or weak enough to shred. Be cautious of items decorated with lead-based paint. Do not underestimate the effectiveness of a puppy's little teeth. Because anything you give a puppy is going to be chewed and chewed hard, it must be made of a material that will resist being torn apart and swallowed, which would cause a blockage in the stomach or throat. This is especially true of objects made of wood, cheap plastic, glass, thin-gauge metal, clay, etc. Avoid broom handles and tree branches. The best materials for dog toys are hard leather, rawhide, and a commercially manufactured bone-shaped object called Nylabone. If a toy looks as if it won't endure a puppy's hard play, then chances are you're right. Don't buy it. Rubber and rubber synthetics are harmful if swallowed. Toys that squeak have a small metal whistle that can be gnawed out and then swallowed. Only the largest and hardest animal bones such as the knuckle or shin should be given to any dog of any age. Make friends with your butcher, and he may give them to you.

If you don't want your puppy to grow up and eat your expensive leather shoes then it is suggested that you do not buy him a toy shoe. Giving your puppy a toy shaped like an actual object in your home is to teach him to destroy the real thing later on. Bones, balls, and barbells are among the better toys for a dog. Pet supply stores are jammed with thousands of items that are offered as dog and cat toys. Think carefully before you buy any. Ask yourself if it can be chewed apart or swallowed whole. Will it teach the puppy unwanted adult behavior? Can the material harm the dog if ingested, even in small pieces? Does the toy aid in play concerning *prey capture, fighting,* and *escape behavior?*

An empty cardboard box will keep any puppy busy for hours, as will a large shopping bag. Old socks tied into large, hard knots are fine as long as they don't appear in their original form (a sock chewer is just as upsetting as a shoe chewer). An old lampshade is a great toy providing there are no synthetic cloth fibers on it such as nylon, etc. Things that make good toys are things that are hard enough to resist being chewed apart, offer some cavelike shelter (a metal bucket, a box, a bag), and objects that move such as a ball, metal bucket, or discarded cooking pot.

Another aspect of toys has to do with the claiming of territory. Allow a dog to claim a few things that are his exclusively and it will greatly enhance his sense of security not to mention a feeling of contentment. Among his toys allow for a bit of blanket to wrap and curl himself into. A security blanket, if you will. This bit of blanket serves many purposes. Naturally, it will make him more comfortable when sleeping. But it offers a substitute for the loss of the little dog's mother and litter mates. It is soft, warm, gentle, and cuddly. Do not underestimate its value. As you can see, toys are a serious business. They're nothing to play around with.

FOOD

Careful consideration should be given to your puppy's menu before he enters your home. Having his food on the shelf the night before is not only convenient but essential. A complete discussion on nutrition can be found in Chapter 6 ("Chow Time") and a more immediate, concise dietary plan in this chapter under the heading *The First Day*. Read these sections of the book before the little dog is brought home and make sure that the proper food is in the house.

PUPPY-PROOF THE HOUSE

Unless you have owned a dog, you cannot imagine the difficulties that a puppy can get itself into. Every little dog is a troublemaker and must be assumed guilty until proven innocent. The most common household objects may become life-and-death hazards for a small puppy and this must enter your pre-puppy game plan. The night before the blessed event, there are things you can do to prevent serious accidents to the puppy.

The first consideration has to do with the areas in which the puppy will be allowed to roam. Remove all electrical wires that can be reached. Believe it, the dog will chew them. If a wire is plugged in, the dog will receive a shock when he bites it. A sustained electrical shock can stop a small heart, causing injury or, in rare instances, even death. If a wire cannot be removed, at least unplug it whenever the puppy is in the room. Unplug or cover electrical outlets that the dog can reach. Don't forget the puppy's height when standing on his hind legs. Even if the dog does not chew through a wire completely, he has still created a hazard—perhaps a worse hazard. The puppy may have taken much of the insulation off. When the wire goes into use, the remaining insulation will soon wear away and either cause a short circuit, thus knocking out all your power, or set your carpet or baseboard on fire. Get the wires out of reach or check them every day for chew marks.

Be aware of cupboards, closets, and drawers that contain common household poisons such as laundry detergent, ammonia, bleach, disinfectants, lighter fluid, cleaning fluid, paint, paintbrushes, mothballs, insecticides, roach and ant traps, flypaper, antifreeze, etc. Be certain that there is no way a puppy can get into these storage places. Remove mousetraps and loose thumbtacks, nails, staples, brads, and other sharp fasteners that the puppy can chew on and swallow. Watch out for paint chips that contain lead. If a glass or other piece of crockery has been broken on the floor, vacuum the area thoroughly so that no tiny particle can get into the puppy's paw or mouth. Take several slices of white bread and pat the area with them to get up the tiniest of glass fragments. The broken bits will adhere to the bread.

Be warned that puppies love nothing better than poring over a good book or curling up with it and nibbling away as if it were a box of cheese crackers. In many homes, bookshelves start at floor level—and that's trouble. You can tack on a piece of screening at the bottom of the shelf and hook the top of the screening onto small nails driven into the lip of a higher shelf. It's not very aesthetic, but it does protect your books until the dog grows out of his need to chew.

Beware of your puppy's desire to swallow your pills and medicines, sewing supplies, small toys, and exotic foods. Three ounces of Beluga caviar will only upset a small dog but its disappearance will make you sick.

Do not allow the dog the opportunity to jump from any height greater than eight inches. A puppy's bones are fragile and will break or dislocate from too high a jump. Do not place the puppy or his bed on a chair, table, bed, couch, or any other object that is high off the floor. Without a doubt, the little dog will jump and possibly hurt himself.

Make sure the new puppy is going to be sequestered from other house pets. An older dog and a puppy or an older cat and a puppy will eventually work out the terms of their relationship. However, it could be a traumatizing experience for a new puppy to have to adjust to the curiosity or hostile treatment of an older pet. Give the little guy a chance to adjust to being away from his previous home before subjecting him to new and terrifying experiences. Keep other pets away for several days if you can.

Puppy-proof your floors, too. Stock up on old newspapers. Gather as many as you can and keep them in a neat stack in the puppy's living area. See "Housebreaking" in this chapter under the section entitled *The First Week*.

SELECT A VETERINARIAN

Before buying a dog, it is important to know which veterinarian you will be seeing for your animal's needs. It is best to choose a veterinarian before you choose the dog. The puppy is best examined before he enters your home where you and your family will immediately become attached to him. If the dog has a serious medical problem, return it at once and start over. Despite the fact that it seems cold-hearted, it is best. There is no experience more emotionally wrenching than coming to love a small dog only to find that he has hip dysplasia or some other ailment that may require euthanasia or long, protracted medical procedures that will cost a great deal of time, money, and anxiety. It is also wise to select your veterinarian in advance in case of injury or an emergency situation. It is no time to start hunting for a doctor while a dog is in the throes of sickness or physical stress.

Because most people find a veterinarian by word of mouth, you should speak to dog owners and get a consensus of opinion about the best veterinarians. Price is a big factor; cleanliness is another. The ability to relate to dogs and cats is something important to experienced pet owners. Find out if a veterinarian is compassionate, if he or she will answer your questions adequately, if you will be given the help and consideration that you need. Is medical service available over the weekends and during holidays, especially if it's an emergency? Doctors of Veterinary Medicine can be found quickly in your Yellow Pages under two headings: "Veterinarians" and "Animal Hospitals." You can also call your local veterinary medical society and ask for recommendations.

WHEN TO BRING THE PUPPY HOME

Friday afternoon is the best time to bring a puppy home. The dog is going to howl and whine during the first few nights. Neighbors are less likely to complain over the weekend. If you're very lucky, the neighbors will have gone out in the evening, giving the poor dog the opportunity to cry and carry on without causing complaints. By Sunday night, the puppy is likely to have adjusted to his new home, and that is when most people need an undisturbed night's sleep in preparation for work on Monday morning.

Friday afternoon also gives one the opportunity to see the veterinarian and have the dog examined before going home. Stores are open at that time for any conceivable need you or the dog will have. The breeder or pet-shop owner can still be called on the telephone for any last-minute information. The family will just barely have time to meet the new addition before dispersing for dinner, thus giving the little fellow time to rest and recuperate from the shock of leaving his last home.

It's a good idea to chat with your family the night before the puppy comes about how they are to behave. Let it be understood that no one is to make too great a fuss the instant he comes into the house. The house or apartment must be kept quiet, and after a brief introduction, everyone should go their own way until the next day. Rehearse the way it is supposed to happen so that there can be no doubts in anyone's mind as to how they are to behave. This is especially important if there are children in the house. See the section entitled *The First Hour* in this chapter.

If you follow these suggestions before the big event, you will be more prepared for dog ownership than most dog owners with years of experience. It may be said of you that you are dogmatic but also goodhearted and humane.

The First Hour

Many breeders watch you leave their kennels, puppy in hand, with the dejected feelings of a bride's father unable to stop the honeymoon. If he's smart, the groom waves good-bye from the car. The caring breeder secretly hopes you'll change your mind and restore the little orphan to his proper home. The pet-shop operator counts out your change and hopes you won't come back (for a while). In either case, you're on your own and the puppy's health, happiness, and very existence are in your hands. More than that, his future behavior patterns are about to be shaped according to what you do to it and for it.

GOING HOME

If you are driving home from a country breeder's kennels, be prepared with a roll of paper towels, a plastic trash bag, an expendable blanket, and the ability to withstand spillage. If you're lucky, all of these items will be unnecessary. Assuming you are not the driver, place the blanket over your lap and hold the puppy on top of the blanket. If the little dog is excited, frightened, or carsick, he will do one of three things and maybe all three. Use your paper towels and plastic trash bag efficiently but gently and without anger or disgust. It's all part of owning a dog.

For those in the city returning home from a pet shop, do not take a subway, streetcar, or public bus. Be a sport and take a taxi. That way the puppy will not be mentally wounded by the sudden harsh noises of city life. It will also spare him the terror of traveling in a brutally dark, cardboard carton, bouncing around in an alien environment. Once inside the taxi, take the puppy out of the carton and place him on your lap, holding on gently. It is important to maintain a neutral attitude if the dog cries or whines. When you pet a dog that is whining you are teaching it that whining gets results. This may become a lifelong habit and a means of manipulating you. Stroke the dog at any time during the ride except when it yips, howls, or whines. Do not scold or push the dog around. Simply hold on gently and give no reward for unwanted behavior.

This is the foundation of the teaching process and it begins immediately. If the little dog squirts or messes or heaves, remain calm and simply clean it up. Remember, neutrality will get you everywhere. Petting is a reward and is given only for accomplishments and genuine expressions of affection. Forget about notions of hitting or rough treatment no matter how many dogs were owned by the man who said, "You gotta show 'em who's boss right from the beginning." The person who beats a dog or even hits the dog on a consistent basis is violent, repressed, dictatorial, and not without psychological problems. The battered puppy, like the battered child, becomes a violent creature gnawing at the underpinnings of society. It is true that a dog can be beaten into submission and thus rendered absolutely obedient—but only at the cost of the dog's potential as an engaging companion enjoying mental health and canine dignity. If you think about it, the same applies to human beings.

Home at Last

So many dogs and dog owners fail in their relationships because of what happens at this very important moment. The dog is led into the house as a prize lion entering the Colosseum to the cheers of a thrill-seeking mob falling all over itself in a deluge of mass hysteria. It is a great mistake to induct a puppy into its new home in this fashion. A puppy's earliest experiences have a lasting effect on his behavior and mental hygiene.

Here we have an infant mammal of about seven to twelve weeks of age, perhaps leaving his mother and litter mates for the first

time and entering the society of humans. All that was warm, secure, and known is gone, evaporated with the slam of a car door.
The puppy's world has suddenly and without warning expanded
to unmanageable proportions inhabited by large, vertical
creatures stripping it of all choice and freedom. These mammoth,
two-legged monsters reach down from the heights and grab and
clutch and squeeze while uttering the most terrifying, unbeautiful
sounds. We are left with a fear-ridden, overexcited victim with no
means of escape or ability to adapt. This can only result in the beginning of abnormal behavior which, in human terms, is called
neurosis. It is not healthy. It is not fair. It is not necessary.

EARLY LEARNING

If the new dog owner understands that everything happening in
the first year of a dog's life is a learning experience, then he or she
might be more careful when relating to the dog. Puppies and
babies have so much in common in their infancy period that
science has taken advantage of this and learned a great deal about
humans by studying canines. Like human babies, young puppies
develop their behavioral patterns very early in life by imitating
those that are around them the most, parents and litter mates
(brothers and sisters in humans). This form of learning is called *allelomimetic behavior.* Don't even try to pronounce it.

Allelomimetic Behavior.   This form of behavior is defined as
doing what the other animals in a group do, with some degree of
mutual stimulation. According to Dr. John Paul Scott and Dr.
John L. Fuller in their monumental work, *Dog Behavior: The Genetic Basis,* puppies first do this at five weeks of age, when the litter begins to run in a group. It is a basic part of the social life of
dogs and wolves. This behavior has its origins in pack hunting and
defense of the den. When the pack is threatened by an enemy,
they all work in concert to defend themselves. When a puppy
comes to live in our home, he accepts the human family as his
pack and the house or apartment as his den. The puppy then imi-
tates our attitudes and emotional and physical actions. This happens with infants as well. A baby and a puppy begin to shape their
personalities early in life by adopting the behavior of those in
charge. How a dog owner treats his dog in the early stages pretty
much determines what the dog will be like with that owner. There
are other factors that will be discussed later in this chapter.

A new puppy from the human's perspective. *(The Photo Works)*

LET HIM ELIMINATE

Once the trip home has ended, the puppy will probably want to urinate or defecate. Do not go directly into your house. Walk to the outdoor place that is going to be the toilet area and ease the small dog down to the ground. This only applies if you intend to housebreak the dog as opposed to paper training him. A housebroken dog is one that eliminates outdoors exclusively. A paper-

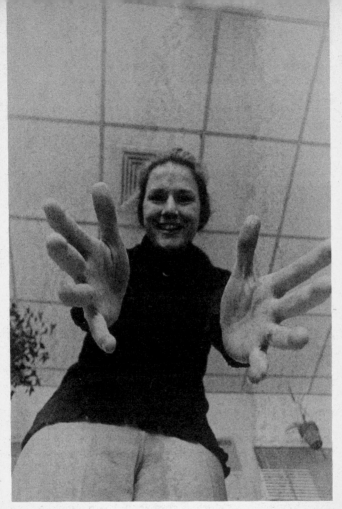

What the puppy sees. A human from a puppy's perspective appears to be a mammoth creature from another world. Hands become tentacles and smiles become threats. Give the little dog time to adjust to his new family of humans. *(The Photo Works)*

trained dog goes indoors only, over several layers of newspaper. This first action begins the dog's toilet training and makes that training much easier. Give the puppy at least ten minutes to eliminate. Once he does, shower him with loving praise. Pet the dog and tell him what a great thing he has accomplished. Point to the evidence as you offer your congratulations. Allow the puppy to sniff at his great achievement so that he can begin to associate your praise with his own accomplishment. If the dog is to be paper trained, do all this immediately upon entering the house, at the paper-covered toilet area, of course.

INTRODUCING THE PUPPY

When first entering your home with a new puppy, the objective is to complete the disturbing transition for the dog with as little trauma and overstimulation as possible. It is certainly impossible to bring a puppy into a house where children live and deprive them of meeting the new member of the family. This applies to the adult residents as well. In order to satisfy this urgent need, you may offer a quick but gratifying peek. Devote five minutes for quick introductions and one or two *calm* pats on the dog's head. Make it clear that the family—especially the children—are not to stimulate the dog with loud squeals, giggles, hugs, kisses or other physicalized or overly vocalized expressions of delight. Remember, it's the dog we are concerned with at this point. After the brief time allotted for introductions, chase the family into another part of the house for at least an hour and perhaps the rest of the day.

NOISE

By prior agreement with the family, keep the noise level to a bare minimum. Loud sounds interfere with the puppy's ability to accept the new environment as his own. Obviously, a high-pitched phonograph or television set, or the squeals of children at play will scare a puppy. It will be more difficult for him to adjust to your home and to his new "pack." This idea is not far removed from the theories of Dr. Frederick Leboyer expressed in his book, *Birth Without Violence.* He theorizes that the trauma of birth can be eased by avoiding as much as possible the sharp transition from the environment of the mother's uterus to the delivery room at the hospital. Silence and low-key lighting help toward that end and are suggested here for the first hour with your puppy.

Criticism.   Do not be discouraged by those who advocate the "harsh realities of a dog's life." They are either uninformed or living with dogs on a basis other than that of companionship and member-of-the-family status. You may also find yourself criticized by dog owners who do not wish to make this much of an effort or emotional investment. That's fine—for them. It is not distorted behavior on your part to make every effort to create a long-lasting, pleasurable relationship with your dog. The "treat a dog like an animal" idea does not stand up against the reality that we, too, are animals and that human contact with a dog demands humane considerations in that dog-human relationship. Even theories of child rearing conflict with one another and set off heated debates in the scientific-medical community as well as among parents faced with the actual responsibility. Like a new parent, you will have to do what you think is best for yourself and your dog and then stick to it no matter what anyone else has decided for you.

A Friendly Voice. It is absolutely impossible to predict how the new puppy will feel at this point in his journey. It depends on his breed, the way he's been handled in the first eight weeks, and many other variables. He may have been quite frisky when you got him but is now wilted or dejected from the great change. The most sensible goal for the new owner is to gain the dog's confidence. You have already begun by keeping the introductions short, lowering the noise level, subduing the lighting, and not forcing the pup to relate to anyone other than yourself. And this brings us to the question of how you can relate to the dog so that he will trust you and his new surroundings.

It has to do with communication. Everything you do or say has an effect on the dog. Ideally, you want to do and say those things that communicate safety, affection, and comfort to the baby dog. This is accomplished by avoiding sudden moves around the puppy, especially those motions that are directed toward him. Move slowly and smoothly and do not grab or clutch. Although most dogs come to understand some words, they don't at this stage of puppyhood. Your puppy will respond positively to a soothing, gentle tone of voice. Do not be inhibited about talking to your dog. You will eventually talk to him anyway. You may experience direct communication at this early point if you start talking in a soft, friendly manner. Once you gain a dog's confidence you will have it all his life—providing you don't abuse him. Having a dog's confidence means you will have little difficulty in shaping him into the kind of creature you want.

EXPLORING THE LAY OF THE LAND

The next step during this hour is to let the puppy explore the house, investigate anything he wants, providing it is safe. Here you will have to use your judgment. If the dog heads for the area where the family is, he may be allowed to do so providing that no one pays too much attention to him. If that's impossible, then restrict his movements. After the dog has satisfied his curiosity about his new quarters, take him back to his sleeping and eating area and confine him there, preferably with a gate. Give him one of his new toys, perhaps a Nylabone, and let him play with it for a while. Once it has been established that this toy is his possession, take it from him and place it in his bedding. If you're lucky, the dog will appreciate the soft sleeping area and take his first nap.

CONFINEMENT

There is certainly less emotional stress for a puppy who is not confined or isolated from other members of his new family. There are two options. If the puppy is not confined, the owner must stay with him for the remainder of the day and evening. The dog must not be allowed to get into trouble. He must also be watched for signs of body elimination. The puppy will eliminate soon after eating, drinking, awakening, playing, or chewing. He must then be taken outdoors to the first place he was allowed to eliminate. If the dog is being paper trained, he can be taken to an area of the floor covered with newspapers. Confining the puppy is very convenient for the owner, but you can be certain that the dog will whine and try to get out of the closed-off area if left alone. If the dog is to be confined and left alone, do not confine him in the first hour. (If you choose not to confine the dog, he must never be left alone; it is too dangerous.) If the hour before confinement has not yet ended, give the dog a little water. If he drinks, take him outdoors for immediate toileting or take him to his newspapers. Try to get him to take a nap by placing him in his bed. He may be tired by now.

The First Day

Out of the goodness of their hearts, novice dog owners serve their young puppies huge meals. This is hardly correct.

THE FIRST MEAL

No matter how subdued you have made your house, the puppy

is still in a very excited state of mind, and the transition from one home to another is very sharp. It's quite likely that the dog will not be too hungry, if at all. A dish of water is necessary, but don't over-indulge the puppy with too much food or very fancy food. The dog may show no interest in dry cereal but gobble up caviar canapes, bacon-wrapped wieners, or sautéed chicken livers in dry sherry. This cocktail-party mentality will bring nothing but digestive trouble, not to mention very poor eating habits for the future. Most exotic foods meant for human consumption will never agree with the canine digestive tract. Large quantities of food are also hard for a little puppy to digest. Your dog must be placed on a properly balanced diet determined by his weight and age, and he should be fed on a regular basis according to a set schedule (see Chapter 6, "Chow Time").

What to Feed the Puppy. During the first day, do not stress the dog's bowels with milk; with rich foods such as beef, horse meat, or organ meats. Dry dog foods, slightly moistened, are excellent, but the puppy might not eat them right away. Keep his meals bland with light meats such as chicken, lamb, veal, or turkey. You can mix small quantities of dry puppy chow in with the meat. This will enable you to reduce the meat intake gradually and increase the dry cereal in the dog's diet. The sooner the puppy's diet includes dry food, the better. Maintain a consistent schedule of meat reduction as you increase the dry food portion in the food bowl. Start with three-fourths meat to one-fourth cereal and reduce the meat by one-fourth every day. If the dog was purchased from a breeder, you might want to continue the diet the dog has been fed since weaning. Ask the breeder for advice and dietary information.

Digestive Stress. The state of a puppy's bowels indicates the amount of stress he is under. Stressed bowels in the healthy puppy come from emotional sources, rich food, too much food, a change of diet, or any combination of these. If the puppy is under emotional strain, he might develop diarrhea no matter what he'll eat or how much. When the puppy first comes into your home and develops diarrhea, it must be cured immediately or it may continue for a long time and become very difficult to clear up.

Diet and Remedy for Common Diarrhea in Puppies. Diarrhea can be defined as a loose or watery stool that is discharged frequently during the day or night. Anything beyond that, i.e., blood or mucus in the loose stool, indicates more than a simple digestive problem and requires the attention of a veterinarian.

The following diet is suggested for a puppy afflicted with common diarrhea. Prepare a mixture containing one cup of cooked white rice and one tablespoon of cooked chicken meat (cut in small pieces). You may replace fresh cooked chicken with canned chicken parts for dogs or chicken baby food. Feed the puppy one-third of a cup of the chicken and rice mixture four times a day. If the puppy wants more than one-third of a cup, you may give it to him. Keep him on this diet for three days.

If the dog has also vomited, do not give him water for twenty-four hours. Give him several ice cubes to lick after each feeding. The dog that has diarrhea and has also vomited should be fed the rice and chicken mixture for three days and then a soft-moist dog food for the next three days. Any burger-type dog food will do. After that you may start the dog's regular diet again.

In addition to the above bland diet, administer a small amount of liquid Kaopectate. For every five pounds your dog weighs, give him one teaspoon of Kaopectate three times a day. Continue this treatment for two or three days. If the diarrhea is still present after three days, consult your veterinarian. It is important to understand that diarrhea can be a symptom of almost every known dog disorder including distemper, canine hepatitis, or obstructions of the digestive tract by foreign objects. Therefore, after three days, diarrhea must be taken very seriously.

PRACTICING FOR THE LONELY NIGHT AHEAD

A useful way to take up part of this first day with the new puppy is getting the dog accustomed to the idea of being left alone in the dark, away from its litter mates for a night's sleep. For a complete discussion of this subject, see the next section in this chapter entitled *The First Night.*

When a very young puppy is left alone for these first nights in your house, he feels alienated and isolated. The puppy has no inner resources to fall back on such as an established pattern of *lights-out, humans leave, sleep comes, the next day begins, and humans reappear.* Dogs are creatures meant to live in a socially structured society. This need to be part of a pack is both instinctive and learned from birth by the time spent in a litter. Whether your dog has come from his breeder where he recently left the litter or from the pet shop where he stayed in the front window with fifteen other pups, he is going to have difficulty not having other dogs to sleep with. The puppy will be frightened and will feel trapped in a strange and dangerous situation. But it is possible to teach puppies to adjust to this new situation.

Gather one or more of the puppy's toys and place them in his bed. Gently lift the dog and place him next to his toys inside the bed. Lower the shades, pull the blinds, or close the curtains and make the room as dark as possible. Leave the room, closing the gate behind you. Make certain that the puppy cannot get out. Walk away and go to another room. It is most likely that the dog will whine, howl, bark, or cry. Stay away from the room for at least five minutes. If the dog settles down, stay away for ten minutes. Return to the puppy's area, open the door, turn on the lights and calmly say hello. Offer the dog a little water (no food) and then lead him outdoors to his toilet place or indoors to his newspapers. Repeat this procedure once every half hour or so until it is bedtime.

It is highly possible that the teaching procedure described here will have absolutely no effect on the dog. He may just howl and whine for the full five minutes that you're out of the room and behave that way each time you leave. If this is the case, you cannot profit from this technique. Read the next section, *The First Night,* for other ways to cope with this disturbing behavior.

The Rest of the Day

If the puppy was brought home on a Friday afternoon, and if you have followed the prescribed suggestions, it is safe to assume that the day is almost over. You are now ready to have your dinner. Because you do not want to upset the dog on this exciting first day, don't feed him until you have had your own dinner and it's somewhat closer to his bedtime. If the dog's area is in the kitchen and a large family is going to dine there, it is advisable to separate him from the noise and hubbub. Either plan a sandwich dinner that can be taken in the living room or remove the dog to another part of the house or apartment. *A tiny closed-off room such as the bathroom is not suggested.* The puppy should not feel imprisoned, especially while it's still time to be awake. It might be a better idea not to take dinner with your family that night and remain with the dog in another part of the house until the family has eaten. Afterward, go to the kitchen with the puppy and let him play while you dine.

After your dinner, you might want to give the dog an opportunity to investigate the house once again. All that was suggested before still applies about maintaining a subdued atmosphere, quiet and dimly lit. Give the dog more time than he had earlier in the afternoon to explore and learn the new terrain.

Look for signs that the dog is about to urinate or defecate. Sniffing around and turning in circles is a sure sign that the puppy is going to defecate. If he squats, he is about to do one or the other. If the puppy has just eaten or had water, awakened from a nap, or chewed on a toy, he will probably have to eliminate. Get the dog to follow you along the shortest route to his outdoor toilet location or to his newspapers. You will avoid a small mess and constructively add to his toilet training.

It is now possible for the puppy to spend just a bit more time with the rest of the family, but on a one-at-a-time basis with no vigorous play activity. Keep things on a calm, gentle level with expressions of affection and loving acceptance. If you live alone, you may allow the dog to explore, play, and relate to you as he chooses. Do not leave him alone during these first days or nights. And do not leave him alone to go into another room unless he is in his own area, confined. You are now ready to cope with the problems of getting the puppy to sleep for the night.

The First Night

The majority of professional opinions in the dog establishment recommend confining the puppy alone in his area until he can be trusted in his new home even if he cries all night, for the entire first week. The theory is that to do anything else is to teach the dog that crying will get him anything he wants. Therefore, they hold that giving in to the dog's demands is to teach him how to cry and thus create a lifelong behavior problem. They claim that this "spoils" the dog. It is not necessarily true.

This same principle is taken as gospel in coping with human infants' crying in the middle of the night. How often have we heard that to go to a crying baby in the middle of the night is to spoil the child forever and create a selfish, demanding brat who will not give you a night's sleep for years.

In early infancy, most crying is based on hunger. If the baby is on a scheduled feeding plan rather than feeding on demand, crying does not get him the food he wants. The baby cries and no one comes. The results can be devastating on that baby's personality. According to child psychologist Dr. Fitzhugh Dodson, in his book, *How to Parent**:

> He [the baby] may react to this situation with anger or he may become listless and apathetic, as if he had given up on getting his needs satisfied. This baby has "learned" to choke back his anger and to substitute for it a dreadful resignation. But whether the baby chooses continued anger or apathetic resignation, what he is learning is the same: a basic distrust of life. Can you blame him? To him, life is a frustrating, hateful affair.

It is important to understand that all babies cry in the night for a reason. It has to do with hunger, cold, pain, or discomfort. Many child specialists now believe that it is impossible to "spoil" an infant with cuddling, hugging, and other forms of attention. They believe that this attention helps the baby feel loved and gives him a strong and secure self-concept. It is a matter of making the investment in time and energy for a healthier and happier child. Now, you say, that's fine for humans, but does the same apply for puppies? The answer is a definite *maybe*.

When a dog whines, barks, bites, jumps on people, or attacks, it is referred to by psychologist and dog expert Dare Miller as anxiety behavior. Anxiety behavior comes from mounting tension which can turn into frustration and eventually change the dog's personality. In his book, *Dog Master System*, Miller says:

> Some owners confine their dogs behind a fence, not recognizing or correcting the anxiety behavior that ensues and then wonder why the dog digs up the yard or attacks a neighbor, the postman or anyone active on the other side of that fence. These are the ramifications of the BARRIER FRUSTRATION SYNDROME: (a) The dog which is fenced or tied up, away from activity experiences mounting frustration. This develops into a sense of hatred which he then directs against the person who is most frequently seen or heard on the other side of the frustrating barrier. (b) He relieves his tension (frustration) by digging, barking, pacing, chewing or even biting.

One may ask if this applies to young puppies. The answer is yes and no. No young puppy is going to turn into a vicious biter during his tender years because he was isolated for the first few nights. However, if the experience is traumatic, it could be the basis for a neurotic fear of being left alone which will create anxiety behavior that results in whining, barking, jumping on people, and biting. Therefore, a small puppy, left to howl through the night behind a barrier, may have behavior problems later as an adult dog. Obviously, many dogs survive the trauma and live to be wonderful pets. But the risk of developing neurosis is always there. The first night seems a terrible time to add the element of isolation and confinement to your puppy's distress.

A sound way to meet this predicament is to take the puppy's bed with you for the night. Allow him to sleep in the room with you but not in your bed. The dog is likely to sleep through the night without interruption. Puppies need lots of sleep and will get it if they are not anxiety ridden. The bed can then be moved back to his area the next morning. Once the dog is housebroken, you will be able to leave the bed in his area throughout the night and let him decide where to sleep. Most housebroken dogs are allowed the run of the house, and that is as it should be. With very few exceptions, most experts will disagree with this technique and accuse you of "coddling" or "spoiling" the dog and treating him like a baby rather than a dog. If what is written here makes sense to you, then ignore the criticism and do what you think is best.

After thinking the whole thing over, you may still feel that the best method for you is to leave the dog in his own area, confined from the rest of the house or apartment. One cannot deny that every household has its own unique problems and that may necessitate the use of older, more conventional methods of dealing with this problem. Even then, it is helpful to have a complete understanding of why the puppy is crying throughout the night. In *Dog Behavior: The Genetic Basis,** Dr. John Paul Scott and Dr. John L. Fuller say:

> For a highly dependent and helpless animal like a young puppy, the most dangerous possible situation is one in which it is completely alone in a strange place. Under natural conditions a lost wolf puppy would be vulnerable to any predator as well as in danger of eventually starving to death.

*From *Dog Behavior: The Genetic Basis* by John Paul Scott and John L. Fuller. Copyright 1965. Published by University of Chicago Press, Chicago. Used by permission.

In other words, your yelping puppy has been taken from its familiar locale, removed from the protection of its mother, and has lost the comfort and warmth of its litter mates. Because of this, it fears being attacked in the night from a predator without benefit of family protection and is not sure where its next meal is coming from. Place yourself in that situation or, better still, imagine a small child in that predicament. It's not difficult to understand the puppy's terror in those terms. One cannot dismiss his crying and yelping as merely expressing a "bit of loneliness."

For those dog owners who are going to confine their new puppies in an isolated area and not answer the puppies' cries, this will be the longest night. However, there are still some things to do without biting the bullet in ear-piercing agony. The object is to create some of the conditions that the puppy feels it has lost. For example, feed the dog before bedding him down and then take him out to his toilet place. If he does not feel hunger pangs in the early part of the night, it will be one less panic-provoking element.

Take a towel to the puppy's kennel or pet shop the day you pick him up and place it in the enclosure with the other dogs for a short time. It will pick up the scent of the entire litter. Before you put the puppy to bed on the first night, tie one or two large knots in the

To sleep: perchance to dream . . . An alarm clock, a hot water bottle, a transistor radio may all help the new puppy get his first night's sleep in his new bed. When the puppy cries, it will be the longest night.

towel and curl it in the corner of his bed. The towel will not only feel somewhat similar to one or two litter mates, but it will have their odor as well. This may help when you leave the room.

Even though it's been suggested in every book about dogs ever written, and even though some dog people dismiss it, the old hot-water-bottle trick still works. Fill a hot water bottle halfway with lukewarm water and pin a towel around it. Place it in a corner of the puppy's bed just before leaving him. The soft, warm, mushy effect may feel like his mother's stomach and give him some comfort. Another version of this is to use a large jar of warm water wrapped with a towel and fastened with safety pins. You may also add a ticking clock, which may resemble the sound of the mother's heart. It's worth a try.

The late Robert Michell, director of New York's Bide-a-Wee Home Association, one of the great animal shelter systems, swore that he was able to cope with his first-night blues by confining his Scottish terrier and Sealyham terrier puppies with a portable transistor radio playing. Somehow the news, music, and weather were of some comfort to his dogs during their time of stress.

There is another technique worthy of your attention despite the fact that there has been no scientific research conducted in its application to puppies: using the sound of a heartbeat as a means of diminishing anxiety. Some limited experimentation was done with human babies with good results by Dr. Lee Salk, Professor of Psychology and Pediatrics, Cornell University Medical College. His findings were published in the *Canadian Psychiatric Association Journal,* Volume 11, 1966.

In *How to Raise a Human Being,** written with Rita Kramer, Dr. Salk says:

> We can only surmise that the newborn baby misses the accustomed sound that was transmitted by the mother's aorta as it passed through the womb, and that he derives security from being held close to his mother's body, where he may hear—or feel—it again. But experimental evidence does show that this sound has a remarkably soothing effect on newborns. When amplified heartbeat sounds were played in a hospital nursery for newborns for the first four days of their lives, they cried less and gained more weight (probably because they used up

---

**How to Raise a Human Being* by Dr. Lee Salk and Rita Kramer. Copyright 1969. Published by Random House, Inc., New York. Used by permission.

less of their energy crying) than control babies who did not hear the heartbeat sound.

This certainly suggests that the sound of the maternal heartbeat reduces the anxiety of tension felt by the infant.

It would be an interesting home experiment to attempt to alleviate the anxieties of a puppy's first nights in a new home with the nocturnal sounds of a heartbeat. The rhythm of a dog's heart is an irregular one when the animal is resting. As the animal becomes more excited, the heartbeat becomes more regular especially during periods of exercise and excitement. The variation of the normal dog heartbeat is known as *sinus arrhythmia*. The heart rate is regularly accelerated and then retarded. When the irregularity is very pronounced, the heart seems to skip a beat at intervals. Unlike humans, this is the sound of a healthy dog heart and abnormality is indicated when the heartbeats are otherwise. But where, you ask, does one procure the sound of a heartbeat? Unless you can record a dog's heartbeat through a stethoscope, you will have to work with existing recordings of the human heart. No one can be sure if a puppy will be soothed by the sound of the human heart but it is worth a try. This author has experimented with one middle-aged Siberian husky with good results. However, that particular dog lives with a toddler and values his sleep.

One known recording company has produced a 33⅓ LP of the human heartbeat at normal rhythm. One may write to: Heartbeat Lullaby, 3131 Antelo Road, Los Angeles, California 90024. This idea may be a bit exotic, but it is certainly an interesting experiment for the more adventurous dog owner.

If your puppy is confined during his first week and whines throughout the night, it is certainly not productive to run downstairs, shout, or holler for him to shut up. Terror tactics offer very limited results but do have enormous, long-range negative reactions. You will be teaching your puppy to fear and mistrust you and all other human beings. This can result in abnormally aggressive behavior later in the dog's life.

Giving in to a puppy's whines is not recommended either. If the puppy whines and you take him to bed with you because you cannot stand the noise, he will immediately learn that whining gets him everything he wants. If you want to stop the whining, try any of the techniques offered on these pages and expect good results because they attempt to alleviate anxiety at its root cause rather than offer rewards for negative behavior, punish, inhibit behavior, or terrorize the puppy.

The First Week

By now the full impact of owning a puppy has been felt and second thoughts are creeping into your brain. Forget it. There is no turning back. During this first week, your responsibility to your puppy increases and continues to do so for another month or two. After that, it is pleasurable coasting for the next fifteen years. Therefore, dear dog lover, accept your fate, work hard, think of it as an experience with nature, and enjoy the satisfaction of domesticating your puppy.

In this, the first week of dog ownership, many things will continue as they did during the first day and night. The feeding schedule, play and nighttime routines will remain the same. It is still a time for the puppy to become acquainted with the various members of the family and for further investigation of his new home.

THE MASTER OF THE HOUSE

It is of the utmost importance to form the basis of the relationship that will exist between you and your dog at this time. If it is clearly established from the beginning that the dog is a subordinate member of the family and that you are the dominant figure, your training problems will be reduced as will many negative behavior situations. Every human member of your family must also be in a dominant position in relation to the dog. If one human fails to take the lead position over the dog it will be an invitation for the dog to take it, even if it's just with that one human. This is a very common occurrence in many households and should be avoided where possible. It is typical of dogs and wolves to assume a leader position if no one else will take it. They are insecure without a leader and will fill that role if necessary. Once a dog takes the dominant position, it is hard to pry him out of it. A sort of fascist state develops and the family finds itself in the clutches of the irrational needs and desires of a canine. A dog that dominates in a human society is doomed to anxiety and frustration because that society is too complex for him. The result will be neurotic behavior that fast becomes destructive to all. A neurotic dog might chew up the house, bite a visitor, deliberately vomit, or otherwise soil the house in an escalated approach to coercion for something it neither understands nor can achieve.

Please do not confuse being dominant with being violent or abusive toward the dog. Hitting a dog never achieves positive results unless you are defending yourself in a life-or-death situation.

Even then a human is likely to lose. To hit your dog with your hand, with a newspaper, with a hard object is to destroy permanently the dog's trust in you. It is also to teach your dog to "hit back" with his teeth. William E. Campbell, dog behaviorist, states in his book, *Behavior Problems In Dogs**:

> If the puppy is eight to ten weeks of age, a permanent fear imprint may result from being hit. The outcome may be a dog which is forever unsure of its relationship with the owner and/or is panicked by fireworks, auto backfires, and other loud noises. Meantime, the lesson is rarely if ever permanently learned, and the owner's relationship with his pet deteriorates, since such treatment does not mean "no" in canine language.

Never hit your dog. *Period*. The way to gain the dominant position with him is easy. Teach the dog that your commands are consistent and that you mean what you say. If you tell the puppy no when he heads for the garbage can, follow it through and carry him or shoo him away. Do not say no and then let him do what he wants. In this situation call the puppy to you in a playful manner. As he runs to you, turn around and walk in the opposite direction. Make the puppy follow you. When he catches up, bend down and pet him and tell him what a good dog he is. Repeat this many times during the day until the dog comes to you every time you call him. What you are doing is teaching the dog to come when called. Unfortunately, it can only be taught in this manner when the dog is a puppy. The tone of your voice is another way of taking the dominant role. A firm, no-nonsense tone tells the puppy and adult dog that you must be obeyed. Do not confuse a firm tone of voice with shrieking hysteria. It is not recommended that you holler at your puppy. It will terrorize him and do irreparable damage to your relationship with him. Giving the young puppy a call name as soon as possible allows you to gain the dominant position quickly and apply these techniques. The guideline to successful dog training is gaining the dog's confidence and trust while behaving in a leader-like manner.

There are several valid approaches to dog training depending on your needs and desires. The majority of dog owners are primarily interested in simple dog obedience while others are intrigued with American Kennel Club obedience trials. Dogs can be

**Behavior Problems In Dogs* by William E. Campbell. Copyright 1975. Published by American Veterinary Publications, Santa Barbara. Used by permission.

trained for the show ring, for field trials, for hunting, for party tricks, for guard work, for tracking, for show business, and for other sophisticated functions. Please refer to the Suggested Reading List for a random selection of books available on the subject of training.

HOUSEBREAKING A PUPPY

In the beginning, there is the piddle. Later in life, it turns into a puddle and then a deluge. And that's only half of it. Of all the problems of keeping a dog, this is the one that turns the corner for most dog/owner relationships. If a dog can be housebroken or paper trained early, he is going to keep his home and enjoy a full life of comfort and happiness. More than one canine home has been broken up over this subject, and it is therefore of vital importance to all concerned. A fully grown dog's housebreaking problems are a training matter exclusively, assuming he is healthy. But the novice dog owner must realize that a puppy has a very small stomach and an even smaller bladder, not to mention undeveloped [sphincter] muscle control, and needs a great deal of help to become housebroken. You must be patient and sympathetic with a puppy's limitations when attempting to housebreak him. (You would also be well advised to obtain from the US Government Printing Office a USDA booklet [Home and Garden Bulletin No. 62] entitled "Removing Stains from Fabrics.")

Housebreaking (as well as paper training) becomes somewhat more bearable and easier to accomplish when the dog owner understands the nature of canine elimination and how it works. For the first three weeks in a puppy's life, his brain is confined to performing only the most fundamental tasks such as seeking mother's warmth and milk. There is little mental activity. During this period, the process of urination and defecation is accomplished by a reflex promoted by the mother's licking of the puppy's stomach, genitals, and anus. This stimulation begins the involuntary act of elimination. To keep the nest clean, the mother ingests the puppies' waste. On the twenty-first day of life (the end of the third week) the puppy's brain develops further. Its organs begin to function independently allowing sight, smell, hearing, taste, and independent elimination. At this stage the puppy can walk out of its nest, eliminate, and then return. At first the puppy leaves the nest to eliminate on any spot it finds. During the eighth week the puppy begins to use specific spots for elimination. It has been indelibly imprinted in his brain by the example set by his mother not to eliminate in his own nest. The puppy will wait many hours during the night and soil the nest only out of desperation. During the day the puppy exercises less control and eliminates more frequently. Until the little dog is twelve weeks old, he is going to eliminate at least every hour or two, as long as he is awake, according to Scott and Fuller.

There are two important behavior patterns in all puppies that help dog owners immeasurably when trying to housebreak their pets. First, no puppy wants to dirty his own nest and will try hard not to when confined there. A dog needs a certain amount of space to turn around in when he's going to eliminate. He makes circular movements before releasing. When confined to the small area of his nest, it becomes more difficult to turn around in circles. Second, the eight-week-old puppy (and older) looks for his scent or that of another dog's before urinating or defecating. This is the beginning of more adult behavior known as scent posting. Once a puppy (or an older dog) has established several toilet locations, he is always drawn back to them unless they have been deodorized and voided of his scent. This is extremely useful information for housebreaking because it enables the dog owner to allow the scent to remain in a desirable place and eliminate it in a less desirable place.

Dog researchers believe that scent posting has to do with marking off a territory as that which belongs to the dog that marks it. When one dog urinates on top of another dog's urine spot, he is imposing his presence and sense of superiority on top of the other dog's mark. This represents a sort of infighting for territory without actual combat. It is interesting that in a wolf pack only the leader lifts his leg and marks off territory. Our dog may accept us as the leader of the pack, but he takes the full responsibility of marking territory because we are very remiss in performing that important function. From the dog's point of view, no pack is properly established without claiming territory by scent posting. Marking the area with urine has also to do with mating, declarations of one's presence in the area, and of pack domination.

Female elimination is somewhat different from that of the male. She will be directed to scent posts, but not too far from home. Female dogs squat to eliminate as puppies of both genders do. The female goes into two periods of heat a year and will wander a little farther from home at that time. During estrus the female scent-marks with her urine, which has a special odor to it. A male dog becomes excited when sniffing the urine marking of a female in heat. Here, the point to scent posting is for the purpose of mating.

Techniques. There are, as one might expect, several approaches to housebreaking a dog. With the exception of the "rub-their-noses-in-it" method most techniques are effective, some more quickly than others. There isn't a housebreaking method available that doesn't demand of the owner a great deal of time, patience, and energy. Beware of those that would try to convince you that a harsh, physically abusive manner is the only way to housebreak a dog. These methods are inhumane and destructive to both the human and the canine. Here again, do not hit your dog—not for any reason, not under any circumstance.

When you hit a dog because the dog soiled the house, you are punishing the animal for obeying its most natural and necessary instinctive behavior. As stated earlier, besides ridding the body of waste material, dogs urinate and defecate for the purpose of claiming territory, asserting pack leadership, mating, etc. To physically punish him for doing what he was born to do creates neurotic behavior and asks the dog to behave unlike a dog. When housebreaking a puppy, attempt to manipulate the dog's environment rather than reshape his behavior.

In the section titled *The First Hour,* you were instructed to pick a toilet spot outdoors and let the puppy eliminate before taking him into the house for the first time. From then on you were to return to that spot whenever the dog awoke in the morning, after each meal, after chewing, after extensive play periods. You were also instructed to watch for those signs that indicate the puppy has to eliminate. If you have been diligent about this, your puppy is half housebroken (or paper trained) already.

Most living creatures function rhythmically according to the settings of a biological clock. Therefore, it is no accident that various parts of the body function in the same way, at the same time, from day to day. The beating of the heart, breathing, eating, digesting, eliminating, etc., are all accomplished according to the dictates of the biological clock which is effected by periods of daylight, darkness, actions of the sun, the moon, and the earth.

In a young puppy or dog, the process of housebreaking is enhanced by setting the biological clock in terms of eating, digesting, and eliminating. By feeding your puppy a precise amount of food at a precise time every day and night, the biological clock dictates the rhythm of digestion and elimination in a set pattern that helps both dog and owner during the housebreaking period. The intriguing aspect is that you do not take the dog outside when you feel that his food has digested. You take him outside immediately after a feeding or a watering. The reason is simple. Every time the

dog ingests food or water, it triggers a reflex along the entire digestive tract and sets in motion the complicated mechanics of digestion which ends in fecal or urinary elimination. This activity can
be deliberately set in motion and patterned. By feeding the puppy
the same amount of food at the same times each day and by taking
him outside to eliminate immediately afterward, you are creating
a digestive pattern that will work for the rest of the dog's life.

See Chapter 6 ("Chow Time") for specific details on what and
when to feed your dog. For the purpose of housebreaking, the
puppy must be taken to his toilet spot the first thing in the morning and allowed to eliminate. Thereafter he is taken each and
every time he finishes eating and drinking, exercising, playing vigorously, or chewing. He should also be taken to his toilet location
just before bedding down for the night. The dog's digestive reflex
is stimulated after each of the aforementioned activities, and you
can take advantage of that by taking the puppy to the locale that
he now associates with elimination.

Accidents. Without a doubt, every puppy is going to soil in the
house during this time of housebreaking. It cannot be helped, and
one should be resigned to that reality. For that reason the little dog
must be confined in a small area or room when he is not being supervised. This will make it undesirable for him to eliminate because of his natural instinct to keep his nest clean. It will also limit
the areas that get soiled.

Eradicate the Scent. When the puppy has an accident in any area
of the house—even his own—the spot must be deodorized thoroughly so that he is not drawn back to the scent of his own urine or
fecal matter. It is important not to allow scent posts to be established anywhere indoors. There is a product that is superior to all
others for this purpose: *Nilodor.* This is a highly concentrated odor
neutralizer. Only a few drops placed directly over the soiled area,
a fast mopping, and the scent is eradicated. The dog's smelling
mechanism is much more efficient than we realize; he can smell
odors that humans can't. For that reason do not rely on plain soap
and water, ammonia, bleach, or detergents to rid the floor of the
dog's urine scent. You must use an odor neutralizer.

Punishment. Whenever the subject of housebreaking accidents
arises, many people immediately think in terms of punishments
for the puppy—as though that was going to help matters. Your objective is to *teach* the puppy to relieve himself outdoors, not to

take revenge on him for making a mess in your house. When toilet training children, nothing could be more destructive to a child's psyche than hitting him because he soiled his pants when he should have used the toilet. The child may, in a fashion, thereafter remember to use the toilet but he may develop constipation difficulties for the rest of his life. He may have digestive difficulties, and he may develop a neurotic love-hate relationship with the parent that hit him. Child psychologists keep emphasizing over and over again to new parents the importance of gentle, unpressured toilet training for children. It has lifelong ramifications. And don't forget: it takes as much as a year or two to successfully toilet train a human being. The dog owner is very fortunate in that the process, when done properly, takes between one and four weeks depending on the age, breed, and temperament of the dog along with other life-style variables.

Unless you actually see the dog eliminate in your house there is absolutely nothing that can be done about it as far as teaching housebreaking is concerned. Some dog experts recommend that you leave the spot where the mistake occurred, call the dog to you, praise him for coming, walk back to the dirtied area and holler no at the mess itself. Take the dog to his toilet area outdoors and give him the opportunity to relieve himself fully. Clean up and deodorize the scent in the house and be prepared for the next accident. There are now solvents available that have been formulated to remove urine stains from carpets and upholstery. They can be obtained from pet supply shops and some hardware stores.

In the event that the puppy begins to relieve himself in front of you or has all the signs that he is about to, scoop him up and run him out to his toilet location. Do not get hysterical. Do not become overbearing. Be efficient and expeditious. For many apartment dwellers a time-consuming elevator ride is involved. It is still beneficial to use the elevator and remove the dog from the apartment. Eventually the puppy will associate the trip outdoors with elimination.

Praise. In all phases of dog training—and that certainly applies to housebreaking—praise is your most valuable tool. Tell your puppy or dog what a wonderful creature he is each and every time he obeys your command or does what you expect him to do. This is positive reinforcement of the teaching process. Praise the dog every time you walk him to his toilet spot and he does his duty for you. The dog's praise must always be given when he obeys your commands. When you call the dog to you and he comes, lavish him with compliments and joyful acknowledgment of his good behavior. This is the foundation of all good obedience training for dogs. Contrary to past ideas, dog obedience can begin with a seven-or eight-week-old puppy. There are several excellent books on the subject and they can be found in the Suggested Reading list.

One last note on the subject of housebreaking has to do with the puppy's diet and state of health. If the dog has internal parasites such as roundworms, etc., and many puppies do, or if he is ill, he cannot possibly be housebroken at that time. A sick dog is not able to control his need to relieve himself. See your veterinarian and get the dog cured before proceeding with housebreaking.

It is also difficult to housebreak a dog that is not on a carefully thought out diet that is balanced and controlled. Table scraps, indiscriminate feeding of commercial or homemade food, too much food, mixing diets, too little food all contribute to upsetting a dog's stomach and causing random bouts of diarrhea. Obviously, it is impossible to housebreak a dog that is suffering from diarrhea. See Chapter 6 ("Chow Time") for a properly balanced diet or consult your veterinarian.

Paper Training. It is a good idea to decide as early as possible whether to have a housebroken dog or a paper-trained dog. With a few exceptions, the two methods used off and on tend to confuse the young dog. Paper training your dog is not very difficult. Everything written about housebreaking applies to paper training except that the puppy is taken to his newspapers rather than to his outdoor toilet area. The added methodology is to cover the floor of the entire toileting area with newspapers so that the animal cannot possibly make a mistake when he is taken there. On each new day one spreads out less paper so that by the end of a week the dog is only utilizing one portion of the room. This saves on newspaper and narrows down the toileting area to manageable proportions. As in housebreaking, the dog is guided to his papered area in a direct route and should be allowed access as often as possible. If convenient, it is best to have papers on the floor, ready at all times during the training period. If the dog has difficulty in the beginning of training and does not understand why you have placed him on the papers, save out one soiled sheet of paper each time he urinates. Place it on top of the fresh paper when you're ready to have the dog use the papers again. His own scent will attract him and stimulate his need to void.

What is confusing about going back and forth between indoor

use of newspapers and outdoor use of the street or yard is the surface material the dog feels under his paws when he eliminates. Remember, elimination has as much to do with marking territory as it does with the need to rid the body of waste material. This is especially critical with adult male dogs. Just like the leader of a wolf pack, the male dog marks the area he just defecated on with his paws. He makes a kind of signature with a digging or scratching gesture. This is a visualized mark that serves the same purpose as the scent post. If the outdoor toilet area is grassy or hardened asphalt, the dog's mind becomes accustomed to it as he digs his signature into it. Newspaper has an entirely different feel and may puzzle a dog if he is asked to eliminate on both kinds of surfaces from time to time. Saving one soiled sheet of paper and using it outdoors may assist a dog in making the transition from newspapers to outdoor surfaces if he is having difficulties in making the adjustment.

The advantages of paper training a dog, especially a smaller dog, are many. As a matter of convenience, one need only consider having to walk a dog in inclement weather, dangerous city areas, and heavy traffic areas to understand the positive side of paper training. It is also a great gesture for civic pride in knowing that you are not contributing to the unaesthetic problem of dog feces in city streets. Your dog remains cleaner and is less likely to become involved in serious dog fights. This is not to say that the dog should not be walked for exercise. However, a paper-trained dog will save all his wonderful treats for you, at home, on his newspapers.

THE PUPPY'S SAFETY

The first four months of a puppy's life are fraught with physical dangers lurking behind the smiles of every human being the dog comes in contact with. Like a young baby, a puppy is fragile and vulnerable to injuries of every description. Children are often accused of mishandling a small dog. Although it's true that young children, and many older ones, too, do not have the slightest idea about puppy handling, it is the entire family that needs information on this vital subject.

There are guidelines that every adult and child coming in contact with the puppy should follow. First and foremost, understand how frail his little body is and how little he can withstand rough treatment. Second, many new sensations can represent stark terror to a young pup. Third, if there is the slightest possibility that the dog might be dropped, he should not be picked up. This refers to children and elderly persons.

Here are some cautions that must be observed if your dog is going to survive his infancy and juvenile phases of life. There is nothing more important for a puppy than eating and sleeping. A dog does all of his growing (or most of it) in his first year, and that requires his ability to eat in peace so that he can digest his food and metabolize it. This is hardly possible if he is disturbed while eating or if he is played with immediately before or after his meal. Never, never disturb the puppy when he is sleeping. His rest is of great importance, and he must get all that his body dictates. When a puppy sleeps, it's because he must.

Pride goeth before a fall. Puppies in high places fall fast and hard.

Avoid placing the dog on high places such as chairs, tables, beds, or counter tops. If he falls, he just might break a bone, dislocate a joint, or tear a muscle. Affect no loud noises designed to get a rise out of the dog. Because of a puppy's need to learn pack behavior, he is going to behave pretty much like those around him. If you are nervous and excitable, that's how he is going to get. Do not play rough with him. Do not play for extended periods of time. This is the main charge against children. A child's endurance and stamina are far greater than those of a small dog. Teasing a puppy is a sure way of losing his confidence. A mentally healthy dog is one that feels positive about his abilities. If you tease him into thinking he can have something and then don't deliver, you are undermining the dog's confidence in himself and in you.

Learn how to handle a young puppy and then teach everyone else how to do it. It is really very easy. Place one hand under the dog's chest and the other under his rump and hind legs. This gives you a firm grip and makes it difficult to drop him. Please instruct everyone who plays with the dog never to grab him by any single leg or combinations of the four. The puppy's legs are frail, and permanent damage can be done by violating this rule. Forget the classic image of a puppy being held by the scruff of his neck. That's out. It's humiliating and is the puppy's least favorite way of being held.

There are two other cautions. Do not play running games with the puppy if the floor has a very slippery surface such as polished hardwood or waxed linoleum. The little dog can easily slip and pull a tendon or worse. Use an area rug on the slippery surface to prevent injury. Last, there is nothing more natural than dogs and children (see Chapter 3, "Dogs and Children"). But a dog is usually at such a great disadvantage because of the disparity in size that the child must be supervised until he or she has learned how to be gentle and kind to the puppy. Do not leave a puppy alone with a young child.

The First Year

These first twelve months with your dog can very well be the happiest days of your life. It is a time when you will be the envy of those who know you. Do not be misled; there is much ahead that will be unpleasant and inconvenient. But the sheer joy of watching and helping a puppy grow into a mature dog and allowing him to

Incorrect way to hold a small puppy.

Correct way to hold a small puppy.

become part of your life is surpassed only by human parenthood. It is one of the great pleasures life has to offer.

WEANING TO THREE MONTHS

This time in a puppy's life is referred to as the "critical period of socialization" by Scott and Fuller as a result of their important research at the Roscoe B. Jackson Memorial Laboratory in Bar Harbor, Maine. The point to understanding this time in the puppy's life is to be able to produce a well-balanced dog that will adjust easily to humans and dogs. They contend that the time to develop a close human/dog relationship is between the third and twelfth week of the puppy's life. At this period they suggest that the dog be removed daily from the litter and brought into contact with human beings. Puppies three weeks and older respond favorably to handling and cuddling several times a day by humans. This is the process of socialization and enables the dog to realize his maximum potential as a domestic house pet and companion.

The puppy must remain with its litter until the eighth week if it is going to adjust easily to other dogs during its lifetime. If the puppy remains with the litter past twelve weeks of age, it will be well adjusted to the society of dogs but may be timid and insecure in the presence of human beings. This is not to suggest that most dogs, no matter when they've been introduced to humans, cannot enjoy a happy existence as a companion. But a dog that is removed from its litter between the sixth and eighth week and placed in the hands of a human protector will be more secure, confident, well adjusted with humans and dogs, and more adaptable to training and other experiences encountered with human beings. In *Dog Behavior: The Genetic Basis,* Scott and Fuller profoundly comment, "The young puppy from eight to twelve weeks is a highly malleable and adaptable animal, and this is the time to lay the foundation for its future life work. Dogs left in a kennel until four months of age or older are frequently poorly adapted to any other life."

During these early weeks in your puppy's life your job is simply to feed him, protect him from harm, handle him several times a day, and, in a word, love him. Have the dog examined by your veterinarian and discuss the puppy's inoculations. (See Chapter 8, "In Sickness and in Health.") Begin the little dog's housebreaking or paper training. You may even introduce the fundamentals of simple obedience training. Read a good book on the subject or obtain the services of a professional dog trainer. Pay careful atten-

How to create a good dog. Socialize the puppy between three and twelve weeks. *Hold me, touch me* sessions, several times a day, is how it's done.

tion to the nutritional needs of the puppy. (See Chapter 6, "Chow Time.")

THREE TO FIVE MONTHS

This is one of the most delightful times to enjoy a puppy. At this age the dog is fully aware of himself and his environment. He wants to explore, examine, test, and get up your nose if he can. His desire to play is very great as is his curiosity about you and his human family. You are the dog's environment. Everything that he will be is determined by how you behave toward him. This is exactly the period when the closest ties are made and the deepest relationships between dogs and humans are developed. If you are sensitive, kind, soft-spoken, and loving, that is how your dog will be. However, never forget that *you* are the leader of his pack.

Medically speaking, this is the period to watch out for teething pain and symptoms of internal parasites. (See Chapter 8, "In Sickness and in Health.") If you have been living with the dog for more than a month, he should be housebroken or paper trained by now. Basic obedience as a way of life is just around the corner, and the puppy should be partially trained, at the very least. This is especially true for off-leash training.

On the negative side, be cautious about a puppy's desire to chew, especially when left to his own devices. From this time until the end of the first year, a young dog is capable of chewing up expensive furniture, household appliances, and even baseboards when left alone or unsupervised. Destructive chewing is caused by one or more of the following reasons: (1) allowed and encouraged to chew fingers and objects as a small puppy because it seemed cute; (2) teething pain; (3) boredom; (4) insufficient nutrition; (5) frustration born out of anxiety. If your dog begins to chew objects, the answer is *not* to leave him alone, confined in an extremely small area. This is the sort of thing that causes anxiety and then frustration. Think the problem through and determine why the dog is chewing; then make the appropriate changes in the dog's environment. Many dog owners are unaware that a ringing telephone may be scaring the wits out of their dogs when they are left alone. If your dog is barking excessively or chewing, test for telephone fright. If this is the case, the solution is at your fingertips. Take the phone off the hook while you're out, turn the bell volume down, or place the instrument under a thick blanket to muffle the sound. This is the methodology for solving most of your dog's emotional problems. Only the most skilled authorities can turn a dog's behavior around. But a dog owner can solve many problems by simply adjusting the dog's environment. Do not punish the dog for his behavior. It does no good.

FIVE TO SEVEN MONTHS

You can no longer refer to your dog as a little puppy anymore. He is now in his juvenile stage and fast moving toward adulthood. Of course, many dogs of this age are still teething and experiencing the painful discomfort of losing their milk teeth and breaking through with permanent ones.

If your dog is still not housebroken, see your veterinarian and have the dog examined. If your dog is healthy, seek professional help from a dog trainer.

This is a deceptive time for the novice dog owner living in the city and keeping an indoor dog. Here you have a dog that appears to be older than a puppy and almost fully grown. It is a mistake to treat a dog of this age as you would an adult. His body is still in a state of growth, perhaps its greatest stage of physical development. The dog's coat is not fully grown in yet, and he may not be fully protected from drafts, chills, and inclement weather. If it is winter, provide him with a warm sweater for going outdoors. Dry the dog well if he gets wet. You may not have to be this cautious if your dog's coat is long and full. In some breeds, the fur is fully developed at an early age. This is true of Siberian huskies, Alaskan malamutes, Samoyeds, and similar breeds. If it is summer, keep the dog cool by *not* clipping his long-haired coat; it acts as insulation.

The outdoor dog who usually resides in rural areas need not wear a winter sweater or be dried off when wet. If the dog is outdoors most of the time, even his puppy coat will suffice. Of course, you must judge how long a dog should stay outdoors on very cold days.

At this age, give serious consideration to grooming and personal hygiene. It will be helpful to consult a grooming book on your specific breed. (See Chapter 8, "In Sickness and in Health.") In this chapter you will find basic grooming information as it applies to good hygiene.

SEVEN TO TWELVE MONTHS

These may be referred to as the frisky months because at no other time will your dog be as playful, as mischievous, as amusing, or as irritating (depending on your point of view) as he is at this age. At the end of the first year most breeds are approaching their full height and weight and are what they will be for the rest of their lives, both mentally and physically. Your dog's curiosity and audacity will be at full peak and (if you have behaved properly) he will be fully confident of his place in the family structure. It is hoped that his subordinate position has been well established, and he is happy with that arrangement.

The dog's milk teeth have all been replaced by the permanent ones, and his stomach is large enough to accept two full meals a day unless he is on a self-feeding program. This is the period to have a female spayed or a male castrated if that has been your intention from the beginning.

In many cities, six months is the age by which the law requires the dog to be licensed. According to American Kennel Club regulations, breeding is out of the question until the dam is past eight months and the sire is past seven months, but not past twelve years. A female goes into her first heat sometime between the sixth and twelfth month depending on the breed and the individual dog. Male dogs are capable of mating during the same age range.

The one-year-old. An adult dog with a mischievous sense of humor. He bears watching.

By the twelfth month, a dog is definitely an adult by any standard (with the exception of some large breeds). Of course he still has many adolescent traits that will fade away like a child's old toys. The dog is still capable of creating mischief and must be firmly dealt with if and when he tries to take the dominant position in the household. Although your dog is now a fully accepted member of the family and sometimes behaves like a human being, he must not be treated like a human being unless he is being used for some human substitute purpose. In that case, nothing written here will affect that one way or another. How and why some humans relate to their dogs is a private matter and is no one's business providing the dog is not being abused or treated in an inhumane manner. But of course, dear reader, it is understood that you are a good and kindly dog owner in pursuit of a decade and a half of civilization's great dog-human equation. Good hunting!

3. Dogs and Children

Kids and canines are nature's music in simple harmony. The image of Tom Sawyer walking a picket fence for Becky Thatcher while a devoted dog trails behind is a favorite daydream about children and their four-legged companions. It's one of straw hats, freckled faces, and out on the raft with Huck and Jim. However, like most fantasies, no matter how nourishing, it never matches up with reality. Without information, neither parent, child, nor dog can come together in happy counterpoint. A toddler with a mouth full of dog is just as unacceptable as a dog with a mouth full of toddler. We are not always at one with nature and sometimes need a little help from a friend. Dogs and children together must be guided with love, intelligence, sensitivity, and a keen sense of justice. What is correct for both child *and* dog is crucial.

The Bond

Dogs and children enjoying each other only seems like magic. One might take a purely clinical view and suggest that because of a child's limited experience and young intelligence, he and the dog share a mutual perception of the world. Or, one might say that children and young dogs are in a constant state of learning, which is manifested by the activity of play. Another idea has to do with pack behavior on the part of the dog and socializing behavior on the part of the child. Both are trying to establish their positions in society as well as reinforce those positions. While the child attempts to understand his environment, the dog instinctively accepts it. This may be the main difference between the two. Luckily, the child's curiosity and the dog's perception of nature fit hand-in-glove and form a profitable partnership.

The bond that forms between a dog and a child is a firm, hardened linkage that can only be broken with the consequences of emotional pain. Child-dog relationships are extremely durable. A kid bites his dog's tail and the dog knocks the kid down and

The bond between children and dogs is a tender one but stronger than welded chain.

steps on his face. They may both end up wailing, but that is really between the two of them. By no means does that indicate a divorce is in order. They will work it out quickly. Nothing short of violence can come between a child and a dog. They seek each other out and quickly become good friends as long as circumstances will allow. It is in the understanding of this bond between children and their dogs that parents can help shape a successful relationship between the two. In doing so they will be giving their children and their pets a great gift: each other. How to do that and what the dog and child derive from it is what this chapter is all about.

Responsibility

There are many different circumstances bringing together children and pet animals. The most common one is when the child asks for it. Sometimes they beg and plead. Many parents in this situation agree to keeping a dog with the condition that the child must assume full responsibility for the animal. The child always agrees. Whether this is right or wrong, good or bad, practical or otherwise, is a matter of opinion. Two of this country's most eminent child psychologists were approached on the subject. Their responses were varied and altogether fascinating. However, every parent is going to make a personal, subjective decision no matter who says what. Becoming acquainted with the issues and various approaches can be helpful to formulating that subjective decision.

Dr. Lee Salk, professor of psychology and pediatrics, Cornell University Medical College, is the author of *What Every Child Would Like His Parents to Know* and *Preparing for Parenthood.* On the subject of a child's responsibilities for the care of a dog he states:

A dog is a living thing that requires care. It has feelings and a certain quality of individuality. I think it's fair for parents to require a child to assume responsibility not only for the physical care of the animal but also for providing it with comfort, security, and protection. Domesticated animals taken away from their natural habitat sometimes lose the quality of their very primitive kind of defenses.

I think it's an opportunity for a parent to give a child a sense of responsibility about something. A dog needs to be cared for, fed, walked, and attended to. There is an inherent reward, the recognition that the animal shows to the child which gives the child a sense of self-esteem and a feeling of importance. There is nothing more gratifying for a child than coming home and finding a dog jumping with great glee and happiness. I would say that in exchange for that the child whose pet it is has to assume the kind of responsibility anyone has to assume for any other living thing. In some ways you can interpret this as being preparation for parenthood.

I never put things in terms of timetables. When an infant is an infant you can't expect it to care for a dog. In fact the dog's reaction is more one of protecting the child. They almost look upon the child as their own ward. There comes a point when the animal is dependent upon the child (for example) to open doors and get from one place to another. A lot of that depends on the development of the child, but I can't say that there is any special age when this takes place. There are a lot of things in life that you may enjoy. But unless you are prepared for the commitment, then you may just have to forego the pleasure.

Expressing another point of view is Dr. Fitzhugh Dodson, the renowned psychologist and author of *How to Parent, How to Father,* and *The You That Could Be.* Dr. Dodson has practiced both as a psychologist and educator for over twenty-five years and is the founder of the famous LaPrimera Preschool. Here are his views on the subject:

> A child cannot assume the full responsibility for a dog. I think this is a most unfortunate thing when parents assume that a child is going to take over much more responsibility than he or she can, in effect, take over. The general model that I would suggest for parents and children and dogs is for the parents to assume the responsibility for feeding the dog, training, housebreaking, exercise, etc. and encourage the child to witness the parent in action. Often when the child witnesses the parents in action, the child then wants to help. It's just like painting a house. This usually works much better than asking the child to do it. Even if the child does not volunteer to help in any of these activities, he or she will be learning something from watching the parents do these things in an intelligent manner.
>
> The only thing, I would say, that the child can do on his own, in a completely unrestrained way, is to play with the dog. Then it will depend upon the individual child and the age of the child as to what things he wants to do with the dog. Some children will be fascinated by the idea of training the dog while other children might want to just romp and play. It's a matter of individuality. If the parents take the lead in doing all these things, they will very quickly find out how much of it interests the child and the kind of things the child wants to help the parents do.
>
> For most children, dogs make the best pet for various reasons. Dogs are not as independent as cats. Dogs are more responsive to both adults and children. They become the closest companions that children can have. Most children have times when they want a pet who will never let them down, will not be mean, will not be competitive, and will be there to be enjoyed for emotional companionship. For this a dog is ideal.

It is only reasonable and fair that the child who asked for a dog be required to take care of it more than the child who has had the dog thrust upon him as a gift. When requesting a dog, few children realize the extent of the effort involved in its care. As time passes, many children become more and more negligent of their dog's needs. A parent's options in this situation are (1) to assume full responsibility themselves; (2) to dispose of the dog (in a humane

Good playmates work their differences out. It is a private affair.

manner, such as finding a new home); (3) or to make greater demands on the child. A sensible approach would be to taper the child into the responsibility by gradually introducing the various activities on a one-at-a-time basis. Sooner or later, every child is given some household chores. One or more dog-care chores in addition is not unreasonable and may help strengthen the relationship between dog and child. In addition, it may afford the child a sense of satisfaction and ego gratification. Praise and slight rewards for a job well done reinforce the child's sense of pride in taking care of the dog.

For the sake of both dog and child, parental guidance and supervision are absolutely necessary when it comes to dog care. No matter how much or how little responsibility falls to the child he or she must be taught what to do. It is definitely a parent's responsibility to instruct and supervise. One way or another parents are going to be immersed in dog care.

When there is more than one child, responsibility for the dog's needs can be shared. Sometimes a puppy is given to only one of several children in a family. Whether this is good or bad depends on the circumstances. Dr. Salk says:

I can imagine a configuration where one child just doesn't like dogs and the other loves them. Under those circumstances I would say I cannot see any harm [in giving a dog to one child]. If you have two children who absolutely love dogs, who both want them, and you give the dog to only one, obviously that's unfair. It is feasible to give one dog to two or three children. Then it becomes a member of the family. When you have a little baby, you don't divide the baby for one member of the family and not the rest. A dog should really be a family responsibility rather than an individual possession. Incidentally, anybody who plans to give a child a pet ought to consult in detail with the parents of that child before doing so. It could be a disaster any other way. It's a big responsibility and should not be looked upon like bringing a box of candy to someone.

The highly unique qualities of individual human beings and the many variables of life-styles and environments render formulas for dog-care instruction less than perfect. However, how-to formulas have their usefulness to the totally inexperienced, dog-owning parent or to those who are befuddled by it all. The following is a schedule for children's dog-care responsibilities. It must be viewed as a guideline only and not taken as the last word on the subject. Remain flexible and do what is possible. Some children will be able to take on more responsibility and some less than what is indicated in the schedule. It is best to follow the dictates of the child in this respect. The schedule has been developed so that the parent might have a general idea of which dog-care responsibilities children can assume at a given age.

Schedule for Children's Dog-care Responsibilities

INFANCY

From first breath to eight months, it would seem that there is nothing that a baby can do for a dog. If anything, the dog does much more for the baby in terms of protection and adding another dimension of awareness. The presence and availability of a dog for an infant offers a unique opportunity for sensory stimulation of sight, sound, touch, and smell. Sensory and intellectual stimulation during infancy play a major role in a child's ability to realize potential intelligence. So much for what the dog can do for the infant.

Believe it or not, there is much the infant can do for the dog. Next to new fathers, there are no creatures more insecure than dogs with new babies. Because dogs instinctively require an organized social structure (pack behavior), the introduction of an infant is upsetting and disruptive to the pack order. If the dog is given the opportunity to meet the baby and the baby is encouraged to relate to the dog, it can be valuable for both. Naturally, great care and caution are required. Being given the chance to sniff and examine an infant allows the dog to claim it as a member of the pack and, therefore, feel at ease about its presence. Once a dog understands that its position in the pack (family) is unchallenged, it can accept a new arrival without those negative behaviorisms that dog owners refer to as "jealousy." Therefore, an infant can be helpful in easing a dog's anxieties simply by being introduced. This refers only to normal house dogs that are not overly neurotic about their human family. A gradual and cautious introduction is advised. This is a matter of personal judgment.

Another thing a baby can do for a dog is something that has longrange effects. If a young baby is carefully encouraged and taught to gently pet a dog and be sensitive toward it, that baby will probably develop a love of animals all its life. A child taught to relate to animals in a healthy sense is usually one who can comfortably relate to most human beings. A child who loves and respects animals is one who loves and respects life, and that has got to be good for any dog.

TODDLERHOOD

Roughly, this period lasts from nine months to three years. So much is happening in a child's development during these months that one would hardly think dog-care responsibilities are appropriate. Not true. There are some dog-connected activities that provide an ideal outlet for a toddler's boundless curiosity and desire to discover the world. There are no dog chores for a child of this age that can be competently achieved without a parent's assistance. But the rewards for allowing the toddler to participate in the family dog's activities are very great. Self-sufficiency, creative play, a sense of individuality, feelings of competency, being a part of the world are just some of the benefits derived by a toddler who helps her parents or brothers and sisters take care of their dog.

When a toddler is past eighteen months, she is able to help empty the grocery bag and carry the dog's food from the bag to the table. The same applies to the shelf on which it's stored. The simple act of handing you the can or box of dog food may not seem like much, but is certain to make her feel truly accomplished.

At two years old a child can help you with other tasks connected with the dog. For example, when you wash the dog's food and water bowls, your assistant can attempt to dry them (if you show him how). It would be a good idea to check the work and point out the moisture he didn't get. Once the bowls are completely dry, both you and the toddler can pour or spoon the dog food and water into them. Caution: Do not allow a toddler to hand the food to the dog or get very close to the feeding area on the floor. Many dogs misinterpret the child's presence at their food and take defensive action. To avoid getting bitten, the child should never get too close to the dog while he is feeding. This may upset the dog and make him snap, growl, or bite. It can be dangerous.

A two-year-old can also help a parent tidy up the dog's area, be it a kennel, a doghouse, or a corner of the kitchen with a blanket on the floor. Minor tasks involving a cleaning cloth or whiskbroom are ideal. You might even give him a turn with the mop. At this age many children love to help out with chores as a way of testing their competency by imitating their parents. It is a rare opportunity to develop in the child the pleasure and gratification of responsibility.

From nine months to three years, children understand so much more than adults realize. This may be because of their limited use of speech. Their powers of comprehension far exceed their desire or ability to use language actively. If you speak slowly and simply, at eye level, a toddler will understand what it is you want him to do. Once the request is made, it is up to the parent to take the child by the hand and begin the assignment. Remember, the child is only assisting you and must be instructed and supervised. Once the task has been completed (or seems so to the child), inspect the work and offer your praise and congratulations. Tell the dog what a good job your little girl or boy has done and solicit some enthusiasm from the pet. Dogs get excited when their owners get excited. They quickly perceive human emotions and get caught up in them. It is therefore not difficult to make the dog appear to praise your toddler for a job well done.

THREE TO FIVE

Children of this age group may help prepare their dog's meals (although they should not feed the animal directly). They may continue to help clean the dog's utensils, equipment (leashes and collars, etc.), dog's areas, and house areas where the dog has shed fur or knocked things over. During this period most children develop a greater attention span and are capable of more difficult tasks. They are more self-confident and able to exercise greater patience. Language has become fluid and understandable. Children between three and five can take a more dominant position over the dog. This dominance is highly desirable because of the dog's difficulty later in accepting status changes in members of his pack (family).

Three-to five-year-old children stand well above eye level of a medium-sized dog. This is not necessarily threatening to the dog providing the child's behavior does not indicate a challenge to his position of dominance. Let us not forget that for three years (one-sixth of the average dog's lifetime) the family pet has viewed the young child from infancy to toddlerhood as a puppy or subordinate member of the pack. If the dog has always taken a leader's position in the family, then there may be trouble ahead for a growing child. Even a dog that has been subordinate to other members of the family may feel threatened by the transition of a child's size and behavior as the years pass. In a wolf pack, the alpha wolf (leader) may be forced to step down from his dominant position by a younger and stronger male. But, as one can imagine, it does not happen without a physical confrontation.

Although it has not been ascertained scientifically, it is safe to assume that there is a time in the family dog's life when he accepts the fluctuations of pack structure and resigns himself to the idea that there is one less subordinate member in his family. Prior to acceptance, there may be a defensive-aggressive action resulting in a young child's getting bitten. There is no reason why parents cannot prevent this type of incident if they intelligently shape the relationship between dog and child. It is during this period of childhood (three to five) that the preventive measures can be taken.

A child in this age range is still learning from parental example. Therefore his parents must relate to the dog in a loving but firm tone of voice when giving commands and instructions. The child can be guided to relate in the same manner. Everything must be done to encourage the child to take a leadership position in relationship to the dog, but it must be done gently and as smoothly as possible. If the dog is taken out for a walk, a four-or five-year-old can accompany his parent and even hold the leash for a moment or two. Anything that places the child in a dominant position over the dog is desirable providing the parent is there to prevent the dog from rebelling. Teach your five-year-old how to hook the leash to the dog's collar before going outdoors. Make that one of his responsibilities, but never without your presence. If the dog has been obedience trained, start teaching your child how to execute the various commands. Remember: a three-to five-year-old is too frail in demeanor and physical presence to truly dominate the average adult dog.

A loving but dominant attitude toward puppies helps shape the ideal relationship between children and dogs.

Take things slowly without expecting too much of the child or the dog. This is merely the beginning of a slow transition in their relationship. It is very encouraging to note that most dogs adore their young family members once they are able to spend time together without adult supervision. That comes later. But a dog and an older child hanging out together is a joyous sight. This is the time to prepare for that time.

SIX TO TEN

There seems to be general agreement among child experts that the age of six is a difficult one for many children. According to Dr. Dodson, "Six is an age of [emotional] extremes. A confusing mixture of baby and child, parents often find him quite difficult to handle."

This is a time when a child is breaking away from total dependency on his home and parents and is forcing himself to explore the world outside. It is also the time when most children begin formal schooling, which can be an emotional drain. It is probably not a good time to make very many demands in regard to dog care. A six-year-old can be obstinate, easily distracted, and insistent on doing things his own way (whether right or wrong). However, his need for a dog's love may be greater than ever. It is probably best to allow a child of six to accept whatever responsibilities he can handle for his dog and not push things too far. For the sake of the dog's needs, other members of the family should assume full responsibility for the animal's care until this difficult period is over.

Seven to ten is quite another matter when it comes to dog care. At this age there are few chores connected with a dog that a child cannot accomplish. Still, you must supervise and, at times, assist in various activities such as grooming procedures, baths, medical treatment. A young child in this age range should not have to take a pet to the veterinarian's office unescorted. It's a good idea for a young dog owner to share that responsibility with a parent. It is a question of the seriousness of the dog's illness in relationship to the degree of sensitivity of the child to such situations. If a dog is extremely sick or near death, it may be a good idea to allow the child to witness those events and procedures leading to euthanasia or natural death. Bearing witness to the truth is a good rule to live by and applies to the unhappy aspects of life as well as any other. It is, of course, a matter of parental discretion.

An eight-, nine-, or ten-year-old is mature enough and strong enough to walk the average dog alone and should be given that responsibility. This may not be true in certain urban areas and certainly does not apply to long walks that turn into hiking excursions. Short walks close to home are an excellent chore for the young dog owner. A child of these years must be instructed about desirable outdoor toilet areas for the dog. Children are often oblivious to the amenities of being a good neighbor and might allow their dogs to relieve themselves on lawns, sidewalks, or building walls. This must be discouraged.

An older dog needs time and patience when asked to accept a five-year-old as a dominant member of the family. Learning to walk the dog on a leash is the best way for a child to take a leadership position over the dog.

Children between the ages of six and ten may now participate in feeding the family pet but must still exercise caution with dogs that are extremely territorial. If this type of dog is used to being fed by the adults of the household, it may become snappish if the food is handled by a younger member of the pack (family). In the natural state the entire wolf pack participates in the hunt for food. But once the kill is made, the dominant members of the pack eat first while the subordinate members wait their turn and take what's left. This is especially true in the winter, when game is scarce. Unless the family dog has come to accept a child as a dominant figure, it is going to be uneasy about that child being near its food. It takes a while for the dog to understand that the child is not taking—but rather giving—the food. You must remain present as the child feeds the dog. Ideally, both parent and child together should position the food in its proper place. This helps the dog to fully accept the child's shift in status from subordinate to dominant pack member.

Another responsibility for children of this age is the dog's need for exercise, which does not mean just walking the dog. Most walks are for toilet purposes, anyway. There is probably no greater exercise for a dog than a good romping play period with children. Every house or apartment offers its own set of physical limitations on this kind of play. But there is always room enough for some degree of physical play between a child and a dog, and it is such a desirable activity that it is well worth the noise and inconvenience. Here is a responsibility that every child will enjoy and benefit from at the same time. Both dog and child are not only exercised but enjoy the development of strong bonds of friendship as they interact. They will play and then they will relax and enjoy each other's company in a way that few adults can experience. A ball, a stick, a bone, or a cardboard box are almost all that is needed for this purpose. Of course the child must be guided so that the dog is not hurt or overstimulated. Some dogs really want to call it quits but the child continues, unaware of the animal's exhaustion or oncoming irritability. This problem is easily solved by parents setting a time limit on the play-exercise period and also by confining it to one room.

Eleven and Twelve

This stage of childhood is referred to as preadolescence. Many physical and mental developments are taking place at the same time and they are often in collision with one another such as the

When the world closes in, an eleven-year-old and his dog can cling to each other. Each depends on the other.

normal dependencies of any child clashing with the great need to be independent. Large, overpowering emotions can erupt from eleven- and twelve-year-olds. Sometimes those feelings are not fully expressed but just seething under the surface. Emotions range from one extreme to another, and one can see joy and despair, elation and dejection from day to day, or sometimes from hour to hour. Children of this age are often moody, suspicious, or irritable. Because this is in part a difficult period for adult and child alike, the pleasures of dog ownership can be especially beneficial. Being totally responsible for the needs and desires of a dog offers the immeasurable reward of self-confidence and an understanding of your child's competence. With the exception of the dog's medical needs (veterinary examinations, home-nursing procedures, and home diagnoses) and, to some extent, obedience training, an eleven- or twelve-year-old child can assume all responsibilities for a dog.

The thirteen-year-old is more than capable of teaching dog obedience commands once he understands them himself.

The right dog with the right child can offer the ideal private relationship that does not have to be shared. With luck and parental skill, an eleven- or twelve-year-old might just find in a dog the middle ground between emotional turmoil and family love. It is important here to consider the well-being of the dog. Therefore it must be made clear that with the comfort the dog brings must also come a dedication to its care. If the child cannot enter into such an agreement, it is best for all concerned to forgo the relationship and allow the animal to become the family pet. However, it is difficult to imagine a dog not being able to burrow beneath the barriers of preadolescence and relate lovingly to any child.

THIRTEEN TO FIFTEEN

Probably the most important liberty for the early teenage child is the freedom of choice. Finding out what he prefers and letting him make his own decisions in regard to dog ownership is essential. Allow for the inconsistencies between declarations of independence and quiet requests for money and other kinds of assistance. Once your teenager takes on the burden of dog care, don't be surprised if a little neglect or abdication of some responsibilities creep in along the edges. Discussions and adjustments of dog-care responsibilities will probably be in order. The many benefits of a relationship between a human and a dog have all been stated before and apply to a greater degree with a teenager.

A girl or a boy between thirteen and fifteen years old can take on any and all aspects of dog care providing he or she understands that the dog's very life is in his or her hands. Probably the most worthwhile and rewarding responsibility for a child in this age range is teaching the dog basic obedience. There is much to be learned through this activity by dog and child. With the help of a competent dog obedience book or classroom instruction, both dog and child learn to bring order from confusion and chaos. For the dog there is the security of affirming his position in the family pack order. For the child, dog obedience offers lessons in leadership, self-discipline, and responsibility.

The Fear of Dogs

Children of every age sooner or later express fear or terror. Very often the object of the fear has no basis in reality or no apparent reason. But fear and terror are no less real to the toddler or somewhat older child. Child psychologists believe that these emotions are to be respected and dealt with by the parents. Among the most common childhood fears is the fear of dogs. It is not unusual for a child to suddenly and unexplainably fear dogs (even while growing up with one at home). Like fear of darkness or ferocious monsters under the bed, the fear of dogs is a short-lived fright but one that is often rooted in a kernel of justified emotion. It is possible that the appearance of a strange dog was overpowering; perhaps an attempted nip or showing of teeth set in motion a series of nightmarish fantasies. Influences from television or motion pictures may be at the heart of the matter. One rarely gets to know for certain what creates a specific fear in a small child. Therefore it is more productive for parents to help the child cope with the fear rather than attempt to hunt it down.

It must be stated from the outset that if a child appears to manifest more than the ordinary expression of various fears, professional help should be sought. Psychologists, pediatricians, and child health counselors are in a better position to discern stark terror, hysteria, and extreme emotional disturbance from the temporary fears that arise in the lives of all children. The fear of dogs most often falls in the category of temporary fears.

When your child expresses a fear of dogs, accept the fact that the fear is real and then offer comfort and protection. Shaming, teasing, or pretending that the child is not really frightened will only prolong the irrational emotions, in some cases for a lifetime. It is best to show your child that you will assume the full responsibility for his or her safety and will not allow any dog (or feared monsters) to get him. Be gentle and believing so that your child will be reassured that he is safe and in protective custody. When an adult is in control of the situation, the child begins to loosen up and let go of the terrible emotion.

If we are dealing with a child who has never lived with a dog and is terrified by the sight of them, it is best not to thrust him into the company of dogs. Go slowly, therapeutically, with the idea of stripping away the child's fear by demonstrating that dogs are not as dangerous as he thought they were. The parent may start with children's picture books on the subject or magazine articles with photographs of dogs that make wonderful pets and friends. Toddlers and small children might even be given a stuffed toy dog to be used as a *huggy*. Just about anything will serve that depicts dogs as friendly animals that want and give love. The child that has eased up in his fear of dogs is ready for a more direct approach, such as being introduced to a puppy. He may even want to have a puppy of his own, and that's good.

Fear of dogs in children can manifest itself in several ways. Some children accept small dogs but not large ones. Some children do not fear walking up to a dog but are terrified if the dog walks up to them. Some dogs are viewed without fear from a distance but not close up. Sometimes the dog is not so terrifying if the adult is holding the child. It is useful to know the exact dimensions of the child's fear and respect them. It is useless to consider a child's fear of dogs as cowardly, and it is counterproductive to force the situation. You can only gently, slowly, and respectfully guide a child through the maze of his own fear.

Fear of Children

It is seldom that one comes upon a dog that slinks away in fear when in the presence of a child, but it does happen. The reasons for this behavior are obvious. If a dog's early experiences with a child are negative, reminiscent of pain and other abuses, then that dog is going to be difficult to convince that all children aren't malevolent. Dogs and children occasionally need to be protected from one another just as some children need protection from other children. The main qualities that dogs and children share, apart from freely expressed emotions, are lack of restraint and poor judgment. It is very rare that a dog or a child behaves sadistically or with extreme anger. If a child frequently behaves in this manner, medical attention may be required. If a dog behaves in a ferocious manner, then get professional help from a trainer or handler. The alternative is to rid yourself of such an animal before someone is hurt seriously.

To best prevent fear of children in dogs, we must teach youngsters of all ages how to behave properly with a dog. Parents can set up guidelines of behavior for children to follow when they relate to the family pet or with strange dogs. Although we are concerned with the well-being of the dog, there is a question of safety for the child. Children are often attacked or bitten by dogs that were frightened by childlike, unrestrained behavior.

How to Behave with the Family Pet

From infancy to adolescence, it is never a waste of time to use the word "gentle" in a gentle tone of voice to illustrate to a child how to relate to any pet animal. One can even demonstrate how to pet and stroke a dog (in a gentle manner, of course).

Children must use the dog's name in a friendly tone of voice and never shout or yell or scream at the animal. Any form of physical abuse is out. The dog must never be hit or yanked or dragged. Do not allow a child to pull the dog by a limb, by the head, or by the tail. Aside from the possibility of the child's getting bitten, the dog may be seriously injured. It is helpful for parents to understand that all children accumulate a certain amount of aggression or hostility and attempt to cover it up by hugging the dog too tightly. It can be anger disguised as a desire to be affectionate with the dog. This can be avoided along with the deceptive practice of accidentally dropping the animal by forbidding the child to lift the dog.

One of the most distressing activities for a dog is being chased around the house by a small child when all the dog wants is to be allowed to rest. It may seem amusing, but there are serious consequences in relation to the dog's emotional balance. It is possible to create a neurotic, aggressive, shy, or terror-ridden animal from a gentle creature who started out as a happy pet. The inevitable outcome of a child's chasing a dog around the house is for the dog to

get cornered. One of the primary needs of all animals—dogs especially—is an avenue of escape. If it is denied, even a field mouse
will stand on its hind legs and start fighting back. Be warned.

One technique for preventing this situation is to establish a play
period every day. Make it no longer than half an hour at a time.
Confine both child and dog to a room where excessive running
and chasing are impossible. Small children and puppies should
both be seated on the floor. Do not leave very small children alone
in a room with a dog. Create and guide the play with games described in the next section. If a toddler physically abuses a dog, it
does no good to holler or punish the offender. Either distract the
child or start a positive play action between the two, such as rolling
a ball on the floor. The keynote should be to create a happy,
healthy interaction between dog and child. Romping together
should be confined to the play period only. After playtime, allow
the dog to drink water, go to his toilet area, and take a nap.

It is possible to guide the child into a responsible, leadership
position with the dog. As stated previously this will help avoid future stress for the animal as the child grows. Parents can create the
relationship by teaching the child to execute some simple obedience commands and practicing walking the dog indoors hooked to
his leash and collar. *If the child is very young, they must never be left
alone in a room together.* This is crucial!

The best dog-child relationships develop when the intelligent
parent takes into consideration the individual dog's temperament
when conducting play periods. The dog may be nervous, shy, stubborn, sedate, aggressive, or normally playful. The activities between a dog and a child must take these factors into consideration
in order to avoid as much friction as possible. Naturally, a shy or
sedate dog is going to want to be less active than a playful one, and
a nervous dog is going to require gentler handling than a stubborn
one.

The best objective for a parent is to teach the child that *a dog is
an object of love and will be a devoted friend if treated properly*. All
activities and behavior involving the dog should reinforce this
idea. It will not take very long for the child to accept it and enjoy
the rewards of humane attitudes and behavior.

How to Behave with Strange Dogs

Next to mailmen and meter readers, children are the largest
group to experience dog attacks, and it has a great deal to do with
the uninhibited manner in which most children approach strange
dogs. It is unfortunate that a child's purest intentions are often met

Coming up behind a dog is a serious mistake that can lead to terrible consequences. If the dog is frightened enough he will bite first and be sorry later.

with canine distrust and aggression. But let's understand the situation from the dog's perspective. If an extremely territorial dog is
with its master and a strange child approaches, the animal will
snap or bite if it views the child as a challenge to its dominance or
possession of the human master.

Another example has to do with the fearful or shy dog. The fear
of strangers often results from shyness in a dog. That is exactly the
type of animal that will bite a child or anyone else that does not
recognize shy behavior and relates to the dog overtly. Most dogs
exhibiting shy behavior have been punished too severely and
therefore distrust strangers. They become fear-biters and are dangerous. In all fairness, shyness can also be the result of inherited
traits. Either way, shy dogs, aggressive dogs, possessive or territorial dogs, must all be approached with caution.

The problem between kids and strange dogs is that there is no
way of knowing in advance how the dog will react to any given
stranger, adult or child. If a child is too young to teach the safe way
to approach a strange dog then it is the parent's responsibility to
prevent such get-togethers *even if the dog's owner encourages it.*
This author has witnessed more than one dog owner dazed and
shocked after discovering his own dog capable of attacking chil-

dren. Children can be severely injured and permanently scarred from facial dog bites. It is just not worth it.

A child must be taught never to approach a dog from the rear. It is impossible to know if the dog is going to be friendly or not. Assume the dog will be unfriendly until proven otherwise. Do not make sudden movements or loud noises. If the dog approaches, the child should stand still as the dog sniffs and records and catalogs the scent of that person. More than likely the dog will wag its tail, slurp, and move about gaily. Under no circumstances should the child offer a hand or extend any limb until certain that the animal is friendly. Do not hold up an arm over the dog's head, with or without an object held in the hand. This is a menacing gesture to some dogs. To a dog that has been trained for guard work, it is a

Once it is determined that the dog is friendly a hand may be extended in this manner.

signal to attack. Make no movement or gesture that could be interpreted by the dog as threatening to its master.

There are certain sure signs that a dog is unfriendly and possibly dangerous. The more obvious ones are bared teeth, snarling, blocking your path, barking. If a dog attempts to stare you down, it is challenging you. Avoid eye-to-eye contact. If the dog stares and its ears are lying flat, it may be about to attack. Standing rigidly with the tail down is another sign of trouble. A crouching dog with a menacing glare, snarl, or stare is also a dog to watch out for. In all of these circumstances, stand perfectly still and do not move arms, legs, or hands. Do not approach such a dog, although talking with a soothing voice can be helpful. Do not let the dog circle behind you. Turn gently as the dog turns and try not to run. That is the worst thing to do. If the dog lunges, fold your arms and cover your face. Standing perfectly still may end the attack. Many dogs lose interest if there is no sign of movement from the victim. Of course, this type of incident does not happen often, but do not be lulled into a dangerously permissive attitude when it comes to children and strange dogs. Keeping them apart is the best preventive action a parent can take. It is hard to accept, but a strange dog encountered in the park or on the street may be frightened to death of your child and might possibly snap defensively. Just as some children fear dogs, the reverse is sometimes true.

Games That Dogs Will Play

Games are the blueprints for the compelling spirit of play. Children and dogs have the undeniable need for play, and suggested games afford parents the opportunity to shape and guide those urges. Games that dogs and kids can play together are healthy and great fun. As suggested earlier in this section, it is time well spent to set up a play period for the dog and the child for thirty minutes at least once a day.

When creating games for dogs and children, bear in mind that play is a teaching process, a release of energy and/or tension, and the physicalization of a mood. For dogs, play is practice for prey capture, fighting, and escape behavior. Puppies and kittens learn how to survive in a wild state (that they almost never experience) through the various forms of play activity. Adult dogs and cats never seem to lose the desire for these survival games, nor do other canids such as wolves or coyotes. This would support the notion that you can teach a dog some new tricks. The following games and activities are mostly based on the three aspects of survival and, depending on the dog's mood and temperament, are sure to appeal. There is no question that a boy or girl will enjoy any number of them.

RETRIEVE

Does anything seem dumber than running after a stick, carrying it back only to run after it again? But if the dog was on a hunting trip, he would be bringing home the bacon (read stick) each time the prey was downed. Retrieving is a time-honored skill that only the best dogs can perform when working the fields and marshes. Many dogs are born with this desire to retrieve. It is more an activity than a game, but it is one that appeals to many dogs, particularly the hunting breeds. It involves a ball, a stick, a rolled-up newspaper, or any object that is not too heavy and shaped so that the dog can get it into his mouth. Simply throw or roll the object to be retrieved away from the dog into a corner of the room. If the dog doesn't quite get the idea, he must be emotionally involved with the child's excitement just before the toss. This is done verbally and also by letting the dog get a taste or brief snatch of the toy. Once the object is tossed, the child calls for the dog to get it. When the dog catches up with the object, the child must call the dog back and offer a reward of praise or, perhaps, a small biscuit. Be certain that the tossed object is no heavier than two or three ounces.

BASEBALL

Although no one gets into the Hall of Fame with this version, it is highly satisfying for both dog and child. Here we have another variation of prey capture. The child gives the dog a smell of the ball and even lets him toy with it as he builds up the dog's enthusiasm. Once he has the dog focused on the ball, the child tosses it lightly in the air with his left hand and swings the bat with his right. As the ball sails in the air (assuming our batter has gotten a good swat), he yells for the dog to retrieve the object. Hopefully the bat and ball are made of plastic so that no one and nothing gets damaged.

VOLLEYBALL AND/OR PUNCHBALL

Yes, we're still involved with prey capture. Here we have volleyball without the net, the two teams, or even the idea of keeping score. One simply hits a large, lightweight ball (or balloon) into the air with the flat of the hand. The dog competes with the child for possession of the ball. Punchball is a slightly rougher version and can be fun for larger dogs, kids, and rooms. The ball is smacked with a closed fist and is sent flying with full force. Once the ball is in motion, both dog and child can race for it.

FRISBEE

Prey capture is the name of the game. A Frisbee is a plastic object shaped like a flying saucer. It is approximately ten or twelve inches in diameter and comes in one of many colors. By holding it flat with the fingers and tossing it with a flick of the wrist from a curled hand, it is possible to make it sail through the air like a

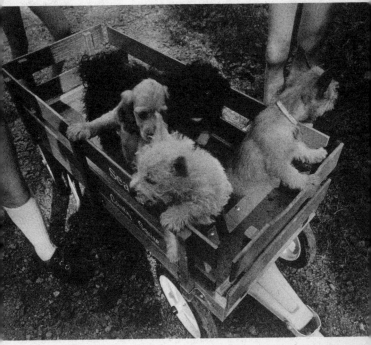

When creating games for dogs and children, bear in mind that play is a teaching process, a release of energy (or tension), and the physicalization of a mood.

What good is a Frisbee if the dog isn't allowed to sink his teeth into it once in a while?

guided missile. Few dogs can resist a good Frisbee chase. When indoors, the Frisbee must be tossed in a gentler manner so that it doesn't go sailing through a pane of glass. Allowing the dog to catch and retrieve the Frisbee keeps him entertained and amused. Do not frustrate the dog by never letting him get his teeth into it. It will damage his pride and his self-confidence.

HIDE THE BISCUIT

Think of a dog biscuit as a prey for a dog to stalk, capture, and consume. The dog's scenting equipment (his nose) is among the finest in nature. It will be difficult to hide food he enjoys so that he cannot find it. Give him a small taste before the game begins just to get the saliva running and his sniffer in tune. Think of some inventive place to hide the biscuit that might confuse his sense of smell such as in a powder box or container with aftershave lotion. Take the dog out of the room and hide his quarry. Bring the animal back and turn him loose. If the dog becomes confused, give him a biscuit. Let him see you hide another and then turn him loose again. Repeat this several times until you are able to hide the biscuit with him out of the room. Once the dog becomes proficient, you can replace biscuits with small items of clothing with someone's scent on them. This is how the magnificent tracking dogs such as bloodhounds and talented German shepherd dogs begin their training. There are several books available about tracking dogs that teach this fascinating activity. Tip: Always reward the dog when he finds the hidden item by letting him eat it if it's food, or by giving him a morsel if it's clothing.

SOCCER

Like volleyball or punchball, the dog and the child compete for possession of the ball. The ball is kicked as in soccer. Clear the room of breakables before starting.

AMBUSH/HIDE-AND-SEEK

The dog is removed from the room as the child finds a good hiding place. The dog is then returned to the room and encouraged to search for the missing playmate. Is it possible for the child to spring up suddenly and surprise the dog before he can find the hidden challenger? Only sometimes. If the child is holding a tasty morsel, the dog will nail him that much faster.

BLINDMAN'S BUFF (BLUFF)

Here, too, we have a game based on a form of prey capture with the addition of an obstacle. Either the child or the dog is "it" and "it" is always blindfolded. With the blindfold tied in place (an even-tempered dog will not object) "it" is spun around three times and set loose. The child makes sounds that give the dog clues as to his whereabouts. The objective is to avoid being touched by the blindfolded dog. Wait for the squeals of laughter as the child tries to dodge away from the pursuing dog. Both dog and child take turns as the blindman. With the completion of each set, offer the dog a small treat. It will sweeten the game and encourage him to play on.

Tug-of-War

Traditionally, tug-of-war is played with two teams pulling on opposite ends of a rope. Each team tries to pull the other across a center line. A game of this type fits into the dog's inclinations to learn how to fight. It is innocent enough as long as the game remains a game. Tie four or more old socks together. Use a pillow, a box, a yardstick, or a drawn line as the dividing point between the dog's and the child's territory. Let them each grab an end of the sock line and begin tugging. Many dogs, particularly terriers, will develop a low, throaty growl as they pull the rope with clinched teeth. This is fine unless the dog loses his playful mood and begins taking things too seriously. In that event, stop immediately and move on to another game. Do not allow the child to pull so vigorously that the dog's teeth may be loosened. Explain to the child that there is great honor in letting the dog win. Always reward both winner and loser.

Boxing

In a boxing match between a dog and a human pal, it is not necessary to adhere to the Marquis of Queensberry rules. As a matter of fact there should be more jabbing and almost no punching. The game lasts longer and remains safer when the child keeps his hands flat and purposely misses the dog. An old pair of gloves will protect the child's hands from accidental nips. This is not a good game for toy breeds or oversized breeds. Be certain that the dog is even-tempered and in a playful mood before starting a boxing match. The match should be divided into four or five one-minute rounds. The winner is determined by whichever opponent manages to control the impulse to hurl his body on the opposite fighter. Biscuits all around are in order after each match.

I'm Gonna Get You

Here is a fighting-wrestling game that has no beginning, middle, or ending. It just sort of starts when the child suddenly crouches and hobbles toward the dog in a mock-threatening gesture. The child growls in a pretended monster voice, "I'm gonna get you!" Every dog responds in a different manner but soon understands that it is another game. The child must understand that he or she is not to terrorize the dog. Explain that it is supposed to be funny. If the dog doesn't feel comfortable, something's wrong. Discontinue the game.

Gotcha. Once the dog understands this game he will look forward to getting caught.

Shopping Bag

Part of a dog's learning process in a play session is the various means of escape he can try from different situations. With a small-to medium-sized dog, you can use a large shopping bag for this escape game. In this situation, give the dog the biscuit before starting. Lay it on the floor and let the dog stoop down to get it. As he does, cover him completely or just his head with the bag. A large cardboard box will also do the trick. Stand back and watch how deftly the dog extricates himself. Give him a treat each time he escapes. If the dog appears upset, discontinue playing it. It must be fun for the dog or it's not valid.

Take a Giant Step

When played traditionally, many kids line up in a row on one side of the street curb and wait for orders from the leader who stands to the side. The leader (or "it") tells each player how many steps he or she may take and what kinds of steps. Sometimes "it" says a child may take three itsy-bitsy steps or one giant step or six mediums. The stepping player must always ask, "May I?" before stepping off. If a player doesn't ask, "May I?" or if the steps are performed incorrectly, he must go back to the curb and start over.

When playing Giant Step with a dog, you must alter the rules drastically. You are going to be hard-pressed to get a dog to ask, "May I?" As a matter of fact, the dog is only asked to do what the child does, more or less. The child calls out how many and what kind of steps to make. The dog, standing next to the child, is expected to step off at the same time as the child. If the dog is willing to stop when the child stops, then they are ready to proceed with the next call until they both successfully reach the opposite wall of the room. However, if the dog fails to stop when the child stops, then they must both start over. Of the various kinds of steps that can be called are scissor steps, baby steps, grasshopper steps, rabbit steps, and whatever the imagination can conjure. The game is over when both dog and friend reach the other side of the room or when mom can't stand the noise anymore.

HOUSE OF CARDS

Here is a game designed to test the most patient child's ability to tolerate a tediously built structure knocked down by a heartless and clumsy canine, insensitive to the architectural skills of the young. All that is needed are one or two decks of cards, a kid, a dog, and a dog's leash and collar. The idea is for the dog to be led out of a circle of houses built of cards without knocking them over. The dog's leash and collar must be placed around his neck. With the aid of a biscuit, the animal is then placed in the center of the room. Once the dog settles down, the child begins to set up card houses around the dog, leaving openings between each card house wide enough for the dog to be maneuvered through.

Houses are built by leaning two cards against a third. There are as many variations as the imagination will allow. One card may be laid atop the standing cards, forming a roof upon which a second floor can be built. Once the dog has been encircled with card houses, the child carefully steps inside the cul-de-sac. She takes hold of the leash and attempts to lead the dog out of the circle through the spaces between the houses.

If a house is knocked down, they can no longer exit from that position and must return to the center. Both dog and child keep trying to leave between the houses without becoming a demolition company. Biscuits and other treats for each round accomplished successfully. Tip: It is easier to build card houses on carpeting or throw rugs than on wooden floors.

Obstacle Course

Appealing to the dog's desire to practice escape behavior, set up a series of barriers, hindrances, hurdles, and various other obstructions for the dog to get through in order to receive his reward (a biscuit) at the end. Stacked pillows, boxes to jump over, tubes to crawl through, and any other imaginative barrier will create a suitable obstacle course. Establish at least five or six barriers for the course and walk the dog through them while held and controlled by his leash. With practice and encouragement he will gladly volunteer his services, if only to receive his treat at the end of the course.

Cardboard Box

For this escape game one needs a large box, the type that appliances come in. The larger the box, the more fun there will be. For the child the box becomes either a ship, cave, house, store, tank, car, bus, truck, or whatever. Both dog and child climb inside and pretend to be driving or sailing, etc. At a certain point the dog will decide he's had it with being cooped up inside an appliance carton and will want out. The high walls of the box and the presence of the child will create enough of a barrier to make it difficult to get out (for small to medium dogs). That's when the fun begins. Rewards for those who get out.

Working Dog

For some medium to large breeds of dog, pulling a burden is natural and pleasurable. Such breeds are from the Working Group and are the Alaskan malamute, Belgian sheepdog, Belgian Tervuren, Bernese mountain dog, Bouvier des Flandres, boxer, bull mastiff, German shepherd dog (only even-tempered), giant schnauzer, Great Pyrenees, mastiff, Newfoundland, St. Bernard, Samoyed, Siberian husky, and almost any large mutt. Obviously, members of other breeds willingly pull carts around, but that is on an individual basis. Do not attempt to burden any dog if he is not the least bit willing or interested in this activity. And certainly a small dog should not be used in this manner.

First purchase a dog harness designed for the specific purpose of pulling. Dog harnesses can be obtained on order from a pet supply shop. *Never—repeat, never—attach a line for pulling purposes to the dog's collar*. This will cause choking and irreparable damage to the dog. A pull rope may be attached to a dog harness and then to a wagon, cart, bicycle, or scooter. This makes it possible for the dog to pull the child around the room, giving pleasure to both.

DRESS UP

This is a game that has nothing whatsoever to do with a dog's instincts or desires. As a matter of fact, if the dog submits to this form of play, it is because of the animal's characteristic forbearance and willingness to please above and beyond the call of duty. The child collects whatever old or discarded items of clothing that he or she can gather (with permission, of course) and attempts to dress the dog for an effect. One might try to create a canine pirate (patch and all) or a gypsy fortune teller or a military hero. The fun lies in creating a specific effect and in attempting to get the dog to sit still for it. Have a camera close by.

PHOTOGRAPHY

A child must have a camera (an inexpensive Instamatic will do), several rolls of film, a nice dog, and a lot of patience. Assuming the child knows how to use the camera, the trick to animal photography is to follow the animal around, keeping him in focus, waiting until something grabs his attention, waiting until he holds still, and then clicking the shutter. It sounds oversimplified, but it is really a combination of persistence, intuition, and luck. The more you work at it, the better you get. Animal photography is one of the most entertaining and satisfying activities there is. It's a natural for a child and a dog.

ARTIST AND MODEL

For the child that can draw, paint, or sketch, his dog is a fine subject. This is a wonderful exploratory activity to find out if he has artistic ability. As a matter of fact, it's great fun even if a child has two left hands and sixteen fingers. Setting image on paper does not have to be restricted to the talented. Psychologists, teachers, and child specialists find that children's paintings and drawings tell adults a great deal about the inner life of a child. They can be useful tools for understanding and communication. But more important than that, sketching is a great deal of fun. Dogs make terrific models and very often strike fascinating poses if they real-

Playtime in a cardboard box. From a yellow submarine to a jungle tree house, nothing can match a bigger-than-life carton for time machine versatility. (*The Photo Works*)

ize that they are being looked at for any length of time. Most dogs love being the center of attention and may even cooperate for a young artist—especially if she's a friend and there is a biscuit in it.

PLAY DEAD

This is one of the most hilarious games that a child can play with a dog. It probably has something to do with one of the dog's instincts—but who knows, who cares. It's fun. The twist is that it is not the dog that lies down and plays dead, but rather the child. In the middle of the play period, it is delicious fun for the child to lie on his belly and close his eyes and wait. If the dog doesn't go bananas and do everything in his repertoire to get the child on his feet again, then it's not a dog at all but some form of plankton! This is a game guaranteed to end up with licked ears, nuzzled noses, and nipped heels. The game goes faster than potato chips.

Follow the bouncing ball and join in. If you raise your head skyward and sing, your dog will accompany you.

SINGING

Deep beneath the fur of every dog is a Caruso begging to come out. If you raise your head and look to the ceiling and begin to sing a song, your four-legged alto will probably join in. Wolves seldom bark as a means of communication (as dogs do) but dogs will howl like wolves in an instinctive response to a distant howl (such as a fire alarm or ambulance siren). Singing an entire song will more than likely entice your dog to accompany you or the child. It is impossible to contain the laughter once it starts. My dog Pete cannot resist singing when he hears "Puff the Magic Dragon."

SHNUFF

Tilt your head back in an exaggerated manner and snap it forward with a pretended sneeze. It seems to amuse all dogs. Some dogs will even sneeze along. When that happens, both child and dog are in heaven.

WAGGING, RUBBING, LICKING, NUDGING

It is quite endearing to watch newborn puppies licked, rubbed, and nudged by a doe-eyed dam, the proud mother of a new litter.

This special attention can be viewed clinically as instinctive or an-thropomorphically as an expression of some form of love. To watch dogs behave similarly with children is to be involuntarily swept up in a scene of natural beauty and tenderness. It is for a lifetime.

Children and puppies will spend the better part of childhood together if all goes well. From the humpty dumpty years to sixteen tons, the boys, girls, and dogs that have lived together will have something more valuable than money in the bank or straight A's. Together they will have shaped the materials of inner resources that will help sustain life in the coming adult years. The free ex-pression of emotion, the desire to live with others, and the ability to accept responsibilities are part of entering the adult world. Children learn much of this from dogs they have known. They also love them and enjoy them. It is a very fortunate dog that spends its life participating in childhood.

When childhood comes to an end, a dog, like retired folks rock-ing on the porch, can finally do those dog things he's been mean-ing to do for so long. There's still a cat to chase, an old bone to find, and a fireplug that needs attention . . . but first a much-needed nap.

4. Dogs and Adults

Beneath the Surface

Biting your dog's face or kissing his tail has more to do with emotional extremities than physical ones. An adult's behavior toward dogs has much to do with attitudes toward animals that have developed over the years in addition to possible human neuroses. These attitudes and neuroses are a key factor in shaping the dog-human relationship. Whether you totally dominate your dog (sometimes with brute force) or allow yourself to be treated as his pet is greatly influenced by how you feel about all animals and yourself. A dog that runs the show is going to be a sort of canine mother-in-law, insisting on having her way, working you over with intimidation, guilt, and other manipulations. The reverse of that situation is the dog that cringes in fear whenever you enter the room because he's not sure whether you're going to yell, hit, or just scowl. In either situation, both dog and human are acting upon each other in less than satisfactory terms. Maybe your dog is not crazy—maybe he just behaves that way because of his environmental influences. Certainly there must be alternative life-styles.

Setting aside the genetic influences and the early socialization factor, your dog's behavior is going to reflect the life-style he lives with his family. If a dog lives in a neurotic situation, you can rely on his being neurotic. For example, many people use food for neurotic reasons that go beyond the need to satisfy their own hunger. If that type of person keeps a dog, chances are good that the dog is portly and relates to food in the same neurotic manner. This is also greatly influenced by whether that adult views animals as something closely related to humans or not. Here again we return to human attitudes toward animals and neurosis. There can be no doubt that animal attitudes and psychological distortion play an important role in shaping pet-owner behavior which, in turn, affects the pet's behavior.

The most desirable life-style for a dog lies between the parameters of his natural or instinctive behavior and the needs and conditions set up by his human family. Dog behavior is, in most instances, a modified version of wolf behavior. When a small puppy leaves his litter and moves into a human situation he simply transfers his pack behavior to the new environment and relates to his human family as another dog or wolf pack. This works perfectly because of the compatibility between family life and pack behavior. In human families as in wolf packs, a social structure based on dominant-subordinate relationships is developed with unusual clarity. Beyond this, the dog's behavior takes on whatever colorations exist in the human condition. Human attitudes toward animals and human neuroses have the greatest influence on a dog's behavior. Basic obedience training makes dogs manageable but does not necessarily alter their neurotic tendencies.

Have you ever witnessed a dachshund having a psychosomatic asthma attack? The poor baby hacks and wheezes and honks in situations where he cannot have his own way. Fat dogs that eat until their eyes cross overeat to feel loved or because they fear they'll never be fed again. Many dogs deliberately disobey commands and rules of conduct as attention getters.

There are dogs that pace, dogs that suffer from insomnia, dogs that fear strangers, dogs that fear other dogs, dogs that are sexually attracted to specific humans, and even dogs that suffer mental breakdowns. There are no known canine chain-smokers. But dogs, in their current state of domestication, are subject to almost all the manifestations of neurosis found in humans. Neuroses in dogs are a matter of great concern for many pet owners. When human neurotic behavior is seen in dogs it can be upsetting for those who love them.

Is there any difference between neurosis in dogs and humans, and is it harmful? In the long run, neurosis in humans is harmful and more intense. Such behavior stems from emotional pain. A neurotic person is one possessed of irrational fears who develops defenses that offer relief and security from those fears. It is these defensive tactics that are distorted and ultimately interfere with a full and happy existence. Neurotic behavior which develops as a defense against fear often creates more fear. These views of human neurosis can also be applied to the emotional life of certain dogs, but to a lesser degree of seriousness, for the most part.

In the immediate sense, neurosis is harmful to a dog only if his behavior is going to lose him his home. It may be harmful to the dog's owner if the dog becomes aggressive or destructive. In some situations, the dog and his human partner make an arrangement of accommodation and live with the status quo. For example, a dog may demand more and more food and the owner will relish doling it out because the human wants an eternal child. This dog becomes totally dependent like a child that never grows up, that never leaves home. In such a case one neurosis serves another in a symbiotic relationship. It is a neurotic arrangement.

A typical canine neurotic is the *fear-biter*. This is a dog that is extremely frightened because of a genetic defect or because of early trauma such as a severe beating. If the dog was continually hit with a rolled newspaper or a human hand, he will irrationally bite anything resembling those objects. A fear-biter will bark with much bravado as long as he is attached to a leash or behind a fence. Release the dog and he will cower. Turn your back on him and he will bite. It is defensive; it is irrational.

To determine how neuroses develop in dogs, one must attempt to define dog neurosis. Dr. Mark W. Allam, former dean of the University of Pennsylvania School of Veterinary Medicine, believes that there is no true scientific discipline known as "dog psychology" and that not much data exists on the subject as it does in the field of human psychology. Much scientific examination has been made on wolf behavior and that, of course, helps understand dog behavior. This is not to say that no scientific work has been pursued in the field of dog behavior as it pertains to genetics and instinctive behavior. When writing on the subject of "dog psychology," however, one is never out of the area of conjecture and opinion. Dr. Allam also believes that it is sometimes difficult to know whether the neurosis rests with the owner or the animal.

He contends:

> Where an animal is born free and clear of disease and has little contact with humans, you're going to find that it develops a very low mentality and that while it may not be neurotic in the one sense, it is from the standpoint that it is afraid to venture forth. It will have been too protected. The hunting dog is a good example. He is never in conversation with the house but rather, tied outside. The dog's mentality develops only as much as he gets in the hunting field. The responses of animals are related in that way. When you get into the neurotic animal, I always find that there is a person in back of it. A widowed lady once purchased a three-month-old Doberman pinscher. She herself was a nervous person and did a great deal of pacing in a circle in the house, smoking cigarettes. This little dog took up pacing after her and by the time the pup was eight months of age, it was absolutely uncontrollable. It took on all of her nervous tensions, all of her nervous reactions.

Dr. Allam and his wife took that dog into their home and retrained it so that it could be used as the eyes and ears of a blind woman.

Dogs develop the canine version of neurosis from their human families who teach this behavior through interaction with the animal and by the example they set the animal. Sibling rivalries, psychosomatic illnesses, and the whole range of neurotic behavior in dogs is often learned from human beings or developed by them into symbiotic relationships. When a dog is used as a substitute for another human being, chances are great that he will become neurotic—as neurotic as that human's need happens to be. Where there is a neurotic dog, look for a neurotic human. After all, a dog will never take his college degree and move away from home and forget to write or call. Dogs are grateful . . . or they lose their jobs.

If a neurotic dog is young, it can be retrained away from abnormal behavior, providing there is no physical or genetic deficiency. Have the dog examined by a veterinarian to be certain that he is not physically sick. Illness can induce irrational behavior. Dr. Allam claims:

> It is possible to bring a neurotic dog back to some acceptable form of behavior. Most neurotic dogs are restless, nervous. They are not responsive to the commands or wishes of the owner. In an advanced neurotic picture, in certain circumstances, they'll have a rather shiny, glassy look in their eyes. They look like they're looking through you rather than looking at you. You must put the dog into a different environment and take enough time and be very patient. You can bring them back to normal again. It can take as long as a year. However, I wouldn't have the success with a five-year-old animal that I might have with one that is twelve or fourteen months of age.

If the family dog is neurotic and it makes you unhappy, then some degree of self-examination is necessary if there is to be any opportunity for change. Ask the question: "Is there anything in my behavior that contributes to this dog's neurosis?" Self-help, psychotherapy, counseling, meditation, yoga, even tennis can be useful. Self-confrontation and the release from anxiety is the only answer. On the other hand, if the dog's behavior is to your liking, stop clutching the leash, relax, and have another slice of chocolate cake.

Human neuroses are difficult to change. Attitudes may be easier to cope with. Discerning your own attitudes toward animals is yet another useful method of helping to improve relationships with pets. Although it is not often easy to be objective about your own attitudes, it is possible to achieve some degree of self-understanding if you are given definitions of generalized attitudes held by others.

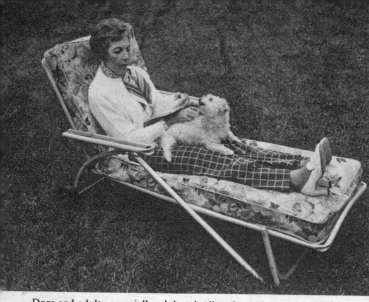

Dogs and adults, especially adults who live alone, share special relationships that are as meaningful and as necessary as any two human beings. Two living beings devoted to one another is more than a compromise arrangement. The relationship becomes as necessary as life itself.

In a study for the Fish and Wildlife Service of the United States Department of the Interior, Dr. Stephen R. Kellert, research associate, Behavioral Sciences Study Center, Yale University School of Medicine, developed just such a set of attitudinal definitions. They are to be found in his prodigious and highly significant study, "From Kinship to Mastery: A Study of American Attitudes toward Animals."

Dr. Kellert interviewed a sample of men and women who were characterized by having a significant level of interest or involvement with animals. He consulted a wide variety of animal-related organizations such as the American Kennel Club, the Fund for Animals, The National Rifle Association, Ringling Brothers, Barnum & Bailey Circus, and twenty-six others for recommended subjects to interview. Of the seven hundred specific persons recommended, the group that was finally interviewed was comprised of artists, breeders, conservationists, ecologists, farmers, horsemen, humanitarians, hunters, ornithologists, pet owners, preservationists, ranchers, rodeo cowboys, scientists, show people, trainers, vegetarians, veterinarians, writers, zoo directors, and others. The group was trimmed down to represent every section of the country, and at least one person from every animal activity mentioned above.

The sample of animal-oriented people were then interviewed extensively so that Kellert might delineate a model of basic types of attitudes toward animals existing in American society today. Over nine hundred pages of transcript were accumulated, analyzed, and interpreted. For the purpose of aiding the adult pet owner in recognizing his or her own animal attitudes, Dr. Kellert's nine basic attitudinal orientations are presented here. It is helpful to understand that few people fall rigidly into each category. Rather, every pet owner is represented by one or more elements in each category. Do not look for harsh judgments, worthiness, or validation. The keynote here is understanding.

Nine Basic Attitudes Toward Animals

I   THE NATURALISTIC ORIENTATION
A. A strong interest in direct contact with the out-of-doors and the natural world.
B. An affection for animals in general, but particularly for wildlife. Wild animals considered superior to domesticated animals.

C. A tentative belief in the superiority of the natural world and a related distaste for the modern, urban world.

D. A spiritual, but not religious, feeling for the natural world.

E. An interest in the primitive in both animals and men. A somewhat atavistic belief in getting back to basics and living off the land.

F. An interest in hunting as a way of being active in the out-of-doors.

G. A view that death is a natural process, important and valuable to understand.

II   THE ECOLOGISTIC ORIENTATION

A. An emphasis on ecosystems—in viewing life-forms as interrelated and interdependent.

B. A great intellectual interest but not necessarily strong personal affection for wildlife. A lack of interest and affection for pet animals. An interest in the species rather than the individual animal.

C. A concern more for habitat than for specific animals.

D. A "naturalizing" view of man, regarding human beings as just another species within an ecosystem.

E. A people-centered approach involving: one, a concern for reconciling the value of habitat protection with the commercial and practical use of animals and the natural environment; and, two, a tendency to support social change.

F. An interest in scientific knowledge and methodology, but a skepticism about relying solely on science.

G. A spiritual and aesthetic feeling for the natural environment, but not a religious belief.

III   THE HUMANISTIC ORIENTATION

A. A very strong emotional affection for domesticated pet animals. Comparatively little interest in wild animals.

B. A view of pet animals as companions and friends rather than as work animals.

C. An interest and involvement with specific animals rather than animal species or broad animal and environmental issues.

D. An abhorrence of pain or suffering being inflicted upon animals. An interest in animal but not social welfare.

E. A tendency to idealize the capacities and attributes of animals, particularly pet animals—at times, a romantic and anthropomorphic tendency.

IV THE MORALISTIC ORIENTATION

A. A stress on ethical issues involving the proper treatment of animals.

B. An abhorrence of cruelty, pain, or harm being inflicted upon animals.

C. An intellectual interest in general issues regarding animals more than an emotional involvement with specific animals.

D. A feeling of equality and kinship with animals.

E. A negative attitude toward utilitarian exploitation and domination of animals.

F. A tendency toward social reform and advocacy of social change.

G. A skeptical attitude toward modern society, its reliance upon science and technology, and its commercial emphasis.

H. A tendency to believe in particular philosophies of life and to correlate these with attitudes toward animals.

I. A highly spiritual and religious feeling for animals and the natural world.

V THE SCIENTISTIC ORIENTATION

A. A tendency to view animals as objects of study rather than as subjects for affection or ethical concern. An intellectual interest directed toward problem-solving.

B. A "mechanistic" tendency to regard animals in terms of how they work and function, rather than in terms of how they think and feel.

C. A "reductionist" tendency to view all animals, including man, in terms of certain basic principles and processes.

D. A belief in ethical and emotional neutrality regarding animals. Little personal involvement with animals or concern for broad issues of animal welfare. A lack of spiritual or philosophical feeling for animals and the natural world.

E. An emphasis on details of animal morphology, physical characteristics, and biological functioning, rather than on behavior in natural habitats.

F. A belief in the power of science to improve man's world.

VI THE AESTHETIC ORIENTATION

A. A view of animals according to the premise of artistic beauty and taste as a fundamental standard.

B. A willingness to exploit animals for aesthetic purposes.

C. A tendency to regard animals as objects of beauty rather

than as subjects for affection or ethical concern. A kind of objective detachment from animals.

D. An aesthetic pleasure in animal activities such as hunting, pet shows, and horsemanship.

VII THE UTILITARIAN ORIENTATION

A. A perception of animals in terms of their practical or profitable qualities—largely for their material benefit to humans.

B. Not necessarily marked by a lack of affection or interest in animals, although such feelings are usually subordinated to the more predominant interest in the usefulness of animals.

C. While many utilitarian-oriented persons own pets, for example, most believe they should be trained for specific tasks and not kept just as companions or friends.

D. A view that tends to be indifferent to issues of animal welfare which do not affect the animal's performance or practical value.

VIII THE DOMINIONISTIC ORIENTATION

A. A view involving a sense of superiority and a desire to master animals are the defining features of this orientation.

B. Animals are mainly regarded from the perspective of providing opportunities for dominance and control, and expressions of prowess and skill in competition with animals are typically emphasized.

C. Considerable attachment to animals may accompany the dominionistic attitude, but usually in the context of dominating them as, for example, in rodeos, trophy hunting, and obedience training.

IX THE NEGATIVISTIC ORIENTATION

A. The most common feature being a desire to avoid animals.

B. Typical of this orientation are such feelings as indifference, dislike, fear, and superstition.

C. This viewpoint is quite often marked by a fundamental sense of separation and alienation from the natural world.

D. For many, an utter gulf in emotion and spirit distinguishes animals from humans.

E. This orientation is obviously very much people-centered,

involving little, if any, empathy or kinship with animals and the nonhuman world.

In a paper presented at the forty-first North American Wildlife and Natural Resources Conference Dr. Kellert stated:

The nine attitudes have been presented as ideal types and should be regarded as conceptual constructs of general human tendencies rather than specific descriptions of actual behavior. Most people typically possess more than one attitude toward animals, feeling and behaving a certain way in one situation while manifesting a different attitude under other circumstances. Additionally, when individuals express a particular attitude, rarely do they exhibit every characteristic of this attitude. In other words, not only do people have multiple attitudinal orientations, but they also vary considerably in the intensity of their commitments. In general, however, it is possible to identify in most individuals predominant characteristics of a primary attitude toward animals, with elements of secondary and tertiary attitudes present as well.

The Four-Legged House Plant

No matter why anyone starts out wanting a dog, it is always possible to reevaluate and change those reasons. And for those who never sought an explanation or understanding of their motivations, here is an opportunity to develop a point of view that may present their own dogs to them in new and more meaningful terms.

No matter how domesticated dogs are, and even though they almost never experience the lust for freedom that their wild canid cousins enjoy, they are a measure of nature. Dogs are connective tissue with the unpaved world of plains, forests, deserts, mountains, and jungles. Stroking the nape of a Labrador retriever can conjure a feeling of rushing water and roasted fowl on a crackling spit. The bloodhound's cry from a distant woods and the aggressive basenji on a jungle hunt are there for the imagining. The darting lope of a saluki racing on the sands of the Sinai can easily transport a sidewalk daytripper. The German shepherd dog and his fellow worker, the collie, bring to skyscraper apartments the smell of grass and the image of sheep grazing in a pasture. The dogs have all been there at one time or another and keep us in touch with nature because of their uninhibited lives.

We walk on carpet, we hear the low hum of motors, we smell lubricating oil, we move about on rubber—and only once in a while realize that we are natural beings. All that's left are house plants and dogs. In our synthetic society, dogs remind us that we are part of nature and also live off the land. Keeping a dog is a civilized and convenient way to live with some tiny fragment of the natural earth. It's a better reason than most and is more than likely the hidden point of it all.

5. Dogs and Dogs

The World from Twenty-five Inches

Despite the fact that humans control the destiny and hour-by-hour behavior of family pets, domestic dogs do have some autonomous aspects to their behavior. Dogs live in another world then we, or, putting it another way, experience our shared world from a totally different perspective. The dog experience is so different and unique from the human experience that to be unaware of it is to not know your dog at all. How can one understand, control, and enjoy a dog if that dog's perspective is a mystery? In the human community there is also a dog society, and dogs in the plural can be a pure delight or a nightmare riding a human.

The genetic traits derived from the wolf have been explored as a means of clarifying canine behavior. Another aspect of dog behavior has to do with sensory perceptions, particularly as they apply to relations with other dogs. It can be said that human understanding of the world is an intellectual one with an emphasis on visual perception. This is not the case for the domestic dog.

There is very little intellectualization in a dog's mind about the environment in which he finds himself. Part of the reason for the incredible adaptability of the domestic dog is his willingness to accept conditions as they are and make the necessary adjustments to survive. It can also be said that visual perception is probably one of the least developed sensory perceptors that dogs possess. With limited intellectual capacity and underdeveloped vision, the dog must rely on other means for maintaining himself in a sometimes dangerous and difficult world.

The average dog sees the human society from approximately twenty-five inches above the floor. By getting on all fours and crouching, you may begin to understand more about a dog's-eye view of his home and surrounding terrain. In the human home, the dog has no choice but to learn to communicate in order to satisfy his needs. Eye contact, touching, and vocalizing must all be put into play if the dog wants its dinner or to be let out for toileting, etc. Unfortunately, these are the dog's least natural abilities and require great effort to utilize adequately. Things are quite different when a dog communicates with another dog.

Vision is practically unnecessary when dogs have a need to communicate. Even so, the sight of another dog is usually the first perception, though a limited one. Visual proficiency varies from breed to breed and sometimes from dog to dog within a given breed. The best example is the difference between sight hounds such as whippets, Afghan hounds, and greyhounds and scent hounds such as beagles, harriers, and bloodhounds. When comparing a dog's visual capacity with a human's, there are two aspects. The dog's peripheral vision is almost twice that of the human's, however, the human's ability to focus sharply is greater than the dog's. These are important differences. The result is that a dog is acutely sensitive to motion and sees it faster than a human. He must then rely on sound and smell to discern what he has just seen. Because dogs are essentially prey seekers, they respond on a hair-trigger mechanism at the first sight of strange and sudden motion. This could account for car chasing, cat chasing, running away, and a long list of tiresome behaviorisms.

Dogs can hear better than humans but not quite as well as cats. They can hear sounds that we cannot and can listen for a familiar footstep long before it comes within human earshot. The so-called Galton whistle or silent dog whistle is not silent at all. It is pitched at a frequency too high for the human ear but quite clear to the canine or feline ear. According to Dr. Maurice Burton in his book, *The Sixth Sense of Animals,** "Another way in which a dog's hearing differs from ours is in its better sense of rhythm. A dog can tell if the beat of a metronome changes from a hundred to ninety-six beats a minute. A man can only detect this if he is timing the beats with a stopwatch." This is an ability that has great use in seeking prey and coping with natural enemies and prey. The dog not only has sensitive hearing but is able to determine breathing rhythms and possibly the quantity of footsteps and at what speed they are moving.

In dealing with friend, foe, or prey, the dog's front line of defense is his olfactory receptor (smelling apparatus). All mammals possess an olfactory mechanism under a membrane. In humans it is about the size of a postage stamp. Under the membrane are thousands of nerve fibers terminating in olfactory hairs. The various scents (in gas form) pass over these nerve fibers and send messages to the brain concerning the nature of the scent. In the average dog the olfactory membrane, when spread out, is fifty times greater than that of the human membrane. However, a dog's nose

---

The Sixth Sense of Animals by Dr. Maurice Burton. Copyright 1972. Published by Taplinger Publishing Co., New York. Used by permission.

When dogs get together they perceive each other in a totally different manner than we imagine. Smell and sound are the identifying factors.

is not necessarily more sensitive than a human's. The dog excels in the variety of smells he can detect.

In the receptor area of the dog's olfactory mechanism, the receptors are interspersed with glandular cells which secrete a mucous substance. The odor molecules of one odor are thought to separate differentially in the mucus and therefore cause different spacial stimulation of the receptor field than other odors. This is the physiology of odor reception.

The key to a dog's perception of his world lies in his smelling abilities. Scent posting and scent perception are among the main activities of all dogs. Through this unique set of mechanisms and behaviorisms a dog seeks and finds food, obtains a mate, claims territory, fights for his rights and his life (if need be), procreates, performs parental functions, and maintains an instinctive integrity within his social structure. All of this depends largely on a dog's ability to use his incredible nose. When a dog sees another dog, his smelling apparatus immediately goes to work, probing for information and various signals. His hearing also comes into play, but the dog's behavior from that point on is very much influenced by what his nose tells him. In addition, dogs have an uncanny ability to catalog and remember thousands of odors and their associations with people, animals, places, and events. One could call it scent memory. The greatest of the dog's smelling talents is its capacity to discriminate one odor from hundreds of odors, from great distances, and over long periods of time. These are the abilities that make great trail, tracking, bomb, and drug detector dogs.

A long-time trainer and breeder of Brittany spaniels, Tom Martin of Leverett, Massachusetts, says of his dogs' olfactory talents:

> I have seen a dog flush a covey of quail and when given the signal to advance refuse the command and stand on point instead. After another unsuccessful attempt to get the dog to go off point, I advanced to the spot only to find two quail out of fifty or sixty left. The dog was able to sense the remaining two quail with its nose. I have also seen one of my dogs, trained to retrieve, go on point for another bird with the first bird still in its mouth.

Tom Martin's dogs are trained to follow the odor of pigeon, quail, and pheasant *only,* out of all the other smells in the world. Humans cannot even find the kitchen with their noses once they come in contact with cooking odor for fifteen minutes. The dog is universally regarded as the animal with the greatest sense of smell. The truth is that many animals can smell well and use this ability with great efficiency. However, the dog's ability to analyze odor in the central nervous system can be utilized to its maximum advantage by man.

It is not within the purview of this book to fully develop the inner workings of the various sensory receptors in dogs. However, it is necessary for the dog owner to understand the nature of animal senses and how they differ in order of importance for dogs. There have been many cases of dogs losing their eyesight and still managing efficiently with the help of the more important senses, hearing and smell. The order of importance—smell, hearing, and then sight—helps the pet owner appreciate how the dog perceives the world he lives in. It is particularly essential when living under the same roof with two or more animals.

Giving Your Dog a Pet

If necessity is the mother of invention, then certainly boredom is the parent of destruction; at least as it affects dogs. A dog with nothing to do between walks, who is alone most of the time, who hardly ever has the opportunity to relate to other animals, is a dog who can go in one of several directions. He'll become either destructive in his home, totally docile and hence a bore of a pet, aggressive, or perhaps physically ill.

Getting your dog a pet of his own may sound laughable at first, or even ridiculous. It would seem to be in the same category with silver feeding bowls, vicuna pillows, and mink-lined booties. This couldn't be further from the truth. When you compare the cost of a chewed-up sofa, a shredded carpet, scarred baseboards, and destroyed clothing and appliances, boarding another animal becomes a matter for serious consideration if it is an alternative to the above. The animal shelters of America are filled to capacity because many a *former* owner never anticipated the problems that arise in some pet/owner relationships.

All dogs are social creatures owing to inherited instincts that are drawn from pack behavior. The wolf pack is essentially a small family of wolves living together in a very specific social organization. If your dog is left alone much of the time, as many pet dogs are, he is living out an existence similar to that of the lone wolf. It is unnatural and debilitating to his physical and mental state. A lone wolf is one who has become too old or too sick to fulfill his destiny within the pack order. He is an outcast and does not last very long in the remote wilderness.

Think of your dog as a wolf and your home as his den. Then ask yourself how long he would remain there on his own, unless he were prevented from leaving. If he were a wolf, what would be his reaction? Once his frustration mounted, it would become manifest in howling and chewing behavior to enable escape or to express his fear. At the very least, some physical attempt to abate boredom would be made. These and other elements are what the average dog owner faces when a dog is left to his own devices for long periods of time.

Although there is never one cure-all answer, a possible solution that has worked for many dogs and their owners is the introduction of another animal into the environment. There are many variables involved, and matching the right dog with the right companion animal has a great deal to do with the temperament of each animal. Logic and common sense are necessary. For instance, you wouldn't want to introduce an animal resembling a rodent to a terrier or dachshund, nor would you want too small a species for a hunting dog. Giving a cat to a dog that is a proven cat hater could lead to tragic consequences, and so on.

When considering what kind of a companion to get for your dog, the first thought that comes to mind, naturally, is another dog. Ideally, you should consult someone who keeps more than one dog and has the experience to advise you. Ask as many questions about this arrangement as you can think of. The dogs should be of the same sex to avoid the problems of unplanned mating (unless one or more animals are neutered). Some experts believe exactly the opposite. The new dog should be a puppy that has just left his litter. In that way, the puppy will have no problem living with the domination of a larger animal. On the other hand, your first dog must not feel threatened in any way by the arrival of a new companion. Because of their age and size differences, he will clearly have the upper hand. The two dogs will immediately work out their respective status differences in the household. Two dogs in one house could result in jealousy problems in the older dog if the owner is not prudent in sharing the attention. It is not much different from bringing a new baby home when there is an older child. It is important that the older child never feel displaced or replaced by the younger sibling.

The word *jealousy* is used here because it best describes the situation of social rank violation which all dogs feel very strongly. There have been many instances where an exceptionally aggressive puppy grows up with an older dog and eventually becomes the dominant animal. The situation then reverses, and the younger dog finds it intolerable when the older, more subordinate pet is given too much affection (in the view of the dominant dog). Although it appears to be the emotion known as jealousy, it is really something more basic, more indicative of dogs.

Owning two dogs can be twice as rewarding as owning one. Some people acquire two pets at the same time, possibly even litter mates. But sometimes a new pet is brought into a household that has been the exclusive domain of one for many years. The pet owner must be careful not to lavish too much attention on the newcomer. The senior pet isn't likely to welcome a newcomer who takes away such tender loving care.

While a young puppy might require more attention at first, there's no reason why the older pet can't be given reassuring pats on the head, some extra soothing words, or a few additional minutes of play with a favorite toy.

It's also important to have separate food and water dishes for each pet and to feed them in opposite corners of the room to make certain that neither pet feels compelled to protect his food supply or compete for food and water.

If the older pet is a senior citizen, the addition of a youngster to the family can have some very traumatic results. The competition may place too much emotional and physical strain on the older dog. It depends on the temperament of the older dog and how advanced in years he is. A very old dog must be spared the extreme change of a new dog in his life.

Usually, it only takes a short period of time before two pets settle down to a friendly routine under the care of a pet owner who has found that caring for two is no more difficult than caring for one.

There are those who feel that dogs never seek the society of other dogs to ease their loneliness or boredom, but rather would have the human owner all to themselves. This is the exception rather than the rule. That point of view seems to go against the obvious logic of pack behavior. Although dogs are not wolves, they do share this proclivity for a social existence. The problem between two dogs—particularly two males—is one of domination and subordination. The matter of territory is one that has to do with dogs of another *family* or pack. Two grown male dogs will in all likelihood have to fight it out in order to determine the dominant and subordinate roles.

There are so many actual case histories of dogs not only living with other dogs but aiding each other in one way or another. In *Science Digest,* a case of a seeing-eye dog for a dog was reported. It happened in Great Britain. A three-year-old German shepherd dog named Simba appointed herself guide dog for a blind seven-year-old spaniel. Simba leads the spaniel, Minky, by gently tugging on her ear. The German shepherd appears to be devoted to the spaniel. The dogs' owner, Esme Bidlake of Kent, swears that Simba chose her own role as protector and leader purely by instinct, sensing the helplessness of her friend. Whatever the reason, it is an odd sight when Simba appears at the top of the stairs with Minky's ear in her mouth. She leads the smaller dog to the bottom of the stairs, lets go of the ear temporarily while she opens the door with her paws, and then takes the spaniel out for a walk. Behaving like a trained guide dog, Simba holds onto Minky's ear when they approach a road, waits for traffic to pass, and then gently guides Minky across the road, still holding onto her ear. "Simba will even guide her to her feeding bowl," says the dogs' owner, "and sit beside Minky while she has her meal." This is companionship above and beyond the call of duty.

But there is no need to restrict your dog's companionship to other dogs. The next best companion pet is a cat. Because dogs were originally hunters, it is instinctive for them to chase small prey that might serve as food. The domestic dog, no longer in need of catching his dinner, is still left with the instinct to chase without even knowing what it's all for. This does not apply to many sporting breeds that are bred and trained for the purpose of hunting, trailing, chasing, pointing, flushing, retrieving, and sometimes killing.

It is because of this instinct for chasing prey that some dogs and cats fight like cats and dogs. It is rare, however, that a dog chases his own *family* feline. Once another animal becomes a part of the household, the dog accepts it as part of his territory. It quite literally becomes his property. The objective, therefore, is to help the dog understand that this new creature—this cat—is not a wild animal merely passing through, but a new member of the family. Extensive introductions, controlled examinations, patience, and a great deal of time are necessary to pull this off.

A small kitten and a grown dog adjust more easily to each other than the other way around. Again, a caveat about terriers and other hunting breeds. They might very well be tempted to kill a small kitten.

Introducing a dog and a cat for the first few times must be handled with great delicacy. Your obedient dog will not attack the new kitten in your presence, not even a hunting dog, if you order the dog to stay or sit in a firm but soothing voice. Cradle the cat in your hands and allow the dog to sniff all over. Some kittens are fearless; others will hiss and recoil. Do not let the little cat scratch you or the dog. Once the dog and the cat have had a chance to get a look at each other, separate them until the next session. With each meeting, allow the two animals to get physically closer until it is safe to put them both on the floor, unrestrained. You must avoid leaving them alone together during the first two or three weeks of their acquaintanceship.

New theories on the formation of early social attachments are being considered by psychologists as the result of experimentally induced pairing between dogs and monkeys at the California Primate Research Center, University of California at Davis. A report describes how a gentle, accepting dog can be a highly effective mother substitute for young rhesus monkeys, even for those that have had experience with the real mother. When between one and ten months old, the monkeys were separated from their original attachment figures and gradually exposed to adult, spayed female mongrels. The monkeys' immediate reaction was fear, but this disappeared within hours. Eventually each monkey was housed with its own dog. They lived and played together. The monkeys even

Where's my cat? The dog with a working owner becomes a *lone wolf* without companionship. Dogs need other living beings to share their daily pleasures and struggles. A cat will do just fine.

accompanied the dogs on exercise periods and exhibited distress if prevented from doing so. The monkeys clearly preferred the familiar dogs. What the report does not explore is the ease with which the dogs accepted the infant monkeys and their adaptability to the uniqueness of the situation.

If a dog can live with a monkey, then it can live with any form of animal life including tropical fish. Like all forms of life, dogs need other living beings to share their daily pleasures and struggles. It is the only way he knows for sure that he exists. How different is he from the rest of us?

Dogs That Visit

When you and your dog visit a friend who also owns a dog, there are several points that must be kept in mind. Obviously, the same applies to a friend and a dog who pay a call on you. The two dogs, especially if they've never met before, are going to compulsively work out the dominant-subordinate order. In the case of two male dogs it can be quite a hassle, even a vicious fight. Be prepared. It may occur as a gentle tussle on the floor with one dog playfully lying on its back and accepting the subordinate role (the way a puppy would with an older dog). In that event you and your friend are very lucky.

Sometimes the establishment of social position is accomplished in a peculiar form of battle that has to do with scent posting. As you approach your friend's house, your dog will instantly smell the other dog and possibly lift a leg and urinate on a wall, a tree, a bush, a flower bed, or some other vertical object suitable for scent posting. The other dog, if in a challenging mood, will do likewise. Even the best trained dogs will forget all their housebreaking and compulsively mark off a territory with urine.

Other areas of combat have to do with food, water, and symbols of territory not the least of which is the human master. A dog as-

When dogs come calling on other dogs one must be certain that they can get along with each other. Keep them leashed until order is clearly established.

serting itself with another dog can get quite vicious if the intruder goes near its food or water. This dog might also fight over a child's attention or its master's permissive offerings of affection to the visiting animal.

There is very little you can do in advance to avoid these annoying situations because it's impossible to predict how the two dogs will get along. Sometimes things go perfectly, and sometimes the situation deteriorates from dreadful to horrible. The simplest thing is for one dog to stay home. Barring that, all one can suggest is to keep the dog on a leash and exercise tight and meaningful control. Smaller dogs can sit on their masters' laps. Go slowly. Talk soothingly. Do not extend gratuitous affection to the other dog. Do not allow the visiting dog to get at the home dog's food or water bowl. Do not allow the visiting dog to go near any of the other dog's toys, blankets, or other possessions. Carefully observe how the dogs relate to one another. If they appear to get along, release your dog from the leash and turn him loose. If the dogs begin to fight but it is not a serious fight, allow it to run its course so that they might establish the social order of rank. If the fight turns vicious, the dogs will have to be separated and the visit terminated. It is impossible to lock a dog away while another dog is in his house. It is unjust, but more important, it will drive him berserk.

The Dog in the Street

Meeting strange dogs in the street during a walk can be a very pleasant experience for both dogs and humans. The opposite is also true. When dogs collide, it is because of a question about social rank, territory, or matters pertaining to sex. The desire to fight it out is born out of several social signals emanating from each dog. Being able to recognize those signals helps the dog owner know when to tighten up on the leash or to avoid the other dog altogether. The dog owner has little or no control over the situation if one or both dogs are off-leash.

The first stage of a dog fight is usually a contest of physical display designed to *outpsych* the opposing dog. Some fights, therefore, never even begin if one dog is sufficiently convinced that the overpuffed opponent is stronger, bigger, or magically more furious. The antagonistic signals between two dogs considering a fight are seen in the expression of the face, the stance of the body, the position of the ears, the movement (or lack of movement) of the tail, and the sounds emanating from the throat.

When two dogs meet by chance, and there is no inclination to fight, there is usually a sensory examination of each other through sight, smell, taste, and sound. However, two dogs that are either aggressive, overly territorial, or simply in a rotten mood behave very differently. A challenging dog assumes a threatening posture of erect head, fixed stare, pricked ears, taut muscles, stiffened legs, highly erect but usually still tail, and a general increase in size. Sometimes the dog's fur stands up and away from the body, creating the impression of more bulk and height. This is the meaning of the expression *his hackles are raised.* Many dogs then turn sideways to further impress their opponents with a show of even more body mass. If this does not convince the other dog to lower its tail between its legs and look away in submission, the teeth are then displayed in various degrees of menace. From here on, a low, throaty growl can be heard, and an attack is imminent.

If a fight actually ensues, the two dogs attack each other's legs, ears, paws, and especially the neck, or, more to the point, the throat. In order to reach the objective—the throat—an attempt is made to overturn the opponent on his back. Paradoxically, if a dog submits, he does so by offering his throat, which in turn automatically stops the dominant animal from continuing the fight. The question has been settled and both dogs part, ready to go home and heal their wounds. It is the wise dog owner who never allows the situation to progress this far. At the first signs of confrontation, the animals must be separated and both owner and master depart from the scene.

There is no dishonor in avoiding a confrontation between two dogs. When dogs fight, it is based on an instinctive impulse that once, in some primeval time, had relevance. What could be more meaningless than two canines fighting over three feet of curbstone? It is only for the misguided and unbalanced dog owner that this behavior has any charm at all.

Stopping a fight between dogs once it has begun is extremely dangerous. Much advice has been given by experts to grab one or the other animals by the tail or hind legs and pull them apart. This may be effective, especially if both dogs are pulled simultaneously. One is reluctant to offer this as a sound technique because of the dangerous vulnerability to hand and leg lacerations. Even the most loving and obedient dog is capable of inflicting serious wounds on anyone interfering. A thorough dousing with buckets of cold water is certainly more effective and safer. But water, buckets, etc. are not readily available on a city street or country road. Prevention is the only altogether safe means of dealing with dog fights. Learn the signs of aggression and hurry away before the fight begins.

Dogs living together under the same roof are usually happier, healthier, hardier, and more of a joy to their human fellows. A brace of pugs, harlequin Great Danes, or even a gang of mongrels are good to look at and even better to live with if one has the room. A dog and a cat are more natural together than apart, and even caged gerbils can be diverting fun for a dog that has time on his hands. As much as a dog may love his human family, another animal may share his world more successfully and understand the dog experience on a lustier level. More than one dog is a happy thought.

6. Chow Time

In the beginning, Dog was the first Trash Masher. Early dog participated in the hunt, was the nocturnal guard protecting the cave from swooping pterodactyls, and whined when the night fire went out. In return for services rendered, he was not brained, barbecued, and served. Rather, he was permitted to lick fingers and toes and rummage through the cooked bones for nuggets of grilled brontosaurus or prehistoric mule. In addition to his other tasks, the dog was expected to sniff around the outdoor dining room and clean up the mess around the cookfire. It is here one finds the origins of the restaurateur's famous doggie bag. Because the dog did his job so well, nary a sanitation worker was ever called upon to sweep or cart. The humans ate the meat and the dog cleaned up the scraps. Although short on dignity, it was long on survival. It was, perhaps, the first *détente,* and no one complained. In a desperate world, all creatures must seek accommodation.

Prior to this humble arrangement, prehistoric dogs had to fend for themselves and hunt down and kill whatever was available for the once- or twice-weekly meal. Then as now, finding game, maneuvering it into a capture position, and then bringing it down was difficult, especially during the winter months. Some dogs survived and many did not; it all depended on the capriciousness of natural circumstance. No, working for humans and taking their leftovers was far safer and offered some guarantees in an altogether insecure world.

Food sources have always been a critical aspect of existence. To the scientist, the food chain is a delicately balanced ecosystem of animal and plant nutrition. To the modern domestic dog the food chain is the place where those wonderful cans, bags, and cellophane-wrapped boxes come from that fill the bowls of Canine America. Dogs and other pets have come a long way, baby, from those Ice Age campfires and dinosaur table-scraps. Modern dog food is a nutritional miracle hatched from the innovative chemistry of Industry and Science . . . and dogs never had it so good.

The first commercially prepared dog food was a biscuit product introduced in England about 1860. Dry dog foods were subsequently developed with formulas based on the nutritional knowledge of the day, but none approached the nutritious, full-feed rations produced today.

After World War I, canned horsemeat for dog food was introduced in the United States. In the 1930s, canned cat food and dry-mixed meal dog foods were introduced. The fifties saw the introduction of dry expanded-type pet foods. The 1960s were marked with great diversification in the types of food available to the dog and cat owner, which included the newly developed soft-moist products, and dry foods which make instant sauce or gravy when moisture is added. In the 1970s the multibillion-dollar pet food industry has concerned itself with the areas of nutrition and convenience.

The major sources for pet foods are those that are mass-manufactured and nationally distributed throughout the country. A new phenomenon is the self-styled "pet gourmet" shops that are springing up in many urban areas. These shops specialize in fresh meats that have been bagged and frozen, canned specialties such as calves kidneys in cream sauce, and braised ragouts of chicken, beef, or fish. To be sure, they have captured only a small portion of the pet-food market. Of course, there are still many folks who either prepare special meals for their pets or feed them the same meals that they are having. It is a fair assumption, however, to state that most pet owners use one of the many commercially manufactured dog foods.

Commercially Prepared Dog Food

DRY DOG FOODS

These grain or cereal types are made of meal, pellet and expanded forms, and biscuits. Each pound of dry dog food contains between 1,600 and 1,700 calories and 10 percent moisture. Palatability to the dog is increased when the food is moistened. Dogs eat around 20 percent more when water has been added.

Expanded foods are made in larger particles than the meal or pellet forms and are sprayed with fat which adds to palatability. Dogs like it. This is the type of dry food used most often in self-feeding programs.

Another dry-type food is biscuits. Although this form of dry food is often used as a treat or reward, there are still many pet owners utilizing dog biscuits as a staple meal. The manufacturers of the better-selling biscuits claim that the baking process does not destroy any of the nutrient content as was once thought.

SOFT-MOIST FOODS

Most soft-moist products are red in color and hamburgerlike in texture. They give the appearance of ground meat and are high in palatability. They contain close to 25 percent moisture and between 1,400 and 1,500 calories per pound. These are considered complete and balanced foods and are fed as the sole diet or as a supplement to other type of foods, including homemade.

CANNED FOODS

Canned products are produced in three forms: (1) All-meat with vitamins and minerals added. All-meat can contain beef, chicken, or horsemeat. There are approximately 600 calories per pound, but most cans are slightly under one pound. (2) All-meat (without vitamins and minerals added). This type is never served as a sole diet without nutritional deficiency problems developing. When using all-meat canned products, it must comprise only 25 percent of the total meal and be mixed with 75 percent of a properly balanced food. (3) Regular canned dog food. This is the most common canned dog food. It contains mixtures of meats, cereals, and other nutrients to make up a balanced diet. Each can contains approximately 500 calories. Not every brand includes high-quality protein. Poor-quality protein is not recommended for older dogs. Be choosy when buying dog food. The cheaper, nonbrand name products should be suspect because one can assume only that the price is reduced because the protein ingredients (the most expensive part of dog food) are of dubious quality. House brands of some supermarkets are less expensive because they do not advertise. These brands may contain high-quality protein such as beef, eggs, or cottage cheese. Read the ingredients on the label.

HOMEMADE DOG FOOD

There is absolutely nothing wrong with preparing dog food at home using the same foods consumed by humans providing the dog's diet is properly balanced according to his needs. However, it is costly and somewhat complicated if you are going to ensure your pet's health by formulating the correct ratios of protein to carbohydrate to fat to vitamins to minerals. Vitamins and minerals can be obtained from high-quality supplements available in all pet-supply stores. The nutritional values (protein, carbohydrate, and fat) of human food can be found in many books including several weight-reduction books. The quantity of protein, carbohydrate, and fat each dog needs is essentially based on weight, age, size, and environment. If you are planning to feed your dog homemade food, please consult the following charts to compare the complete and balanced diet obtained in high-quality commercial dog foods with the nutritional composition of your own recipes. Your dog's calorie requirements can be found in the feeding chart on page 131. To better understand what some foods offer in nutritional values read *Understanding Your Dog's Nutrition* later in this chapter. The formulation for homemade dog food is also discussed in Chapter 7.

Self-Feeding (ad libitum)

Self-feeding allows a pup to eat whenever it wants to, which enables it to match its food intake with its energy and growth needs. If an animal is never introduced to scheduled meals, it will not overeat or undereat. Self-feeding takes the guesswork out of feeding. Your dog will probably eat the right amount to maintain proper nutrition. Use the major brands of dry foods and consult your veterinarian about feeding puppy food, liver-flavor, or high-protein products. When using lesser-known brands of dog food, read the label and check it against the charts on pages 128–129 which reflect the nutrition required by all dogs. The figures in these charts were formulated by The National Research Council, which is a part of the National Academy of Sciences. Be certain the food products you feed your dog are correct for his needs. Ask your veterinarian.

Self-feeding programs are appropriate for growing puppies, adult dogs, pregnant dogs, nursing (lactating) dogs, and working dogs. All self-feeding programs require dry dog food and a separate bowl of water. However, it is a good idea to add water to dry food for gestating (pregnant) or lactating females with large litters. The same applies for hardworking dogs. Water added to a dry diet negates the self-feeding routine. This mixture will go bad eventually.

There are many pet owners afraid of self-feeding diets because they suspect their dogs will consume all the food that is made available. It has been documented that over 90 percent of all self-feeding dogs take only that amount of food that they require and no more. If a dog devours all the dry food that is put before him for an entire week, he is probably neurotic and should be fed scheduled meals determined by his age, weight, and size. (See Scheduled Meals Feeding Chart later in this chapter.)

How to Implement a Self-Feeding Program

Allow the dog or puppy to feed himself from a bowl in which dry food is always available. Allow the food to remain available on a twenty-four-hour basis. Maintain a large bowl of fresh water twenty-four hours a day near the food. Do not add water to the dry food or it will spoil.

If you are going to try the self-feeding plan, be certain the food selected is a complete and balanced diet and says so on the package. With this in mind, it is important not to unbalance a well-balanced diet with overuse of table snacks, manufactured food supplements, or manufactured dog snacks. Milk in small quantities makes a fine, nourishing snack (if it agrees with your dog), and occasional dog biscuits are also healthy.

Traditional Meal Schedules

As a traditional alternative to self-feeding, you may choose to feed a prescribed amount of food at a set time. The options for this style of feeding program are dry, soft-moist, canned, or home-made dog food. Calculate your dog's dietary needs by matching size, weight, age, and environment with the proper amount of food to be fed. For example, field dogs, sled dogs, racing dogs, cattle and sheep dogs, and others expending greater energy perform most satisfactorily when kept in a lean, muscular condition. A fat dog will not perform as well as a lean, muscular one. Neither will an underfed dog.

Because determining a dog's nutritional requirements involves a complicated set of calculations from various tables and charts, the following feeding chart is provided in order to simplify that procedure. Here you will find calories required, quantity of food to give, and a healthful schedule. Note that this chart does not take into consideration the special nutritional needs of dogs in stress, in unusual working conditions, suffering various illnesses, in gestation, or in lactation. The information provided pertains to average dogs living under normal conditions for domestic pets. The Scheduled Meals feeding chart on page 131 was provided through the courtesy of the Gaines Dog Research Center.

Canned food calories can be determined by checking the chart for your dog's calorie requirements and calculating the quantity of canned contents nearest that caloric figure. Premium canned food contains between 500 and 600 calories per can.

FEEDING PUPPIES (WEANING TO 3 MONTHS)

The alternatives are self-feeding or three meals a day. A growing puppy needs approximately 100 calories per pound of body weight per day. A puppy of this age requires almost double the nutrients of an adult dog on a standard maintenance diet. Your puppy's energy requirements are also increased, so his total food intake will be relatively greater in ratio to his body weight. At this age the protein should be of the highest quality for body growth which takes place at a rapid rate. Pet owners should introduce a high-quality commercial dog food or such protein sources as eggs, meat, and cottage cheese. Carbohydrates, fats, vitamins, and minerals must also be given. Between the ages of eight weeks to four months, the average puppy will require an amount of food equivalent to 10 to 15 percent of his body weight every twenty-four hours. From weaning to three months, your dog should be fed at 7:00 A.M., noon, and 5:00 P.M.

It is very common at this age for the puppy to leave his litter and transfer from the charge of the breeder or pet store to the new owner. If a change of diet is desired, the owner must find out what the small dog's diet has been and try to obtain a small supply so that a gradual change from the old diet to the new one can take place without upsetting the animal's stomach and digestive system. The new foods should be introduced gradually until the old diet is completely replaced. Food must always be served lukewarm or at room temperature. Cooked or dry cereal, cooked rice or toast mixed with warm milk, meat broth, or finely chopped raw beef may be fed temporarily until a high-quality commercial dog food is introduced. If a puppy is infested with worms, he will not receive all the nutrition from his food. Puppies must be checked for internal parasites from three weeks on. (See Chapter 8, section on internal parasites.)

FEEDING THREE-TO-FIVE-MONTH-OLD PUPPIES

Once again the options are self-feeding or scheduled meals, three times daily. When using commercial dog food, supplements may be required to balance the diet with vitamins and minerals unless a premium-quality product is purchased. Homemade

RECOMMENDED NUTRIENT REQUIREMENTS FOR DOGS[a]

(Percentage or Amount Per Unit of Food)

Nutrient		On a Dry Basis	Dry-Type Dog Food	Soft-Moist Dog Food	Complete Canned Dog Foods
Food Solids	%	100	90	75	25
Water	%	0	10	25	75
Protein	%	22	20	17	6.0
Fat	%	5.5	5.0	4.0	1.4
Linoleic or Arachidonic Acid	%	1.6	1.4	1.2	0.4
Carbohydrate (mx)[b]	%	67.0	60.0	50.0	17.0
Calcium	%	1.1	1.0	0.8	0.3
Phosphorus	%	0.9	0.8	0.7	0.3
Potassium	%	0.6	0.5	0.5	0.2
Sodium Chloride	%	1.0	0.9	0.8	0.3
Magnesium	%	0.05	0.05	0.04	0.01

		Per Lb.	Per Kg.	Per Lb.	Per Kg.	Per Lb.	Per Kg.	Per Lb.	Per Kg.
Iron	mg	26.0	57.32	23.40	51.59	19.5	42.99	6.50	14.33
Copper	mg	3.3	7.28	2.97	6.55	2.48	5.47	0.83	1.83
Cobalt[c]	mg	1.1	2.43	0.99	2.18	0.83	1.83	0.28	0.62
Manganese	mg	2.2	4.85	1.98	4.37	1.65	3.64	0.55	1.21
Zinc	mg	50.0	110.23	45.0	99.21	37.50	82.67	12.50	27.56

RECOMMENDED NUTRIENT REQUIREMENTS FOR DOGS[a] (cont'd)

(Percentage or Amount Per Unit of food)

		Per Lb.	Per Kg.	Per Lb.	Per Kg.	Per Lb.	Per Kg.	Per Lb.	Per Kg.
Iodine	mg	0.7	1.54	0.63	1.39	0.53	1.17	0.18	0.40
Vitamin B$_{12}$	mg	0.01	0.02	0.01	0.02	0.008	0.015	0.003	0.005
Folic Acid	mg	0.08	0.18	0.07	0.15	0.06	0.13	0.02	0.04
Thiamin (B$_1$)	mg	0.44	0.97	0.40	0.87	0.33	0.73	0.11	0.24
Riboflavin (B$_2$)	mg	0.98	2.16	0.88	1.94	0.74	1.63	0.25	0.55
Pyridoxine (B$_6$)	mg	0.44	0.97	0.40	0.88	0.33	0.73	0.11	0.24
Pantothenic Acid	mg	0.99	2.18	0.89	1.96	0.74	1.63	0.25	0.55
Niacin	mg	4.80	10.58	4.32	9.52	3.60	7.94	1.20	2.65
Choline	mg	550.00	1212.53	495.00	1091.28	412.50	909.40	137.50	303.13
Vitamin A[d]	I.U.	2268.00	5000.00	2041.20	4500.00	1701.00	3750.00	567.00	1250.00
Vitamin D[e]	I.U.	220.00	484.00	198.00	436.00	165.00	363.00	55.00	121.00
Vitamin E[f]	I.U.	22.00	48.50	19.80	43.65	16.50	36.38	5.50	12.13
Vitamin K[g]	mg	0.64	1.40	0.58	1.26	0.48	1.05	0.16	0.35

[a] The values are based on data compiled by the National Academy of Sciences–National Research Council[3], by the Cornell Research Laboratory for Diseases of Dogs[4] and by Gaines–General Foods Corporation.

[b] Carbohydrates are present in dog foods as a protein saving nutrient; the digested sugars and starches are used for energy and the cellulose for proper elimination. There is no evidence that carbohydrates are required per se but because they are part of many ingredients a maximum is suggested.

[c] Dietary cobalt is not normally required if adequate vitamin B$_{12}$ is present in the diet.

[d] 1 I.U. = 1 U.S.P. unit = 0.344 mg. crystalline vitamin A acetate = 0.3 mg. vitamin A alcohol = 0.6 mg. of betacarotene.

[e] One oz. of vitamin D$_3$ equals 40,000 I.U.

[f] As alpha-tocopherol, 1 I.U. = 1 mg.

[g] Under normal conditions, the vitamin K needs are met through intestinal synthesis.

From "Gaines Basic Guide to Canine Nutrition," Third Edition. Courtesy of Gaines Dog Research Center.

CONVERSION FACTORS FOR TABLES APPEARING ON PAGES 118-119

Units Given	Units Wanted for Conversion				
lb	g	× 453.6	kcal/kg	kcal/lb	× 0.4536
lb	kg	× 0.4536	kcal/lb	kcal/kg	× 2.2046
oz	g	× 28.35	ppm	μg/g	× 1.
kg	lb	× 2.2046	ppm	mg/kg	× 1.
kg	mg	× 1,000,000.	ppm	mg/lb	× 0.4536
kg	g	× 1,000.	mg/kg	%	× 0.0001
g	mg	× 1,000.	ppm	%	× 0.0001
g	μg	× 1,000,000.	mg/g	%	× 0.1
mg	μg	× 1,000.	g/kg	%	× 0.1
mg/g	mg/lb	× 453.6	°F	°C	× °F − 32 × 0.5556
mg/kg	mg/lb	× 0.4536	°C	°F	× °C × 1.8 + 32
μ/kg	μg/lb	× 0.4536			

WEIGHT EQUIVALENTS

1 lb	= 453.6 g	= 0.4536 kg
1 oz	= 28.35 g	
1 kg	= 1,000. g	= 2.2046 lb
1 g	= 1,000 mg	
1 mg	= 1,000 μg	= 0.001 g
1 μg	= 0.001 mg	= 0.000001 g
1 μg per g or 1 mg per kg = 1 ppm		

ABBREVIATION OF TERMS

kg	kilogram(s)
g	gram(s)
mg	milligram(s)
μg or mcg	microgram(s)
lb	pound(s)
oz	ounce(s)

SCHEDULED MEALS

Feeding Chart for Dogs—Various Ages and Sizes

Age No. of Feedings Per Day	Breed[a] Size	Weight In Lbs.	Calories[b] Per Day	Amount per Feeding	
				Dry 1 Cup = 8 Oz. Measuring Cup	Soft Moist 6 Oz. Package = 2 Burgers
Weaning to 3 Mo. Three per day or Self-Feeding	Very small Small Medium Large Very large	1–3 3–6 6–12 12–20 15–25	130–343 343–572 572–943 943–1384 1113–1650	⅛–⅓ cup ⅓–⅔ ⅔–1 1–1½ 1¼–1¾	⅛–¼ pkg. ¼–⅓ ⅓–⅔ ⅔–1 ¾–1
3–5 Mo. Three per day or Self-Feeding	Very small Small Medium Large Very large	3–10 5–15 12–25 15–35 25–50	343–816 494–1113 943–1650 1113–2100 1650–2750	⅓–¾ cup ½–1¼ 1–1¾ 1¼–2¼ 1¾–3	¼–½ pkg. ⅓–¾ ⅔–1 ¾–1⅓ 1–1¾
5–7 Mo. Two per day or Self-Feeding	Very small Small Medium Large Very large	4–12 12–25 20–35 35–50 50–90	426–943 943–1650 1384–2100 2100–2750 2750–4302	⅔–1½ cups 1½–2⅔ 2¼–3⅓ 3⅓–4⅓ 4⅓–7	½–1 pkg. 1–1⅔ 1⅓–2 2–2¾ 2¾–4¼
7–12 Mo. Two per day or Self-Feeding	Very small Small Medium Large Very large	6–12 12–25 25–45 45–70 70–100	572–943 943–1650 1650–2556 2556–3542 3542–4640	1–1½ cups 1½–2⅔ 2⅔–4 4–5⅔ 5⅔–7½	⅔–1 pkg. 1–1⅔ 1⅓–2½ 2½–3½ 3½–4½
Adult Two per day or Self-Feeding	Very small Small Medium Large Very large	6–12 12–25 25–50 50–90 90–175	286–472 472–825 825–1375 1375–2151 2151–3675	½–¾ cups ¾–1⅓ 1½–2¼ 2¼–3½ 3½–6	⅓–½ pkg. ½–¾ ¾–1⅓ 1⅓–2 2–3⅔

[a] Here are examples of weights at maturity:

Very small 6–12 lbs.	toy poodle, Yorkshire terrier
Small 12–25 lbs.	cocker spaniel, fox terrier
Medium 25–50 lbs.	Dalmatian, springer spaniel
Large 50–90 lbs.	Labrador retriever, German shepherd
Very large 90–175 lbs.	Great Dane, St. Bernard

[b] The reduction in calories required per unit of body weight occurs gradually as the dog approaches maturity.

[c] The total daily intake is the amount shown times the number of recommended feedings.

[d] The ideal or desired weight must be determined for each individual dog.

[e] Requirements vary due to differences in size, environment, activity and types of stress.

RECOMMENDED NUTRIENT REQUIREMENTS FOR DOGS[a]

(Amounts per unit of body weight per day)

Nutrients		Adult maintenance Per Lb. of Body Wt.	Adult maintenance Per Kg. of Body Wt.	Growing puppies Per Lb. of Body Wt.	Growing puppies Per Kg. of Body Wt.
Protein	g.	2.3	5.1	4.6	10.1
Fat	g.	0.6	1.3	1.1	2.5
Linoleic or Arachidonic Acid	g.	0.2	0.4	0.3	0.7
Carbohydrate (mx)[b]	g.	7.0	15.4	14.0	30.8
MINERALS:					
Calcium	mg.	115	253	230	506
Phosphorus	mg.	94	207	188	414
Potassium	mg.	63	138	125	276
Sodium Chloride	mg.	104	230	209	460
Magnesium	mg.	5.2	11.5	10.4	23.0
Iron	mg.	0.6	1.3	1.2	2.6
Copper	mg.	0.076	0.167	0.152	0.334
Cobalt [c]	mg.	0.025	0.056	0.051	0.112
Manganese	mg.	0.05	0.11	0.10	0.22
Zinc	mg.	1.2	2.5	2.3	5.1
Iodine	mg.	0.016	0.035	0.032	0.070
VITAMINS:					
Vitamin A	I.U.	52	115	104.	230
Vitamin D	I.U.	5.0	11.0	10.0	22.0
Vitamin E [d]	I.U.	0.5	1.1	1.0	2.2
Vitamin B_{12}	µg.	0.21	0.46	0.42	0.92
Folic Acid	µg.	1.9	4.1	3.8	8.3
Thiamin (B_1)	µg.	10.1	22.3	20.2	44.6
Riboflavin (B_2)	µg.	22.5	49.7	45.1	99.4
Pyridoxine (B_6)	µg.	10.1	22.3	20.2	44.6
Pantothenic Acid	µg.	22.7	50.1	45.5	100.3
Niacin	µg.	110	243	221	487
Vitamin K [e]	µg.	14.6	32.2	29.2	64.4
Choline	mg.	12.7	27.9	25.3	55.8

[a] The values are based on data compiled by the National Academy of Sciences–National Research Council[3], by the Cornell Research Laboratory for Diseases of Dogs[4] and by Gaines–General Foods Corporation.

[b] Carbohydrates are present in dog foods as a protein saving nutrient; the digested sugars and starches are used for energy and the cellulose for proper elimination. There is no evidence that carbohydrates are required per se but because they are part of many ingredients a maximum is suggested.

[c] Dietary cobalt is not normally required if adequate vitamin B_{12} is present in the diet.

[d] As alpha-tocopherol, 1 I.U. = 1 mg.

[e] Under normal conditions the vitamin K needs are met through intestinal synthesis.

From "Gaines Basic Guide to Canine Nutrition," Third Edition. Courtesy of Gaines Dog Research Center.

meals will certainly have to be balanced when formulated or compensated for with a high-quality vitamin and mineral supplement. Check with your veterinarian in either case. Feed the puppy at 7:00 A.M., noon, and 5:00 P.M.

Dry dog food may be moistened with warm milk or water for each of the three meals. It is desirable for the food, however, to be less moist than before and more crunchy. This is an important time to control the puppy's diet and not allow it to become fat—cute as he may look in that plump state. Of course the young dog mustn't be allowed to lose weight and get too thin, either. Food may be increased or decreased depending on the physical look of the dog. A veterinarian can best make this determination for the novice dog owner. This is also the time to recheck the puppy for internal parasite infestation. Dr. Michael Katz states, "Worms in puppies are so common that it is almost their birthright." (See Chapter 8, section on internal parasites.)

At fourteen weeks the puppy's permanent teeth begin to appear through the gums and this creates teething pain. Your dog will begin to chew anything and everything to ease his discomfort just as a human infant will. Although they have no nutritional value, large beef knucklebones may help satisfy the need to chew. Ice cubes or a damp-frozen washcloth may work better. Do not give any dog smaller or splintery-type bones. These can be swallowed and either puncture tissue or lodge in the throat, causing serious injury or death. Chewed-up bone material also causes constipation.

Feeding Five-to-Seven-month-old Puppies

At this age, your dog can have two or three meals a day depending on his appetite. Because this is a rapid growth period, the dog's food must be increased at each feeding to meet the caloric demands created by growth and body change. His food must be balanced with the proper ratio of proteins, carbohydrates, fats, vitamins, and minerals. Water must be made available at all times. Keep the bowl immaculate. (Self-feeding is still a fine option. During this growth period, this feeding program has its maximum advantage.) Feed the dog at 7:00 A.M. *and* 5:00 P.M. A noontime feeding is optional.

Feeding Seven-to-Ten-month-old Puppies

During this period your dog is beginning to approach his full maturity. This is more true of the smaller breeds, and less true of the slow-maturing large breeds. This, of course, affects dietary demand. For the average dog, two meals a day may be continued. With eating patterns set, you can add various snacks and table scraps of a wholesome nature to the basic food ration. Meat, chicken, cheese, along with fat trimmings (cooked), vegetables, soups, gravies, bacon drippings, and cottage cheese may all be used as supplemental snack foods—but in modest portions. If your dog is on a self-feeding program, avoid snacks completely. Self-feeding dogs must not be indulged with supplemental feeding, or their body clocks will be disrupted and digestive schedules thrown off. Between-meal feedings of dogs on meal schedules must be avoided. Feed the dog at 7:00 A.M. and again at 5:00 P.M.

FEEDING ADULT DOGS (MAINTENANCE DIET)

One cannot deny the many advantages of self-feeding, which include good digestion, healthy metabolism, proper absorption of food nutrients and, in the long run, financial savings. However, high-quality commercially prepared dog foods (dry, soft-moist, and canned) fed on a scheduled-meal basis will keep an adult dog healthy and enjoyable. At ten months of age a dog may be considered adult and fed twice a day: at 7:00 A.M. and at 5:00 P.M. If your dog begs for more food, a small but nourishing snack or biscuit may be given. In cold weather he will eat more. Ask your veterinarian to establish your dog's normal body weight and condition. A well-balanced diet supplying all of your dog's nutritional requirements will establish a good-looking, healthy coat, a well-formed, normal stool, and all the energy he needs for his regular daily activities.

If your dog's appetite falls off it is probably not very serious. There is usually a reason for a dog's appetite falling off. It is quite possible that he ate something which either caused nausea or some other neurologic sensation which was unpleasant. If the dog is still active, wants to go for walks, doesn't get tired, wants to play, just let his appetite be boss for a few days. If the dog refuses to take food for three or four days, a visit to the veterinarian is in order. Some young dogs experience a change in metabolism and need to create their own feeding schedule. When this happens, a self-feeding program is well worth trying, providing the dog is not sick.

Always consider the dog's environment when determining the amount to feed him. The amount fed may not be correct when considering temperature, relative humidity, space, ventilation, or other environmental conditions, especially if they change. A dog kept in an open kennel in cold weather needs about 70 to 90 percent more calories than an identical dog in warm surroundings.

Generalized feeding information applies only to average dogs living under normal circumstances. If your dog loses weight, increase his food. Obviously, if your dog gains weight beyond his established norm, his food intake must be reduced. If your dog maintains his normal weight as established by your veterinarian, you are feeding the correct amount of food.

The following Rate of Growth Chart can be useful for puppy and young dog owners. From toy breeds to oversized breeds, you can obtain a generalized view of how fast a dog's weight will develop over a thirty-month period. Of course these figures are based on mean averages but can help indicate if a dog is overweight or underweight.

Understanding Your Dog's Nutrition

Modern diets for dogs are based on feeding studies conducted in thousands of tests during growth, pregnancy, and lactation. America's dogs and cats, consuming well-balanced commercial foods, receive a better-balanced diet than most of America's children. Feeding and nutrition of developing puppies can influence size (length, height, weight), shape or conformation, temperament, skin texture, health, scenting ability, and skeletal development. Fortunately, most of these factors can be maintained in the normal puppy within acceptable limits, helping him mature satisfactorily through the reasonable intake of a nutritionally complete diet.

Every pet owner can achieve a high level of nutrition for his animals without becoming a nutrition specialist. He can select from the excellent pet foods available and regulate the intake to achieve optimum nutrient intake economically and conveniently. He can model his pet to the flesh condition desired and still maintain a balanced dietary consumption. A nutritional background will help the pet owner to better understand his pet and the problems likely to be encountered.

More has been learned about nutrition in the past forty years than was learned during the previous forty centuries. Nutrition comprises the food given to animals supplying all of the essentials needed during various phases of the animal's life and activities. Food is composed of all of the forty-three-plus nutrients in combinations to supply the body with everything nutritionally needed for the purpose for which it will be used in the body. All dogs, regardless of size, shape, age, or activity, require the same nutrients,

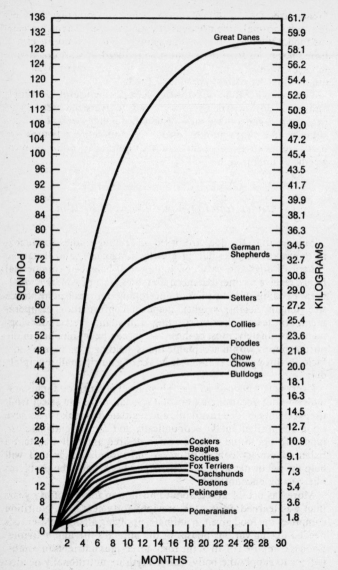

MONTHS

Nutrient requirements for dogs, revised 1974,
National Research Council, National Academy of Science.

but in varying amounts. These are the same nutrients needed by man, except for vitamin C. The nutrient content of specific foods depends on initial formulation, handling during producing and storage, plus the availability and stability of the various dietary components.

The following chart shows all of the best human foods needed to match in nutritive values that which is obtained in one pound of high-quality dog food. In other words, one pound of quality dog food contains the same amount of nutrition as all the other human foods combined.

ENERGY

Dogs expend energy in almost every form of body activity. Their energy is obtained from either oxidation of food or from destruction of their own bodily sources of energy. The utilization of dietary energy by dogs is influenced by food consumed, when the food was eaten, the quantity of food stored in the body, and the amount of exercise.

Energy is obtained from many sources, which can be absorbed and broken down into simpler substances by the body, which includes proteins, carbohydrates, fats, and other organic materials. Most types of fats are more than 95 percent digested in the dog and contribute more than twice as much energy as an equal weight of carbohydrate or protein.

The energy remaining after fecal and urinary loss and increased body heat associated with digestion is available for maintenance, voluntary activity, and production or storage within the body. Since energy comes from proteins, carbohydrates, and fat, the measurement of energy content of a ration is not easy. Not all absorbed nutrients are oxidized by the dog to the same extent. The total energy of a food is measured in a calorimeter in which the food is burned in an oxygen environment.

The energy requirements of dogs vary depending on size, age, and activity of the dog and the environmental temperature. The energy requirements of a dog per unit of body weight decreases as the dog's weight increases in size. This means a small dog requires more energy per pound of body weight than does a large dog. Part of this is related to the extra skin surface in the small dog, through which energy can be lost. This is the same principle that enables crushed ice to cool more rapidly due to the greater surface than that of an uncrushed ice cube.

Hard-working dogs using lots of muscular energy may consume up to three times as much energy as is needed for maintenance.

NUTRITIONAL VALUES OF HUMAN FOOD VS. DRY DOG FOOD

	Amount, Gm.	Water, %	Food Energy, Kcal.	Protein, Gm.	Fat, Gm.	Carbo-hydrate, Gm.	Vitamin A Equivalent In International Units	Thiamine, Mg.	Ribo-Flavin, Mg.
One Pound of Good Dry Dog Food	454	10	1511	109	36.3	218	4340	2.05	2.41
4 strips bacon (crisp)	30	16	180	10	16	2	—	.16	.10
1 egg	50	74	80	6	6	—	590	.05	.15
8 oz. skim milk	245	90	90	9	Trace	12	10	.09	.05
Toast-dry	22	25	70	2	1	13	—	.06	.05
8 oz. fresh orange juice	248	88	110	2	1	26	500	.22	.07
1 chicken drumstick, fried	59	55	90	12	4	Trace	50	.03	.15
6 small green onions	50	88	20	1	Trace	5	Trace	.02	.02
1 ear sweet corn	140	74	70	3	1	16	310*	.09	.08
1 piece celery	40	94	5	Trace	Trace	2	100*	.01	.31
1 peach	114	89	35	1	Trace	10	1320*	.02	.05
Shrimp, 3 oz.	85	70	100	21	1	1	50	.01	.03
Baked potato, ⅓ lb.	99	75	90	3	Trace	21	Trace	.10	.04
Braised beef heart, 3 oz.	85	61	160	27	5	1	20	.21	1.04
4 spears asparagus	60	94	10	1	Trace	2	540*	.10	.11
8 oz. fresh milk	244	87	160	9	9	12	350	.07	.41
2 large lettuce leaves	50	94	10	1	Trace	2	950	.03	.04
	1621		1280	108	44	125	4790	1.27	2.70

*Source of vitamin A equivalent.

Human-type food data from "Nutritive value of foods," Home and Garden Bulletin No. 72. U. S. Department of Agriculture. Revised August 1970. Many values on some vitamins and minerals supplied in dog foods are not available for most human-type foods in published form.

Eight-week-old puppies and heavily lactating females require much more food and energy than normal adult dogs—up to three times as much.

Most dogs fed *ad libitum* will consume the quantity of food and calories needed to maintain their body weight. This amount varies from individual to individual. Some dogs require less than half as much energy per pound of body weight for maintenance as do others. Since individual dog variation makes it imperative that the owner keep track of the dog's condition and adjust the feed intake accordingly, a good rule is to feed one-third to one-half ounce of food per pound of body weight for each dog each day for dogs not working hard.

Protein. Proteins supply amino acids needed by the body. The most commonly known proteins are found in meat, vegetables, fish, and eggs. The amino acid composition of the protein can be influenced by:

- Sources of the protein
- The processing methods
- The combinations of proteins in the diet.

Egg protein is probably the best-known source of balanced amino acids for dogs. However, other proteins from meats, vegetables, and cereals can be combined in commercial rations to almost equal egg protein. Better-quality proteins are well digested and absorbed, and moderate heat treatment, if materials are processed, does not significantly reduce the value of the proteins. Excessive heat treatment will destroy the lysine (an amino acid).

Proteins are used for many purposes and are found within most systems in the dog's body. Protein forms tissues, such as muscle, hair, and ligaments, and is combined with carbohydrates, fats, and minerals in the body to form enzymes, hormones, various body fluids, and antibodies. Proteins enter into practically every phase of the normal dog's bodily activities. A specific level of protein is needed by the normal dog so that effective continuation of the normal body processes is possible. A normal dog consuming a ration containing 18 percent protein (dry food), about 8 percent fat, and 60 percent carbohydrates, is barely meeting his protein requirements. If the level of protein is increased to about 23 percent, then a safety margin occurs which helps cover the needs of those dogs that may have a slightly higher than normal protein requirement. The small amount of extra protein apparently helps increase disease-fighting antibody production. A large excess of protein can be tolerated fairly well by most normal dogs. Excess nitrogen is broken away from the protein or amino acid molecules and is eliminated through the urine. Most of the remaining portion of excess protein is metabolized as energy in the body and may be stored as fat. This excess protein may not be harmful to normal young dogs, but can be harmful to older dogs. Dogs with kidney problems tend to suffer when a high-protein diet is fed. That means too much meat, usually.

Carbohydrates. A large part of most dog foods is composed of carbohydrates which usually supply the most inexpensive source of energy. When properly prepared, carbohydrates are well utilized by normal dogs. Some starches, like those from potatoes, oats, and corn, are poorly digested unless first subjected to heat treatment. Carbohydrates also include the fibrous portions of rations. Fibers have several functions in the digestive tract. Some are digested and used as energy. Other fibers absorb a lot of water and produce a more voluminous dropping than do nonfibrous rations. This is helpful in stimulating and maintaining intestinal action, especially in senile or inactive dogs. Fibers aid in the prevention of constipation and other intestinal problems. Roughage in the form of bran and other plant parts is considered to be relatively indigestible carbohydrates. Although not absolutely essential to dogs, roughages help control the condition of the dog's digestive tract. Without this bulky nutrient, the intestinal tone of inactive and older dogs often becomes sluggish; the ingested material may tend to accumulate and thus precipitate constipation and other intestinal complications.

Roughage helps keep the intestinal contents more uniformly distributed throughout the intestinal tract. Roughage also acts like thousands of tiny sponges that pick up and hold water, helping to prevent diarrhea under normal circumstances and in preventing constipation.

For dogs with some liver and kidney ailments, a well-balanced diet with ample carbohydrates prevents excessive "work" of metabolizing proteins and is valuable in this respect.

Some sugars are efficiently used and tolerated by normal dogs. Others, like milk sugar or lactose, may be poorly utilized by some dogs. Many dogs cannot synthesize adequate quantities of the enzyme lactase, required for the digestion of the milk sugar. This is particularly true of older dogs. When the lactase level is low and milk sugar is high, the milk sugar tends to ferment in the digestive tract and can produce diarrhea. That is often why some dogs tend to scour (diarrhea) when given too much cow's milk, which is high in lactose (milk sugar). Young puppies fed too much cow's milk may scour for the same reason.

Fat. Fat is included in the dog's diet to provide a concentrated source of energy, fatty acids needed by the body (physiological requirement), as a taste factor, and as a carrier for vitamins A, D, E, and K. Fats are made up of smaller components called fatty acids. Most fats contain many different kinds of fatty acids. Some of these have a high melting point. These fatty acids are usually found in the fat from cattle, sheep, and horses. Other fats contain a large quantity of low-melting-point fatty acids which may or may not be liquid at household temperatures. These fats include pork, chicken, and highly unsaturated vegetable fats, such as corn oil. The source of dietary fats influences and helps determine the type of fat deposited in the dog's body to an extent, and the resulting body fat firmness.

The specific fat level required in the dog's diet is related to type of fat and fatty acid compositions being fed. A dog ration containing 4 percent pork fat will supply all of the fatty acids needed by a normal dog. The term "normal" dog used here has significance since some dogs may have had some diseases that have affected their dietary fat utilization. Dogs with pancreatic damage may not have the ability to utilize the fats efficiently. The pancreas secretes pancreatic lipase, an enzyme which aids in the digestion of fats. When this enzyme is deficient, fat may pass through the digestive tract in varied quantities without being efficiently utilized. Such dogs often develop dermatitis, dandruff, lusterless coats, itching, other indications of a dry skin, and diarrhea, due to increased fat in the stool.

Dysfunctional pancreatic activity can be compensated for by adding pancreatic enzyme to the diet so that the fat can be digested or by adding larger quantities of short-chain fats, such as corn oil, to the diet. Corn oil is absorbed through the digestive tract with minimum need for pancreatic activity. This is why corn oil for dogs with pancreatic problems is usually recommended by practicing veterinarians. Another factor to consider is that extra quantities of corn oil in the diet of show dogs will produce a more "oily" coat with sheen. Excess corn oil will, however, decrease food intake. Most fatty acids associated with cereals are highly unsaturated; thus some cereal grains are a good source of fatty acids.

VITAMINS

Vitamins are sometimes referred to as "the spark of life." They are required in extremely small quantities, but are necessary for life. The vitamins are categorized in two groups—depending on their solubility. One group includes fat-soluble vitamins (A, D, E, and K) and the other includes the water-soluble vitamins (B and

C). Some vitamins can be synthesized within the body from other food nutrients while others must be present in the diet. Fat-soluble vitamins tend to oxidize easily. This means that fats becoming rancid, or oxidizing excessively, may be devoid of these vitamins. That is why rancid fats should not be fed to dogs.

Vitamin A. Dogs can convert most of the carotene found in carrots, peaches, green plants, and from chemical and animal sources into vitamin A within their bodies. Many improperly fed animals receive inadequate quantities of vitamin A and cannot see well at night.

Vitamin A is essential for normal growth, reproduction, and physical maintenance of tissues within the body. If vitamin A is deficient, it is entirely possible for dogs to become deaf.

A deficiency of vitamin A leads to tissue malfunction and frequently large, coarse skin lesions. This may be the result of a deficiency in the ration or the dog's inability to absorb the vitamin A and fat from the ration. Extra vitamin A can be supplied to the dog in the ration and even applied topically to the skin lesions if recommended by your veterinarian. Vitamin A can be absorbed through the outside of the skin in some circumstances, although this is an inefficient route. Vitamin A deficiency signs are loss of appetite, poor growth, skin lesions—dryness, scaling and scratching, weak and infected eyes. (Skin problems are not always caused by vitamin A deficiency. Many systems having no relation to nutrition can cause skin problems.)

Vitamin D. Vitamin D is associated primarily with calcium absorption, transportation, and deposition within the body. Calcium absorption from the digestive tract is influenced to a large extent by the amount of vitamin D in the dog's body. Vitamin D is necessary for the effective passage of calcium across or through the intestinal wall into the bloodstream.

Vitamin D may be produced in the skin by irradiation from the sun acting on the skin fats or cholesterol. This process occurs in most animals, including man, although some scientists now doubt that the dog has this ability. Vitamin D^2 from animal sources and vitamin D^3 from irradiated plant sterols are both utilized by the dog.

A severe deficiency will prevent normal calcification of the bones of dogs, even when ample calcium is present. This results in rickets, improperly calcified bones, irregular teeth, and other skeletal defects. An excess of vitamin D may cause calcium to be deposited in abnormal places, including the heart, lungs, muscles, and blood vessels. Very large doses of vitamin D can kill animals, and dogs have died because of excess quantities of vitamin D added to their diets. Some owners have given their dogs excess vitamin D and thus produced abnormalities.

Vitamin K. Vitamin K is synthesized in the intestinal tract of dogs and other animals under normal conditions. When some drugs are included in the diet or specific stress occurs, vitamin K may not be produced in quantities sufficient for normal requirements, including maintenance of prothrombin levels (a plasma protein necessary for coagulation). Vitamin K is necessary to maintain the clotting factor in blood. This is why vitamin K activity, menadione bisulfite, or vitamin K[1] is added to commerical dog foods.

Vitamin E. Vitamin E is usually called the antisterility vitamin. It is a biological antioxidant and is considered necessary for several bodily functions. In a deficiency, the ovum can become fertilized, but apparently fail to become implanted in the uterus. The developing embryo may either die of "starvation" or just pass out of the tract. Too often vitamin E is destroyed in the body by feeding cod liver oil in the process of going rancid, or other oxidizing fats. Vitamin E is very important in reproduction. Forty-five International Units (I.U.) per kilogram of dry food are usually recommended, 37.5 I.U. for soft-moist, and 12.5 I.U. for canned products.

Muscular and nerve degeneration associated with a vitamin E deficiency has been described in cats and mink. A few reports have been made linking this problem to dogs.

Fats in the process of becoming rancid apparently destroy the vitamin E in the ration and in the animal's body. If wheat germ oil, cod liver oil, or other unsaturated fats or oils must be fed by the pet owner, then these oils should be fresh and kept in the refrigerator after the container has been opened in order to retard rancidity.

Thiamine (Vitamin B[1]). Also known as vitamin B[1], thiamine is necessary for dogs. A deficiency may cause loss of appetite, weight loss, and even convulsions. Thiamine is associated with carbohydrate use within the body.

Extra carbohydrates, such as potatoes and bread, given to dogs increase the dog's requirement for thiamine. The need for thiamine is decreased slightly when higher levels of fat are added. The composition of the diet influences the vitamin requirement. Cooking of food destroys part of the thiamine. Some pet owners have fed raw ground fish to dogs. Raw fish has been known to transmit tapeworms to dogs but has probably caused more trouble by creating a thiamine deficiency. Most freshwater raw fish, such as carp, contains thiaminase, an enzyme that destroys the thiamine. Cooking destroys thiaminase. However, the thiamine is usually destroyed by the thiaminase before the fish is cooked. Therefore, fish is a poor source of thiamine. This vitamin is obtained from a synthesis of bacteria in the digestive tract and from pork, beef, and some cereals. Pork, whole wheat, and oatmeal are the best natural food sources of thiamine.

Riboflavin (Vitamin B²).　Riboflavin is used in many body processes, especially those involving skin, eyes, and the lining of the mouth and digestive tract. Fresh milk is a good source of riboflavin, although it is very unstable when exposed to light. When a glass container of milk is placed in the sunshine, most of the riboflavin is lost within an hour. Commercial concentrated sources of riboflavin are available, and there is almost no chance of observing a riboflavin deficiency with modern rations.

Niacin (Nicotinic Acid).　Pellagra or "black tongue" in dogs is caused by a deficiency of niacin. A deficiency also shows up as dermatitis, loss of appetite, ulcers, and other abnormalities, including alternating diarrhea and constipation. Dogs in the Deep South and their owners consumed lots of cornmeal and grits in the past decades, and both frequently developed "black tongue" or niacin deficiency. With today's modern foods, you will probably never see a niacin deficiency since niacin is relatively inexpensive and stable in the dog ration.

Pyridoxine (Vitamin B⁶).　Yeast, liver, cereal grains, and meats are excellent sources of pyridoxine. This vitamin helps make possible the utilization of carbohydrates in the body. Deficiencies cause slow growth, anemia, convulsions, and excitability. A pyridoxine deficiency is not likely to occur in commercially prepared rations even when nonnutritional supplements are fed.

Pantothenic Acid.　Pantothenic acid is found in all animal tissues and is part of each body cell. A deficiency of this vitamin may be associated with depigmentation or discoloration of hair, hemorrhage, poor growth, convulsions, and even with death. Since pantothenic acid is found in most tissues and is not easily destroyed by heat, there is little chance of a deficiency under normal circumstance.

Choline.　Choline is used in the fat transportation within the body and in many biochemical reactions. A deficiency is conducive to deposits of fat in and around the liver. Choline is inexpensive, and there is no excuse for a deficiency ever occurring.

Vitamin B¹². Vitamin B^{12} is of primary importance in red-blood-cell formation. It is essential to prevent and cure anemia and necessary for the development of healthy young pups. Dogs in heavy training need ample vitamin B^{12} to facilitate the development of large quantities of red blood cells which carry ample oxygen from the lungs to the muscles. Some sled dog owners inject vitamin B^{12} into the dogs prior to a race to increase the number of red blood cells. The increase in cells requires several days—this is very effective.

Dogs with hookworm infestations lose blood. Vitamin B^{12} is necessary to help in blood replenishment.

Vitamin C (Ascorbic Acid). Dogs usually do not need vitamin C; however, some dogs deviate from the normal. It is estimated that one dog in a thousand may need added vitamin C in the diet. If the diet is adequate, sufficient vitamin C normally is synthesized by the dog to meet all the needs satisfied by this vitamin. When scurvy does occur, the dogs will respond dramatically to the addition of vitamin C to the diet.

A dog with a vitamin C deficiency frequently shows severe pain after staying in one position for an extended period of time. For example, the dog has difficulty stretching his legs when he wakes up. He will return to normal after a few minutes only to get into this state again during the next nap. Ascorbic acid additions usually help under these conditions.

Pregnancy, lactation, and various sicknesses may require a greater than normal amount of vitamin C. When some females were fed a daily supplement of 50 mg. of ascorbic acid during pregnancy, the survival rate of the newborn puppies increased.

MINERALS

Minerals are very necessary in your dog's diet and enter practically every phase of body activity. Dogs would not live very long with a mineral-free diet. Minerals maintain the acid-base balance within the body and help regulate most body activities.

Calcium and Phosphorus. Calcium and phosphorus occur in the largest quantities in the dog's body. Both in combination and specific ratios, they form the major mineral portion of bone.

Ample calcium and phosphorus accompanied by other minerals and vitamins will help in the formation of good strong bones. When a deficiency or imbalance occurs, poor bone growth results.

Bone formation seems to be optimum when the level of calcium and phosphorus is adequate and associated nutrients, e.g., magnesium, vitamin D, choline, fluorine, and manganese, are present in adequate and balanced quantities. An excess of calcium can produce a phosphorus deficiency, and an excess of phosphorus can produce a calcium deficiency. Some foods are very poorly balanced. Lean meat contains approximately 0.01 percent calcium and 0.18 percent phosphorus. The ratio of minerals (with a ratio of 1.2 parts of calcium to 1 part of phosphorus being desirable) is extremely important. If a dog owner wants to add lean meat, it should be fed with a good commercial dry diet that can contribute the needed calcium. Unless added in carefully calculated quantities, calcium or calcium and phosphorus supplements should not be added to a dog's ration by his owner.

Magnesium. Magnesium in the diet helps to maintain good skeletal growth, deposition of minerals in the right places, and maintenance of body secretions. Deficiencies may cause many abnormalities. The feet of puppies raised on diets slightly deficient in magnesium have relaxed carpal joints or "flat feet." A similar foot condition is produced in pups raised on slick floors. The feet of greyhounds raised on concrete tend to be flat while those on concrete plus a covering of sand to provide good footing are tightly knuckled.

A magnesium deficiency in the dog's diet can also influence the deposition of calcium in soft muscle tissues, such as the heart and blood vessels. The calcium level in the dog's aorta could be increased up to forty times normal by an insufficient quantity of magnesium in the diet. Since minerals are needed in specific ratios, it is easy to see how extra calcium and phosphorus supplementation in a dog's diet can create a deficiency of magnesium.

Manganese. Manganese has long been known to be involved with both bone growth and enzyme production and temperament in animals. Much more needs to be known about all of the effects of manganese.

Zinc. Zinc is a component of hormones and enzymes (such as insulin) and is necessary for normal bones, muscles, and skin growth. Insulin was studied very early in dogs, and the role of zinc in insulin formation is well known. Little zinc is required, and there is no reason for it to be deficient in any good commercial diet.

Iron. Iron incorporated in hemoglobin helps in the transfer of oxygen and other gases in the bloodstream. An iron deficiency results in anemia. This is particularly true in dogs with hookworm infestations or otherwise sustained blood losses. A deficiency of iron is associated with coat color changes in some animals. Very seldom is additional iron supplementation necessary in normal, healthy dogs. About two-thirds of the total iron in the body is present in the blood. The most efficient food sources for iron are liver, heart, muscle, soybeans, and inorganic salts.

Copper and Cobalt. Copper and cobalt are also necessary for good iron utilization in the body and the prevention of anemia. Copper helps in the incorporation of iron into hemoglobin. Cobalt, in the form of vitamin B¹², also stimulates hemoglobin production.

Sodium Chloride. Salt in the dog's diet is one of the most variable and in some ways troublesome nutrients. Fresh meat contains very little salt, while water from some home soft-water conditioners may supply all of the sodium needed by normal dogs. This means that some older dogs with heart problems may receive excess salt, which can result in fluid accumulation around the heart and within the body. Even some older people in some areas receive more salt from the water than they need in their diet.

Salt helps maintain proper fluid balance within the body. An excess can throw a strain on the kidneys in some nephritic (kidney-diseased) dogs.

Salt is necessary for the production of gastric hydrochloric acid (HCl). Higher levels of salt will increase water intake.

Potassium. Potassium is adequate in normal diets, but deficiencies result in poor growth and restlessness. Deficiency impedes transmission of electrochemical impulses in nerve and muscle fibers, and reduces balancing activity of food intake and waste removal from cells. Potassium in the soil accounts for its presence in most food.

Iodine. Iodine-deficient areas occur in some parts of the world, and America produces many animals, including dogs and man, with thyroxine (iodine) deficiencies. Many large thyroids are the result of an iodine deficiency and the resultant growth of the thyroid gland to compensate for low thyroxine production. Use of iodized salt adequately supplies the dog's iodine needs.

Other Trace Minerals. Many other mineral nutrients such as fluorine, nickel, chromium, molybdenum, silicon, selenium, and others are apparently needed by dogs. These occur in such concentrations in normal ingredients that the production of specific deficiencies in animals is not always easy. Although some of the trace minerals are needed in remarkably small quantities, the toxic level of some required nutrients is not high.

Simple specific nutritional deficiencies will seldom be seen in animals outside of the laboratory. Usually any nutritional deficiencies will be complex and may involve a combination of amino acids, minerals, and vitamins; or an interaction with some diseases. Different levels of the same nutrient will produce different responses and degrees of response in dogs. This makes recognition and treatment of some problems difficult, especially when some may result from oversupplementation by the dog's owner.

The owner who is concerned with loving care of his dog should now appreciate the complexity of canine nutrition. Although feeding a dog seems as simple as opening a can or tearing the top of a bag, information and know-how can promote growth, maintain health, and provide all the energy a dog needs for his busy day. Dogs, like people, are very concerned about food. A well-fed dog is a good dog.

7. Weight Watching Your Dog

The four-legged epicure is not a dog breed. It is an eating machine. This kind of dog will consume large quantities of food whether it is hungry or not and create the impression that it savors gourmet cooking. Every home can now have its very own Jaws without all that ocean by simply regarding the family dog as one huge mouth. Of course, a dog must be trained for this. It takes a human being to condition a canine to respond to massive doses of nutrition. *Eat, Eat, My Pet* is a syndrome not necessarily restricted to dogs, but is just as disastrous when inflicted on children or puppies. Wild canids do not capture prey every day they hunt and sometimes eat only once or twice a week. They manage to survive. But the barrel-bellied dogs of many homes have been conditioned to salivate at the mere flick of the kitchen light switch.

People who overfeed their dogs or indulge them in exotic cookery do so out of deep feelings for their animals. They are like loving parents who sit and gaze adoringly at their plump babies as they spoonfeed more food than is necessary or healthy. Such dog owners are kind, sensitive, loving, and very often fat themselves. They mean well and honestly believe they are being good to their dogs. It is ironic and very sad that this behavior springs from love and good intentions.

Another syndrome is one in which the dog is taught to beg for his banana cream pie. In this way no one feels responsible for the inevitable bad results. When the lid comes off the pot, the room is steamed in fragrance from the braised roast bubbling in its own juicy goodness. At that moment, chowhounds and curs transform into waddling wags and heavy-set swains. They float into the kitchen on little cat-feet, courting their owners with meaningful glances, gentle touches, and wily whimpers. The reluctant humans are then seduced by these Casanovas of the kennels. Who can resist a chubby seducer with a hungry look?

Fat dogs are not born; they are created by uninformed, sometimes neurotic, overindulgent human beings. (Of course, this does not refer to you, but the others.) Does a dog really prefer a cheese omelette to kibbled cereal mixed with warm, savory pan drippings? He does not. Food becomes more palatable to dogs when it is moist and warm. You can be certain that the smell of any cooking is going to attract the family pet, but that doesn't mean he must be given a portion.

Pudgy puppies and fatso dogs may be cute and lovable, but they are also in for a bad medical history and a shortened life span. When we give in to the gastronomical yearnings of our overweight dogs, we are literally killing them with kindness. Whether cooking to order or opening a can of dog food, do not allow your dog to get fat. That translates into a sensible diet of measured nutrition or, if started early in life, a self-feeding dry-food diet. If your dog already wears a large corporation around his middle, it is time to trim it down with the help of a weight-reducing diet. It is only through weight reduction and sensible feeding that portly pooches have a chance at true happiness, good health, and long life.

Obesity—What It Is

When a dog carries too much weight, it is attributed to one of two ailments: simple obesity or constitutional obesity. When there is endocrine or metabolic dysfunction, such as hypothyroidism, the result is constitutional obesity. This can only be determined by a veterinarian using the appropriate diagnostic procedures and requires special medical attention.

The most common form of overweight is simple obesity. This is the result of assimilation, over an extended period of time, of calories in excess of current metabolic needs. In other words, the dog takes in more calories of food than it needs in its daily activities and stores them in its body as fat cells for future use. The problem is that it hardly ever uses them and they remain in the body as excess fat tissue. Hence, the fat dog.

There are several other interesting theories explaining the causes of obesity. One deals with the existence of a thermostat-type mechanism located at the base of the brain in the hypothalamus. It supposedly acts as a regulator for the quantity of food stored in the body. The overweight patient is said to have the thermostat set too high, so that more fat is stored than is needed. More research is needed to successfully utilize this theory in the pursuit of weight reduction.

Another idea gaining attention states that some individual mammals are born with, or develop in infancy, an undue increase in adipocytes, or fat-storage cells. Overindulgent parents (or dog owners) offer too much food at an early stage of life and help develop this large mass of fat-storing space in the body. The result allegedly is that one may reduce the size of the cells but not their quantity, thus allowing for a large potential fat-storage area within the body. Some researchers offer this as the explanation for those who lose weight but then gain it all back soon after. Refraining from overfeeding during infancy or puppyhood is more than likely a good preventive for avoiding adult obesity, whether the above theory is valid or not.

Overweight can also be attributed to the sedentary existence of many dogs and humans, especially those getting older. A fat dog lying around the house is a perfect example. In this situation, the quantity of food is not diminished to match the reduced activity of middle or old age. The result is added poundage.

Obesity—What It Does

The largest statement possible about obesity is that it shortens the life of the dog. Do not be fooled by the word "obesity," either. One tends to get off the hook by saying a dog (or human) has to look like Jumbo before being considered obese. Not true. *If your dog is 15 percent or 20 percent over his normal weight, he is obese.*

Among the specific ailments caused by obesity which shortens life expectancy is *osteoarthritis*, which is an inflammatory and degenerative change of the bones at the joints. This is a serious form of arthritis and causes pain and temporary or permanent lameness. Although old age is a primary cause, many young dogs suffer with this disease because of obesity. When the dog's weight is reduced, the dog's symptoms are also reduced. A young dog with no genetic background of osteoarthritis should not suffer from this disease. The overweight dog who is physically active will put abnormal stress on the joints and thus create ideal conditions for producing crippling arthritis. Once the pain begins, the dog stops exercising. This in turn creates a further inbalance between the calories consumed and the calories used, and even more weight is added to the body.

Excess weight can interfere with a veterinarian's ability to make a proper diagnosis of a patient's complaint. Thick layers of fat make abdominal examinations extremely difficult and sometimes impossible. Fat dogs are also poor risks for surgery. An overweight dog's reaction to anesthesia can be dangerous. Fatty tissue can also interfere with surgical access and can cause slow post-operative healing or even infection.

Obesity sometimes worsens already existing illness. These complications can cause loss of coat and other related skin infections, chronic coughing from crowding of heart and lung spaces, heart strain, torn muscles and ligaments, or undue stress on the liver and pancreas. Studies have also indicated that obese dogs have less resistance to viral or bacterial infections than dogs of normal weight.

Fat dogs are neither jolly, cute, joyful, nor good-looking. They are lethargic, listless, and asleep much of the time. The heavy-set swain may be a great lovable huggy, but he sure does have a performance problem.

Obesity—How It Happens

For most dogs, obesity starts in puppyhood with little or no knowledge of nutrition on the part of the owner. The entire situation can be summed up in one word: *overfeeding*. If a puppy or young dog is fed table scraps, then the quantity of food he eats depends on the human appetite and how much has gone uneaten at the dinner table.

Special holidays afford the dog the opportunity to consume huge quantities of leftovers from a virtual cornucopia of very select garbage. Turkey, ham, yams, sweet potatoes, roasts of all sorts, cranberries, duck, goose, stuffing, bread pudding, pumpkin pie (with whipped cream) are all part of the festival foods that dogs grow accustomed to bolting down in ever-increasing amounts. Once the young dog's appetite and feeding habit is established, there's no stopping him if you wanted to (and the table-scrap feeder doesn't want to). By this time even commercial dog food is fed in too great a quantity, and the well-intentioned owner does not believe the manufacturer's prescribed amount printed on the label. If the owner tries to cut down on food consumption, the dog begins to beg and steal to support his habit. Out of pity the owner continues to indulge the addicted dog in increasing amounts of food and continues the spiraling cycle.

There are known circumstances that promote obesity in dogs, and they are worth mentioning. In a 1970 study reported in the *British Journal of Small Animal Practice*, the attitudes of pet owners toward obesity were noted along with the problem as a whole. A similar study was also reported in a 1970 issue of *Modern Veterinary Practice*. They revealed that pet owners seem to accept a degree of overweight in their dogs that is unacceptable to owners of other types of dogs—show dogs, for example. Owners also have conflicting views regarding the condition of their dogs: 31 percent of the persons in the study owning obese dogs considered their pets to be of normal weight.

The *Modern Veterinary Practice* report found 28 percent obesity in over 1,000 dogs observed during a one-year period. Both sexes had a sharp rise in the incidence of obesity after middle age. The report further found that incidence of obesity was 44 percent higher among dogs with obese owners and 34 percent to 37 percent higher among dogs with middle-aged or elderly owners, possibly because these people were unable to give their pets adequate exercise.

The *British Journal of Small Animal Practice* also reported that household pets often are confined to small living premises and have no opportunity for exercise other than that given by their owners. The average working owner has little time to devote to exercising his dog, and urbanization complicates the situation, with fewer and fewer locales in which adequate exercise may be provided.

There are other reasons for humans overfeeding their dogs, and they get as varied as the labyrinth of psychoneurosis itself. The need for love, overcompensation for poverty, problems related to status, oral gratification, deep-rooted insecurities all only scratch the surface.

There is one instance where obesity develops innocently and without fault on the part of the dog owner. It has to do with neutering. Although it is a controversial subject, there are many experts who believe that neutered dogs, possibly because of less physical activity, are more prone to excess weight than normal dogs. Spaying and castration are now encouraged as a logical means of reducing the enormous population of unwanted pets. Once a dog has been altered, it is wise to seek nutritional advice from your veterinarian to help prevent obesity. A healthy exercise regimen for the neutered dog is highly recommended. This is in no way meant to discourage the altering of house pets and rescued strays, but rather a caution about feeding and exercise for the owners of such animals.

How to Determine If Your Dog Is Fat

There is a difference between obesity and slight overweight. No one has difficulty spotting an obese dog. But the overweight dog is more difficult to recognize. How is it possible to place your dog on a diet when you don't even know if he is overweight? If your dog is overweight, how do you determine how much overweight he might be? There are guidelines to help the owner decide whether the dog needs to reduce.

Weighing your dog does not give you sufficient information. Breeds have weight standards as outlined by the American Kennel Club, but individual dogs within each breed vary because of gender, bone structure, degree of activity, weather conditions, and other environmental factors. And what about mongrels and crossbreeds? If a dog is very young, he is still growing and therefore difficult to judge in regard to size and weight.

The first thing you can do is simply look the dog over and decide if he has visible fat protrusions such as a sagging abdomen, a shapeless trunk, or swollen pockets of fat around the body that resemble tumors. These are definite symptoms of excess weight. Another method is feeling for fat tissue under the dog's body. Run your flattened hand over the dog's rib cage, along the underside of his trunk. A dog of normal weight has a very thin layer of adipose tissue lying across the cage and each rib can be felt or seen in outline form. The tissue you feel should be just barely thick enough to

Chowhounds and heavyset swains eventually pay the price for being overindulged with food. A dog on a diet will try to break your heart. If he refuses to count calories you must do it for him.

allow a slight finger indentation when pressed. There should not be more than one-fifth of an inch thickness covering the ribs. If there is more than one-fifth, the dog is overweight to some degree. When the ribs cannot be seen or felt at all by touch, a diet for weight reduction is definitely in order.

A dog of normal weight has a clear demarcation between the stomach and the rib cage. This is called the *tuckup* (a sort of waistline), with the ribs presenting a deeper appearance than the abdomen. However, when there is no tuckup between the two, and the front of the torso is equal in density to the rear, the dog is obese. If your dog is fat, it is time for him to go on a weight reducing program involving fewer calories and more activity (unless a veterinarian decides otherwise for individual health and age reasons).

How to Reduce Your Dog's Weight

A weight-reduction program involves reduced caloric intake (less food or less fattening food), increased physical activity (if tolerable), and a correction of any disease that is current or imminent. Before staring a reducing diet for the old or ailing dog, have the animal examined by a veterinarian. The dog should be examined for heart, kidney, and liver disorders before changing any food intake schedule. Here the veterinarian can determine if the animal suffers from simple or constitutional obesity and can advise how much weight and at what rate the dog should reduce.

In simple obesity or overweight, you can set a goal of visual progress. When the dog looks like his normal svelte self and his ribs are visible and distinguishable by touch, it is clear that the diet has worked and is no longer necessary. You can approximate the amount of weight needed for reduction and use that figure as a generalized goal. However, your dog's visual appearance is the best means of determining if a problem still exists. Weekly or biweekly weighings are useful, especially if the amount is recorded on paper. This allows you to remain aware of the rate of loss which is important to the dog's health. It is helpful to continue to weigh the dog periodically after the dog has achieved his ideal weight.

THE DIET

Some veterinarians recommend a reducing formula which decreases the dog's caloric intake to 60 percent of that required for

Cheating. Turning your head and slipping the canine butterball a between-meal-snack defeats the diet and prolongs the agony.

normal maintenance. (Caution: Some veterinarians may feel this is too drastic a reduction of food in some dogs.) When normal calories are reduced to 60 percent of the maintenance diet a dog up to twenty pounds will lose about one pound per week. Dogs between twenty and forty pounds will lose about two pounds per week. Dogs over forty pounds will lose about three pounds per week. Bear in mind that a forty-pound dog that is overweight is to be considered by the weight he should be carrying when estimating food quantity to feed and the rate of loss. Most dogs on this diet take eight to ten weeks to reach optimal body weight.

Limiting the amount of food the dog eats may reduce the dog's weight but will keep him in a state of hunger. A hungry dog is an unhappy dog, and few owners can resist slipping him additional snacks. This will doom the program from the beginning.

A workable approach is to change the dog's diet to one which contains almost the same amount of bulk but fewer digestible calories, fats, and carbohydrates. A reducing diet should contain no more than 4 percent fat and from 10 to 15 percent fiber, both on a dry weight basis. If fed in wet form, it will increase the acceptability of low-fat, high-fiber diets which are less palatable than the meat-type foods that the dog may be used to getting.

No more than 350 digestible calories per pound of food is acceptable for an effective weight-reduction diet although various experts offer slightly different quantities. Most canned dog foods contain between 500 and 600 calories per pound. Dry commercial dog foods contain approximately 1,600 to 1,700 calories per pound. This extreme difference is because canned dog food is 75 percent moisture and 25 percent solids, while dry food is typically 90 percent solids and only 10 percent moisture. Obviously, a dog on a dry food diet will either have to eat much less than he is used to getting or go off dry food altogether. Dogs on a reducing diet should not be on a self-feeding program.

There are four alternatives for the dog owner who wishes to restrict a dog's caloric intake. First, the veterinarian offers a Prescription Diet called *r/d*. This is prepared by combining low-calorie ingredients such as lean horsemeat, trimmed beef lungs, nonfat dried milk and soy for protein, and wheat bran and cellulose flour for bulk. The fat and digestible energy are restricted and the fiber content increased. By including a small amount of vegetable oil, just sufficient to supply the needed unsaturated fatty acids, and the required vitamins and minerals, a low-calorie, high-bulk diet is obtained. *r/d*, available only from the veterinarian, contains 330 digestible calories per pound.

The second alternative is a commercially prepared canned diet food which is available in most supermarkets and stores and does not require a prescription. This product is called Cycle 3 and is one component of a four-part feeding system designed to meet the nutritional needs of puppies (Cycle 1), adult dogs (Cycle 2), overweight adult dogs (Cycle 3), and older dogs (Cycle 4). Cycle 3, geared for overweight dogs, offers a reduction in calories to 440 per 14-ounce can. The manufacturer (Gaines Dog Food) states that this product is specifically balanced for the overweight, less active dog with 20 percent fewer calories and less fat than other leading dog foods. Cycle 3 is a significant alternative for the dog in need of weight reduction.

A third alternative is to reduce whatever diet is being used until desired weight is achieved. The fourth alternative for a weight reduction diet is to prepare homemade low-calorie dog food in your own kitchen. This is especially attractive for those who are accustomed to cooking for their dogs but want to reduce them.

Here is a basic weight reduction recipe that offers 300 calories to the pound of food prepared.

REDUCING DIET*

    ¼ lb. lean ground beef
    ½ cup cottage cheese, *uncreamed*
    2 cups carrots, canned solids
    2 cups green beans, canned solids
    1½ teaspoon dicalcium phosphate**

Sauté the ground beef until browned. Drain off all the fat in the pan. Add the other ingredients and mix well. This mixture will yield 1¾ pounds of food.

To help satisfy the dog's hunger, feed him half his daily portion in the morning and the other half early in the evening. The quantity of food given is determined by the dog's *ideal* body weight.

FEEDING GUIDE

If your dog's ideal weight is:	*Feed daily:*
5 lb.	⅓ lb.
10 lb.	⅔ lb.
20 lb.	1 lb.
40 lb.	1¾ lb.
60 lb.	2½ lb.
80 lb.	2¾ lb.
100 lb.	3¼ lb.

Snacking and scavenging should be absolutely forbidden during the reducing period. However, since many obese dogs are accustomed to begging, an occasional tidbit of raw vegetable will add only roughage, vitamins, and minerals, not appreciable calories. Give the dog a high-quality vitamin-mineral supplement daily which supplies the minimum daily requirements. This reducing diet consists of 85 percent moisture, 7 percent protein, 1.7 percent fat, and 5 percent carbohydrate.

Once your dog has reached normal weight, place him on a healthy, properly calculated maintenance diet. (See feeding chart

---

*Reducing Diet supplied by Mark L. Morris, Jr., D.V.M., Ph.D. of Mark Morris Associates.

**Dicalcium phosphate, sometimes known as defluorinated rock phosphate, is necessary to maintain the proper amount of phosphorus normally obtained in meat or commercial dog food. This powdered mineral can be obtained or ordered from a pharmacy. It is commonly found in grain and feed stores.

in Chapter 6.) The alternative is to continue the low-calorie diet but in somewhat greater quantity. Your veterinarian can establish your dog's ideal body weight. The breed standard as established by the American Kennel Club is also helpful.

In order to accommodate those who wish to prepare their dog's weight-reduction diet with variety, a limited-calorie chart is included here. Because of space limitations, this listing contains nowhere near the quantity of appropriate food items available and nutritious for dogs. The dog owner can obtain one of many calorie counting books designed for humans and use it for varying a dog's diet.

To use a calorie chart properly for your reducing dog, first determine the quantity of food your dog normally eats and estimate the calories it represents. Next, feed the animal the same quantity if possible but formulate meals that offer more bulk than digestible calories. Feed approximately 360 calories to the pound. This will reduce your dog's calorie intake and consequently his weight. Weigh your dog every one or two weeks and keep a written record.

There will probably be little weight loss for the first three weeks. Do not be discouraged; this is normal. During the first weeks, the fat in the body cells is replaced by water. This creates the impression that no weight reduction is taking place. Stand firm and be confident that fat is leaving your dog's body and will become evident after three weeks' time.

Counting calories seems like an antiquated way to reduce weight in this age of unique diets involving everything from gobs of heavy cream to injections of urine from pregnant women. People object to counting calories because it requires willpower and tenacity to make it work. But let's face it: once you put your mind to it, your dog has no choice! If he won't count those calories, you will. Here then is a calorie chart that may not have everything you need or want but certainly sends you off with a good start from kohlrabi to turtle meat to hot dogs.

YOUR DOG'S CALORIE CHART

MEAT	Calories
Beef liver, fried (4 oz.)	259
Beef stew, with vegetables (cup)	210
Beef, chipped or dried (2 oz.)	115
Beef, ground, lean, broiled (3 oz.)	185
Beef, heel of round, lean, roasted (3 oz.)	165
Beef, round steak, broiled (3 oz.)	330

Beef, sirloin, broiled (3 oz.)	330
Chicken, broiled (3 oz.)	115
Chicken, breast, ½ medium, fried	155
Hot dog, beef or beef & pork (1)	170
Lamb, shoulder, roasted (3 oz.)	285
Pork, chop, cooked (1)	260
Pork, roast (3 oz.)	310
Turkey, roasted (3½ oz.)	265
Veal, broiled (3 oz.)	185

FISH

Cod, frozen fillets (5.3 oz.)	117
Flounder, baked (3 oz.)	174
Haddock, breaded, fried (3 oz.)	140
Lobster, steamed, whole, meat only (3½ oz.)	95
Perch, frozen fillets (5.3 oz.)	133
Salmon, canned (3 oz.)	120
Sardines, canned (3 oz.)	175
Scallops, steamed (4 oz.)	127
Shrimp, peeled, cooked (4 oz.)	103
Turtle, green, raw meat (3½ oz.)	89

EGGS

Boiled (1)	80
Poached (1)	80
Fried (1)	108
Scrambled with milk and fat (1)	110
(Do not feed your dog raw egg)	

MILK

Whole (cup)	160
Skim (cup)	90
Dry, nonfat, reconstituted (8 oz.)	80
Cottage cheese, uncreamed (4 oz.)	100

CEREAL, GRAIN, AND PASTA

Barley, uncooked (3.2 oz.)	349
Cornmeal, cooked (1 cup)	119
Macaroni, spaghetti, cooked (3.2 oz.)	149
Rice, cooked (3.2 oz.)	119
Rolled oats, cooked (3.2 oz.)	63
Soybeans, cooked (½ cup)	130
Soybeans, dried (3.2 oz.)	331
Wheat germ (3.2 oz.)	361

VEGETABLE OILS

Corn (tablespoon)	125

Cottonseed (tablespoon)	125
Peanut (tablespoon)	125
Safflower (tablespoon)	125
Soybean (tablespoon)	125

VEGETABLES

Asparagus (4 spears)	10
Beans, green (cup)	30
Bean sprouts, uncooked (cup)	17
Beets, cooked (cup)	55
Beet greens, leaves and stems, cooked (½ cup)	13
Broccoli, cooked (cup)	40
Brussels sprouts, cooked (cup)	55
Carrots, raw (cup)	30
Carrots, cooked (cup)	45
Cauliflower, cooked (cup)	25
Celery, raw (1 stalk)	5
Chard, Swiss, raw (½ lb.)	56
Chard, Swiss, boiled, drained (½ cup)	15
Collards, raw (½ lb.)	102
Collards, boiled, drained (½ cup)	33
Corn, kernels off cob (½ cup)	78
Dandelion greens, cooked (½ cup)	30
Eggplant, cooked (cup)	30
Kale, cooked, leaves and stems (cup)	31
Kohlrabi, cooked (cup)	37
Lettuce, Iceberg (1 head)	60
Okra, cooked (8 pods)	25
Peas, green, cooked (cup)	115
Spinach, cooked (cup)	40
Squash, summer (cup)	30
Squash, winter (cup)	130
Tomato, raw (1)	40
Turnips, cooked (cup)	35

MISCELLANEOUS

Honey (tablespoon)	65
Peanuts, roasted, unsalted (20 to 23)	114
Popcorn, plain, popped (cup)	52

Among the advantages of preparing your own homemade reducing diet is the emotional involvement with your dog's progress in losing weight. The dog cannot do it for himself and must rely on you to get him back into good shape. Preparing food is fun, and you are assured of feeding the dog the finest ingredients available.

In this spirit the remaining pages of this chapter are filled with recipes that offer low-calorie gourmet fare. Although the recipes are somewhat involved, they do offer food that your dog's digestion can process. The ingredients of the following recipes are wholesome, nutritious, and good enough for canines or humans. The dog owner who enjoys cooking may treat the dog to daily specialties comprised of low calorie, nourishing food best utilized after the dog has achieved his ideal weight. *In no way are these recipes to be used daily as a complete and balanced diet. They are offered as an opportunity for the reducing dog to enjoy an occasional interlude of non-fattening variety.*

The following recipes were prepared especially for *The Good Dog Book* by nutritionist Frances Sheridan Goulart. Mrs. Goulart is an author, lecturer, teacher, health-food expert, and competitive long-distance runner. Her books include *The Ecological Eclair, Bum Steer,* and *Bone Appetit.* All of the ingredients listed within the recipes are available in supermarkets and/or health-food stores.

When you come to an ingredient that seems absolutely revolting, consider the possibility that it is probably delicious to your dog . . . and other health-food enthusiasts. Such ingredients as desiccated liver, brewer's yeast, and bonemeal powder (to be found in Doggie Dinner Balls) are all included in one form or another in the higher-quality manufactured dog foods. They are all exceptionally nutritious for humans, too . . . if they can be gotten down without a blindfold and clothespin. The author assumes no responsibility for any laughter from your dog provoked by the following recipes.

MUTT NUTS
(Unfatty, unfried, unsalted)

1 cup sprouted soybeans*
soy sauce (preferably Tamari** brand)
1 tbsp. vegetable oil
sea salt (optional)

Combine the bean sprouts with the soy sauce, oil, salt (if used). Spread sprouted seasoned beans in a single layer on a greased baking sheet. Bake beans, stirring occasionally, for about 20 min-

---

*Sprouted soybeans are available already sprouted from your natural-foods store, or you may sprout them as you would any other seed.
**Tamari soy sauce is a properly aged condiment free of artificial colorings, sugars, excess salts, etc.

utes in 325° oven. Serve warm and crunchy "as is," or mix into any
dry doggy ration or grind in blender and combine with any
"cooked" canned dog food.

Mutt Nuts taste remarkably like salted peanuts.

CALORIES: 25 per mouthful, approximately.

DOGGIE DINNER BALLS
(Fat-free meatless meatballs)

2 egg whites, beaten stiff
1 cup finely chopped alfalfa sprouts
1 tbsp. finely minced onion or scallion
¼ cup whole-grain flour plus 1 tbsp. brewer's yeast, bonemeal powder, or desiccated liver

Put egg whites in a bowl and carefully fold in the sprouts with a
rubber spatula. Carefully fold in onion and whatever supplemental powder you are using. Add flour a tablespoon at a time until
the mixture can be handled and shaped into tiny balls. (It should
remain slightly moist.) Grease a collapsible vegetable steamer and
set the mini-meatballs inside side by side. Set the steamer into a
deep saucepan filled with water. Bring water to a boil, cover pot
tightly, and steam for 15 minutes.

Serve lukewarm with a "doggy gravy" or cold out of hand.
These are also good when rubbed with olive oil.

CALORIES: Less than 30 per dinner ball if recipe makes 24
balls.

BEEF BRITTLE
(Starch-free, fat-free snack)

½ lb. very lean beef (Round steak, brisket, or a good grade of
   chuck are best. Flank steak may also be used.)
Marinade:
¼ cup Tamari soy sauce
2 tbsps. salad oil
1 tbsp. apple cider vinegar
½ tsp. fresh grated ginger, if possible fresh crushed chopped
   garlic or garlic salt as desired

To facilitate slicing of the meat into paper-thin strips, place in
freezer for one or two hours, until frozen. Remove and cut into
narrow ribbons no more than ¼″ thick. Remove all visible fat and
cut *with* the grain. Prepare marinade and toss the strips of meat in
this mixture until well coated. Arrange strips on a high oven rack

so they are suspended over a drip pan placed below. Dry at 200° for 20 minutes; then turn to 125° for 12 to 18 hours. When dry, store the crispy bacony snacks in a canister. Properly prepared, they will keep almost indefinitely at a cool room temperature.

CALORIES: roughly 25 per 4″ X ½″ strip.

MONGRUEL
(A low-calorie high-potency hot or cold canine cereal)

3½ cups rolled oats
½ cup dry powdered milk
¼ cup sunflower seeds
¼ cup diced fruit or diced dried beef (See Beef Brittle recipe)
6 tbsps. molasses
4 tbsps. salad oil
1 tbsp. water
1 heaping tbsp. desiccated liver powder or brewer's yeast (optional)

Combine all ingredients except sunflower seeds and stir well. The mixture must be agreeably moist without being soggy. Grease a large baking sheet (a jelly-roll pan is perfect, allowing you to stir without spillage) and spread the cereal in an even layer. Bake at 225° for 20 minutes, stir well, and bake an additional 20 minutes. Stir again and bake till just lightly browned. Cool 5 minutes. Then stir in seeds and store in canisters and keep in a cool dry place between feedings.

Cold: Serve with skim milk. *Hot:* Heat equal parts Mongruel and skim milk with a pat of butter. Or serve sans liquid, as a dry "kibble."

CALORIES: Approximately 275 per 1-cup serving.

POOCH PUDDING
(A sort of junket for the jowly set)

4 tsps. cold milk
2 tsps. arrowroot*
1 cup boiling water or skim milk
honey or vanilla extract to sweeten (optional)

---

*Unlike cornstarch, which is a highly refined and processed ingredient, arrowroot is rich in a wide spectrum of minerals and is well tolerated by ailing, allergic, pregnant, or persnickety dogs. It may be substituted wherever powdered milk is specified in these recipes.

Gradually stir the cold milk into the arrowroot and continue stirring until smooth. Gradually add the boiling milk or water and cook over low heat for 2—3 minutes, stirring all the while. Resulting pudding should be thick like junket. Sweeten to suit the dog.

CALORIES: Approximately 60 if recipe makes 2 servings.

GRRRRAHAM CRACKERS

¾ cup coarse graham flour (whole-wheat pastry flour combined with a bit of raw wheat germ may be substituted)
½ cup coarse bran or coarse cornmeal*
1 cup whole-wheat flour
½ tsp. salt
½ cup water or homemade broth
6 tbsps. liquid vegetable oil
1 tbsp. molasses

Combine dry ingredients. Preheat oven to 350°. Combine water, oil, molasses. Stir dry ingredients into wet ones. Form a cohesive ball. Coat the back of a baking sheet with butter or oil and pat the dough out in the shape of the pan. (This saves cleaning up counters and breadboards.) Roll to thickness of ⅛", using rolling pin. Score with knife in desired shapes, and bake about 12 minutes in preheated oven. Cool 5 minutes before removing from baking sheet.

YIELDS: 4 dozen 2" square crackers.

CALORIES: 100 each.

VARIATION: For PEAMUTT BUTTER CRACKERS, substitute ½ cup coarsely chopped (use blender) unsalted peanuts for the bran or cornmeal. Serve, of course, with homemade Peamutt Butter.

BOWSER'S BREAKFAST SQUARES
(Instant cereal or between-meal snack crackers)
2 tbsps. butter or vegetable oil
2 tbsps. unsulfured molasses (blackstrap is best)
½ cup rolled oats (raw)

Heat the skillet in the oven at 350°. Put the oil or butter and molasses into skillet and swish around. Stir in the oats. (Any herb seasoning your pet fancies may be added, including garlic powder or

---

*Bran is almost 100% undigestible cellulose. Therefore, it adds fiber without contributing calories to the diet of the obese or sedentary dog.

onion flakes.) Reinsert skillet and bake until crisp—about 35 minutes. Cool in skillet about 5 minutes before cutting and breaking into snackable chunks or squares.

CALORIES: 400 calories in all, or approximately 40 calories per square.

Muttrecal Loaf
(Low-calorie millet skillet meal)
2 cups ground millet*
5 cups cold water
1 tsp. sea salt or kelp powder
⅓ cup coarse bran flakes

Combine millet meal and cold water. Add salt or kelp. Place saucepan on a flame-tamer or asbestos pad (or use a double boiler). Bring the mixture to a boil, stirring constantly with a wooden spoon until mixture is thick and free of lumps. Reduce heat and continue at a medium simmer, stirring at intervals, for about half an hour or until millet leaves the sides of the pan. Remove from heat and stir in bran flakes. Turn mixture into a lightly oiled shallow baking dish. Refrigerate until stiff enough to cut (3–4 hours). Cut into 16 squares and arrange in a greased baking dish. Sprinkle with onion or garlic juice (optional) or beef drippings and bake at 400° for 15 minutes.

CALORIES: Approximately 75 per square.

Spot's Sprouted "Snails"
(Sugarless but sweet calorie-and-carbohydrate-defused dessert)
½ cup raw whole-wheat berries (available from your health-food store)
1 thin slice whole-grain bread
whole-grain flour or arrowroot (a more nutritious substitute for cornstarch) as needed
1 heaping tbsp. brewer's yeast, dried liver powder, kelp powder, or bonemeal powder (optional)

Sprout the wheat berries by covering with warm water overnight.

---

*Millet is not strictly speaking a grain, but makes a perfect low-calorie low-starch substitute for cornmeal. It is an especially good source of the B vitamins as well as magnesium and potassium. It is tolerated more readily than cornmeal by most animals. If your health-food store doesn't have millet meal, buy whole millet and grind it in your blender. Cracked millet is also suitable.

Drain the next day and put in a large jar. Cover the top with netting secured by a rubber band, and each day for 3 days irrigate the berries twice daily. They should be lightly moist but not wet. When ready to use, tails will be slightly longer than the berries and they will be very sweet-tasting.

Prepare a "sprout paste": Push the sprouts through a meat grinder or food mill, alternating them with torn bits of the whole-grain bread. Add optional supplementation and only enough flour or arrowroot to facilitate handling. Knead the sprout paste dough into a long sausage shape and slice into four lengths. Coil each one into a "snail." Place snails on a lightly oiled baking sheet and bake in a 300° oven on a lower rack for 45–60 minutes (slow baking at low temperatures preserves nutritive values just as sprouting increases them), until lightly browned, thoroughly dried, and naturally sweetened. For even browning you may turn the rolls halfway in the baking process.

CALORIES: Approximately 75 per snail.

Toto's Taffy
(Nonfattening sugar-free fudge)

  2 tbsps. molasses
¼ cup peanut butter or sprout paste*
  3 tbsps. coarsely chopped raw nuts or toasted sprouts
¼ cup nonfat dry milk powder

Combine molasses and nut butter. Add nuts or sprouts. Gradually knead in the milk powder. Roll "taffy" into a rope ¾" in diameter and 12" long. Wrap in wax paper or foil and chill. Slice into bites as needed.

CALORIES: With milk powder and peanut butter, 35 calories per half-inch bite. With sprout paste and bonemeal powder, 17 calories per half-inch bite.

*To make sprout paste (lower in calories, higher in nutritive value) see SPOT'S SPROUTED "SNAILS."

8. In Sickness and in Health

It is no revelation to all the Dogmoms and Dogdads that young Tinkerbell or old Bruce cannot pick up the phone and make an appointment with the veterinarian. Nor can they wince, whine, or complain that a tooth hurts, a belly aches, or they are breaking out in a rash. It is the responsibility of the dog's guardians to be aware of the family huggy and his medical needs. It is no different than taking care of a child.

Small-animal medicine is an enormous subject and requires many, many volumes to cover adequately. Men and women study in universities and hospitals for years to acquire an accredited medical education and hang out the prized shingle. It would be an insult to an honorable and essential profession to even suggest that one could become medically competent from a book of this limited scope. Still, the conscientious dog owner must have some basis of information to know when to see a veterinarian, when to apply a home remedy, when to start worrying, when to relax, and when to take action. It is hoped that within these brief pages that need can be filled.

The chapter is divided into three sections. The first section deals with prevention: those measures which are necessary to promote a healthy, happy dog. The second section deals with medical symptoms and helps the dog owner understand something about the more important dog illnesses so that a veterinarian can be consulted when needed. The third section offers emergency and first-aid techniques as a stopgap measure for those situations demanding immediate medical attention.

Prevention: A Primer for Keeping Your Dog Healthy

PREVENTING INFECTIOUS DISEASE THROUGH IMMUNIZATION

All dogs are vulnerable to the most common communicable diseases. Many young puppies die from distemper because they were not immunized. Vaccinations are a series of "shots" injected into the animal's body which immunize him.

Vaccination introduces a virus into the dog's body so that it will cause antibodies to be formed against it. The virus used is first passed through the bodies of other animals in a series of laboratory techniques and is called attenuated (weakened). By the time it is in its refined state, it will no longer cause the fully developed disease but rather a mild, modified version. This will create an immunity in the animal once it has been injected.

There are many techniques and schedules for vaccinations available, and each veterinarian chooses the one that is the most effective for the prevailing conditions in his section of the country. Different environments influence the procedure, as do the varied circumstances of each dog's life.

When a puppy is first born, it receives with the first feedings of mother's milk a substance called colostrum, which creates a population of antibodies that fights disease for the first two or three months in the puppy's body. It is nature's immunization for young mammals. The problem is that some dogs have greater quantities of surviving antibodies than others. If a puppy is able to maintain a large population of antibodies during this period, it need not be vaccinated until it is twelve weeks old. However, it is almost impossible to determine in any practical way if a puppy has enough antibodies to last the full twelve weeks. Orphaned puppies often begin a vaccination program against distemper as early as two weeks of age.

One method commonly used is to begin distemper vaccinations at eight weeks. This makes certain that the small dog has maximum immunity even though he has received colostrum from the mother's milk. Utilizing the modified live-virus vaccines, puppies under three months are given at least two doses of vaccine and sometimes three or four, depending on the veterinarian's appraisal of the situation. Until a young dog has reached maximum immunity, usually achieved after twelve weeks, it is best to keep him off city streets and out of population centers.

There is a "temporary shot" called antiserum, which can be administered one or two weeks after weaning (before eight weeks). This initial immunization supposedly transfers passive or temporary immunity to the puppy. Serum, rather than vaccine, is used, offering short-term protection until the dog is old enough for vaccine. According to the Counsel on Biological and Therapeutic Agents of the American Veterinary Medical Association, "Evidence to date indicates little merit in use of antiserum either as a preventative measure by a temporary extension of passive immunity, or as treatment of dogs with clinical signs of the disease."

Dr. Michael Katz, who practices veterinary medicine and conducts small-animal research in Amherst, Massachusetts, provides an information sheet for his clients explaining his vaccination procedures. This sheet outlines his schedules and why he adheres to them. It is an example of the many approaches to this complex subject. It states:

Puppies and kittens are given a "passive" immunity when they ingest their mothers' milk in the first few days of life. Antibodies neutralize viruses which cause disease in cats and dogs and are present in the milk. If the mother has a high antibody level against a disease, the youngster will obtain more antibody which will protect it against disease for a longer period of time. The most immune kittens or puppies will lose all immunity by the time they are 13 weeks of age. As soon as a youngster loses its passive immunity, an "active" immunity can and should be produced by vaccination (vaccine viruses "actively" cause the animal to produce its own antibodies). The age at which this active immunity should be provided is as early as the youngster loses the "passive" antibodies. Therefore, kittens and pups are vaccinated for the first time at about 6-10 weeks of age (but, we cannot be sure that immunization has taken place). A second vaccination is administered at 13½-14½ weeks of age along with rabies, hepatitis and leptospirosis (vaccine). At this time an active immunity will definitely take place.

Yearly revaccination for distemper and hepatitis and biannual vaccination for rabies is necessary to maintain the active immunity. Distemper and measles vaccine will be administered to young pups at the first immunization visit. Pups do not become infected with measles virus but, because of the presence of "passive" antibodies in the body of some pups at the time of first vaccination, distemper vaccine will not produce an active immunity. Active production of measles antibodies with measles vaccine will cross immunize the pup against distemper virus until it is 14 weeks of age.

Did you get it? No? Read it again, slowly, and ask your veterinarian to explain it to you. This procedure is one of several formulated by the thousands of veterinarians throughout the country. All veterinarians agree that immunization does not provide permanent immunity. "Boosters," or reimmunizing inoculations, are needed once a year. The vaccine does not harm the dog and offers added protection and reassurance. When annual boosters are not used, the owner is gambling with the pet's life, and the odds are not good. If you have confidence in your veterinarian, it is wise to follow his or her procedure fully.

YOUR DOG'S HYGIENE

Grooming for its own aesthetic sake will not be discussed in this chapter. Dog grooming, when seriously pursued, is a fairly complex business involving equipment, methodology, and an understanding of the many demands of each breed's coat. Few areas of the country are without dog-grooming salons, and they are so busy that appointments are necessary.

Only grooming as it applies to good hygiene will be explored in these pages. A limited grooming effort is absolutely necessary to maintain good hygiene for the pet dog. Grooming for the sake of hygiene not only keeps your dog's appearance attractive, but contributes toward good health and the prevention of disease. Long-

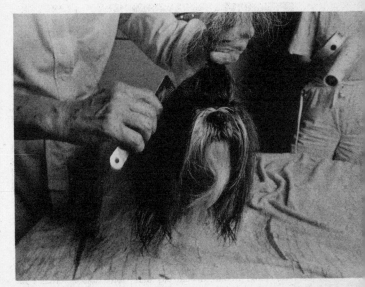

Combing and brushing your dog several times a week is more a matter of good hygiene than canine cosmetics.

coated dogs should be brushed daily with a pin brush to maintain the luster and prevent the fur from matting. Brushing also keeps the coat clean and stimulates the skin. Short-coated dogs need less frequent brushing, but once a week is a good idea with either a curry brush or a lightweight slicker brush. Each breed of dog requires different grooming methods and equipment. A specialized book on this subject should be obtained by the conscientious dog owner.

The Bath.   Nothing makes a dog look more miserable than standing in a bathtub all soaped up and scrawny-looking . . . unless it's dressing him in one of those straw sombreros with a pair of dark glasses. Few dogs like baths. Even fewer dog owners like giving them.

The most frequently asked bath question is *How often is it necessary?* The next most asked question: *Are baths harmful?* Opinion differs on both questions from professional groomers, veterinarians, breeders, and experienced pet owners. It is safe to say that a

Not everybody looks forward to Saturday night. Some dogs experience one bath in their entire lifetime while others are plopped into sinks or tubs more than once a month. It's a question of need and personal choice. Nobody ever asks the dog, though.

bath is necessary when the dog smells bad, is absolutely filthy, has gotten into something greasy or foul, or when a magnificent appearance is desired for some special occasion. Some professionals maintain that once a month is good, while others say that once a year or even once a lifetime is better. *As needed* is probably the best policy.

Baths can remove the oils produced by glands thus drying out the skin and the coat. A dry coat creates undue shedding which in turn can create a problem of insulating the body in hot or cold weather. Dry skin causes itching, and itching can cause minor irritations or infection from scratching. Some dogs are bathed three times or less throughout their lives, while others are bathed more than once a month. It is a personal choice based on the individual dog's requirements.

How Old Before a Bath? Opinion seems to vary from expert to expert. Consider the facts. Veterinarians believe that all puppies are vulnerable to upper respiratory illnesses if they are exposed to drafts or chills. Standing in a tub ankle-deep in water and soaked to the skin can make any dog sick if the room temperature is not warm enough or if there is a draft. For this reason some experts believe a puppy should not be bathed for the first year of its life. Others feel six months is adequate for safety's sake while even others say one day old is a good time to begin baths if the conditions are correct. Dogs with allergies or infections will need to be bathed as directed by a veterinarian, and most country dogs require a flea and tick dip once a week during the summer.

The alternatives to frequent bathing are easy and highly effective. First, you can remove superficial dirt from a dog with a damp washcloth. Gummy substances can be removed with witch hazel on a dampened cloth. Then there are dozens of commercially prepared "dry shampoos" that work well with a good brushing. A simple, thorough brushing every day will do more to keep a dog clean than all the baths he'll ever have.

How to Bathe Your Dog. The most obvious and convenient method is to take him to a dog-grooming salon and avoid the whole mess entirely. But that can be costly unless the salon is also a school for groomers, in which case the price would be somewhat reduced, like a barber college.

In warm weather an adult dog does not need a bathtub. There is entirely too much fuss made over giving a bath. It is more ritualistic than reasonable, and that tends to make it harder. The dog can simply be held in place in your backyard and washed down with a

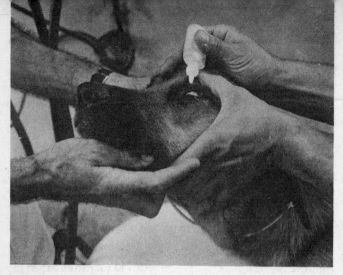

To prevent soap from getting into the dog's eyes, squirt one or two drops of mineral oil into them.

common garden hose. If the weather doesn't permit this, or if the dog lives in an apartment, then the bathtub is used because it has a drain.

You will need an ordinary dog soap or flea soap, a regular or medicated shampoo (obtain medicated shampoos from your veterinarian), a tub mat so the dog won't slip, a shampoo or soap brush (a wooden scrubbing brush will do), Vaseline jelly or mineral oil, two wads of absorbent cotton, a bath towel, an electric hair dryer (optional), a garden hose, or a handheld spray hose.

Whether indoors or out, the dog need not stand in a tub full of water. When using the bathtub, leave the drain open. Standing belly-high in water only makes the experience more miserable for the dog. Use a rubber bathmat so the dog won't lose his balance. Secure him by placing a lead of some type around his neck and tie it to a secure place (other than the hotwater tap). Leave only a short slack in the lead so that he cannot jump out of the tub and hang himself.

The two traumas in bathing are soap in the eyes and water in the ears. Both are painful and uncomfortable and can promote sickness. Place a wad of absorbent cotton in each ear so that water cannot go down the canals. Secure the cotton firmly in the ears so it will remain when needed. With an eyedropper, squirt a drop or two of mineral oil in the dog's eyes to prevent soap from getting in. A pinch of Vaseline jelly will do the same job when smeared in the

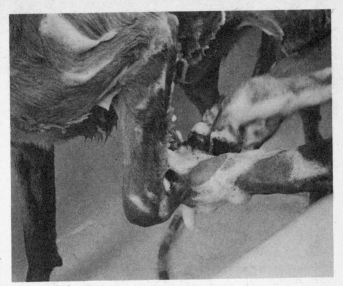

Above: Once the dog has been thoroughly wetted down, apply the soap or shampoo, starting along his back and working the suds into his coat. *Below:* Thoroughly wash each paw, its pads, and between the toes where ticks and fleas like to hide (not to mention city dirt).

corners of the eyes. Place a thin film of Vaseline on the anus and scrotum of a male and on the vulva of a female to avoid soap in these areas. If he could, your dog would thank you.

Wet the dog thoroughly so the soap becomes sudsy. This is the critical moment. The dog may try to run or jump depending on what you do. Use tepid or warm water and start with the paws. Once the paws are wet, work the hose upward along the legs. Spraying against the fur, soak the sides of the torso and under the rib cage and stomach. Wet the top of the body (against the fur) and then the anus and finally, the tail. By now he should be drenched and ready for soap or shampoo. Lather it in with your fingers or a brush and get under the fur so that old dander is washed away along with any wildlife that has taken up residence. Some brushes can be too abrasive for some dogs. When lathering pay attention to the tail, the anus, the hind quarters, and the genitals (careful!). Clean the paws by spreading each toe and soaping inside. This is a favorite hiding place for ticks and fleas.

Rinse the soap and repeat the procedure. It is very important to rinse all the soap off thoroughly or it will cause itching and

Even a sad face must be soaped and washed. If the dog's eyes have been protected with mineral oil or vaseline, it will not hurt if soap gets in his eyes. Still, it's best not to allow soap in at all.

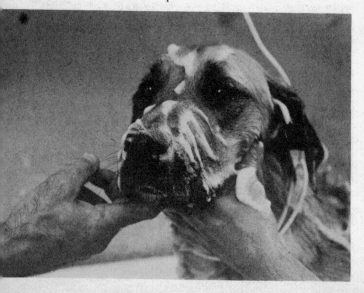

scratching later. If the dog has parasites such as fleas and ticks, a dip is in order. Do not be confused by the term "dip." This is a highly concentrated liquid that must be diluted with water and spread over the body like a shampoo. The dog is not literally dipped into anything. Brush the dip over the entire body as you did the shampoo. Dips are not usually meant to be rinsed off. Many shampoos are dermatolytic, which means they are left on for five to ten minutes. This will reduce bacterially invaded tissue and therefore doggy odor.

Allow the dog to give himself a really good shake (he's going to do it anyway). Wipe him dry with a vigorous toweling. A warm-air electric dryer speeds the drying process and does a thorough job. This is the part of the ordeal the dog enjoys. It makes the fur light and fluffy for brushing and other grooming procedures. In warm weather, allow the dog to dry off in the sun. In cold weather, do not let the dog outdoors for any reason until he is completely dry. At this point, liquid or dry coat conditioners, powders, sprays, colognes, and what-have-you are pleasant options. A good brushing is necessary to complete the procedure.

Toenails.   Clipping nails is often not necessary for a dog who walks the city streets. The asphalt and cement surfaces wear them down sufficiently so that they are not a health problem. Pedicures for the sake of the dog's appearance also have advantages, but they are optional.

Unclipped nails that are allowed to grow beyond the point where they touch the surface of the ground can be hazardous. Extra-long nails sometimes curl under the pads and become painful, keep the animal off balance, and create posture problems.

Nails are either light or dark in color. Light nails are easier to trim because you can see where the transparent area ends and the nerve ending in the quick of the nail begins. Clipping beyond the transparent area is painful to the dog and will cause bleeding. This is especially difficult when the nails are dark-colored. Have your veterinarian show you the proper place to clip. A good rule to follow is cut at the point where the nails begin to curve. The bottom of the nail should be even with the bottom of the pad. It is safer to cut too little than too much. A pliers-type nail trimmer is best for all but oversized dogs. Larger breeds require the guillotine-type trimmer.

Your Dog's Friends.   Any veterinarian will tell you that a dog's health and hygiene are greatly influenced by his living quarters and the company he keeps. A dog that is walked in a controlled situation is less likely to pick up disease, infections, external and internal parasites, and common dirt than one that is let out to run loose. A dog on the loose will sooner or later associate with stray dogs and pick up whatever medical or hygiene problems they are carrying around. A study reported by the *Journal of the American Veterinary Medical Association* stated that the rate of active infection of stray dogs was more than three times greater than that of nonstray dogs. Although this study was part of a report on the incidence of canine brucellosis, it does make one consider the hazards connected with stray dogs. Dogs that have the run of a back yard are as clean and healthy as their environment is.

Odors. Your dog's odors are a barometer for his state of health and hygiene. A healthy, properly fed and well-groomed dog will have little or no unpleasant odors—body, mouth, or otherwise. The attempt to mask odors with perfumelike products without investigating their source can lead to medical problems.

Among the sources of unpleasant dog odors are ear canker, anal gland secretions, and oil secretions from the body glands. Ear infections and anal gland problems should be treated by a veterinarian. Odors from the skin or coat can be removed by bathing and combing and brushing. Use a dog shampoo *before* the dog itches severely, and skin odors can be avoided. The dog's bedding and collar may have absorbed odors from the body and require cleaning or replacement.

Sores covered by matted fur can also be a source of bad odors and must be treated before serious infection begins. Some diseases cause foul odors and can be eliminated only when the animal returns to normal health.

Bad breath can be caused by nasal disease, gastric acid, poor digestion of excess food, or poorly balanced diets. Flatulence, a major source of bad odor, is caused either by poorly balanced meals, parasites, or genetic malabsorption (inability to use food given). Flatulence is gas leaving the body caused by excess bacteria in the bowels. The abundance of bacteria is created by putrefaction of poorly digested food. Sometimes a change in diet is the cause. Mouth odors are often connected with digestive diseases as well as dental problems such as tartar deposits, decayed food caught between the teeth, and diseased gums. Good grooming procedures, clean living quarters, and a healthy body will eliminate virtually all dog odors.

PHYSICAL FITNESS

Preventing disease and physical deterioration, not to mention retardation of the aging process, depends a great deal on the dog owner's willingness to maintain a physically fit animal. Both exercise and mental stimulation will help transform a frail puppy into a dynamic young dog, interesting to be around and fun to play with. There can be no question that physical fitness translates into good health.

Exercise. There has been much talk about exercise but very little research. Most statements on the subject, as they pertain to dogs, are very general and cannot be applied to every dog of every breed. It reduces itself down to the common sense of the individual owner, the owner's personal inclinations toward exercise, and the needs of the dog in question (which varies from dog to dog).

A trip from the TV to the refrigerator is all the exercise most of us get. It may not be good, but that's the reality for a dog living in a household locked in the clutches of "Hollywood Squares," "Love of Life," and spectator sports. There isn't a dog in the world that can compete with the Super Bowl if that's the kind of home he lives in. But even us garden slugs have to move occasionally. And doesn't the electronic cyclops blink its bloodshot eye once in a while, gasping for breath at halftime? Exercising the family dog need not take up so much time that it be put off like waxing your floors or cleaning your closets.

In general terms, a dog's need for exercise should be based primarily on the physical activity that the breed was created for. Sporting Breeds, Hounds, and Working Breeds are strong, muscular, and energetic. In addition, they all performed hard, demanding tasks for their masters of times long past. Exercise is not only important for their bodies but for their mental stability as well. It is sad for the retrievers, setters, and tree hounds that never get an opportunity to run, to jump, to return with a thrown stick. An Alaskan malamute that doesn't get a chance to run and pull is missing what he was born to do. It is not necessary for a dog to do exactly what he was bred for but rather some reasonable substitute. We don't want to witness with horror our elegant Sealyham terriers with their gorgeous white coats running down deep holes chasing badgers. However, several good walks a day and an opportunity to scratch the ground for a while will keep this brilliant dog in fine shape.

Understanding the needs of your breed and your individual dog will tell you how to exercise the animal. Not all terriers need a vigorous workout, but most do. Dogs with short legs must not be walked and run as far as dogs with long legs. Toy breeds need some exercise, if only to work off their nervous energy; but be intelligent about it, and do not strain them.

Exercising the young adult dog is good for him and his owner. Jogging is an excellent way to do it.

Dogs that are exercised as puppies develop better than those that aren't. A dog is considered an elder statesman at eight years old because that is when his metabolic system begins to slow down. Consequently, the food he consumes converts more readily to fat unless it is burned off in a planned exercise program. The middle-aged and elderly dog must be given two, three, or even four walks a day and a good run if he can handle it. Start walking with the dog as often as possible even if it's only for an errand. An occasional weekend of exercise is worse than none at all because it can place too sudden a strain on an older dog. Consistency and regularity are the most beneficial ways to exercise a human being and a dog. A young adult can take one or two hours a day of running, walking, and jogging. A young puppy needs only twenty or thirty minutes a day. Do not jog with a puppy or run it from a bicycle. A dog must never be dragged by the leash or put in danger of getting under the wheels. Jogging is one of the best ways for a human to exercise an adult dog providing both are in good health.

Police and military dogs (mostly German shepherd dogs) work out on elaborate obstacle courses almost every day. Some of them stay on the job until they're ten or twelve years old. A large, vigorous dog can stand a two-or three-mile run every day if you can. Obedience training and training for AKC obedience trials are two

Giving the dog a run by having him follow you on a bicycle is effective, providing he is not held with a leash and is not a puppy. If the dog cannot keep out of the path of the vehicle this form of exercise is a bad idea.

Dogs that work as sentry or police dogs must undergo a constant exercise program to stay in shape. Dog owners may formulate modified versions of these obstacle courses and effectively exercise their adult, vigorous pets.

important and highly beneficial methods of developing a successful exercise program for your dog. Contact the American Kennel Club in New York City for details. If you are still unconvinced about exercise, don't worry about it. Enjoy your dog, your couch, pass the Cheez Doodles, and see if there's a game on the tube. You can always walk him at halftime.

Major Illnesses and Their Symptoms

THE BIG FOUR DISEASES

Canine Distemper.   This disease is the great puppy killer when immunization has not been given. Adult dogs, wolves, coyotes, raccoons, mink, and ferrets are also vulnerable to this virus, which is spread much like the common cold. Pets of all ages may come down with canine distemper but dogs under stress, puppies, and those that have never had follow-up booster vaccinations every year are the most susceptible.

The incubation period is six to nine days, but because the early signs are very subtle, symptoms may not be apparent for two to three weeks. Distemper symptoms appear at first like an upper-respiratory ailment similar to a flu virus in a human. A dry cough, loss of appetite, running nose, diarrhea, watery eyes, and generally depressed disposition are signs of the serious ailment. Advance stages may exhibit a hypersensitivity to light and also convulsions. It is a difficult disease to diagnose. There is no doubt that these symptoms require the immediate services of a veterinarian whether the dog actually has canine distemper or not. Faithfully follow your veterinarian's instructions, but prevention is the only real help. Immunization early in the puppy's life plus annual booster shots offer the best hope.

Infectious Canine Hepatitis.   Known as ICH, it is a major cause of deaths in puppies and young dogs. ICH is a highly contagious virus, and all dogs are sooner or later exposed to it. The virus is passed from all body secretions of carrier dogs, and in the urine of dogs several months after recovery. Dogs of all ages are susceptible. They catch it by ingesting contaminated material.

The incubation period lasts from five to nine days and symptoms vary. The dog's temperature rises from a normal 101.5°F. (average) to 104°F., which may last for six days. The symptoms of ICH are depression, apathy, abnormal thirst, loss of appetite, and excess watering of the eyes and nose. Diarrhea, vomiting, spasms, and heavy and rapid breathing are also symptoms of this painful disease. Because it localizes in the dog's liver, he may arch his back or rub his stomach area to relieve pain. Obviously, with these symptoms, the dog is in dire need of medical attention. Faithfully follow all instructions from the veterinarian—this is critical for your dog's recovery. Be prepared to leave the dog in the hospital or with the veterinarian for at least seven days.

Infectious canine hepatitis is sometimes combined with canine distemper. Early immunization and boosters are important because there is no permanent immunity.

Leptospirosis. Dogs of all ages may be infected by this serious disease. It is fatal if not diagnosed early in its development. Leptospirosis is very difficult to diagnose and requires laboratory techniques available only to your veterinarian.

The infection is spread through the urine of infected dogs or rats. The dog licks the infected urine directly or gets it on his paws and ingests it through self-grooming. The disease is more common in rural areas, where contact with rats or their droppings is more frequent. Certain city locales are also high-risk areas. On rare occasions it can be transmitted to humans.

The incubation period is between five and fifteen days. Many of the symptoms are confused with those of canine distemper and infectious canine hepatitis. The most striking sign of leptospirosis is a change in the color and smell of the infected dog's urine. It develops a strong, obnoxious odor and turns dark yellow or orange. Other symptoms are vomiting, abdominal pain, dehydration leading to great thirst, and a yellowish discoloration of the skin in later stages. The dog's temperature will rise to approximately 105°F. and fall suddenly the next day. Often the dog's stool appears bloody and his gums discharge blood as well. When any of these signs become apparent, the animal must be taken immediately to a hospital or veterinarian's office. Time is vital in saving your dog's life.

Vaccination and annual booster shots can avoid the intense suffering involved in this fatal but avoidable disease. Treatment must be left entirely to a veterinarian.

Rabies. Rabies is a fatal disease threatening all warm-blooded animals. It is caused by a virus existing in the saliva of infected animals. The usual mode of transmission is through a bite from a rabid animal in which the saliva containing the virus enters the victim's body. The rabies virus can also enter the body through contact with an open wound or scratch, although it is less common.

The incubation period varies, but usually is within fifteen to fifty days or even longer. The virus is carried quickly to the central nervous system. It reaches the spinal cord within four to five days and travels upward until it ultimately infects the brain. During this period it also travels to the salivary gland and can then be transmitted to another animal when bitten.

The course of the disease in dogs has three phases, each phase showing its own unique symptoms. The first phase shows a change in behavior. The dog will appear restless and contrary to his normal disposition. A sedate dog will be energized; a friendly dog will become irritable; an energetic dog will become sedate. The next phase is sometimes skipped by some victims. It is referred to informally as "the furious form." Through this phase the dog attempts to bite foreign objects, urinates frequently, and is sexually excited (males only). During this phase the animal may have difficulty in swallowing and may begin to drool excessively. He may also become vicious. The last phase is the paralytic or "dumb" stage, in which the lower jaw is hung open and food or water cannot be injested. Death follows shortly.

Every dog must be vaccinated against rabies to avoid this gruesome disease. There are now new vaccines available that offer immunization up to three years.

If there is the slightest suspicion that your dog has been infected with rabies virus, report it immediately to your veterinarian, the health authorities, the SPCA, or the police. For the sake of your own safety and that of your family's, do not go near the suspected victim, do not touch him, and immediately quarantine the animal. If you have been bitten by a suspicious animal, wash the wound thoroughly and obtain immediate medical attention. Securing the suspicious animal and having it examined and tested for rabies may save you from the protracted and *difficult* treatment necessary for rabies victims.

INTERNAL PARASITES

Almost all internal parasites that collect in a dog's body are called worms, with the exception of the protozoa, which are one-celled animals detectable only with a microscope. Worms vary in kind, size, effect, and seriousness to the health of the animal. Although all worms can do harm to the dog's body, few create permanent or irreparable damage with early detection and treatment. When treated promptly, the dog returns to good health. Depending on the degree of infestation, the condition runs from mild to gravely serious.

Internal parasites are among the most common ailments of dogs and other animals. Almost all puppies have them, and adult dogs get them at one time or another in their lives. They must be treated as expeditiously as possible by a veterinarian. There are many patent remedies for worms, but they should not be used without professional advice. Some worms are more dangerous than others, and the proper identification is necessary to know which treatment to administer to your dog. Some patent drugs may be too strong or too weak for your dog.

All worms have some symptoms in common that can alert the dog owner and get him or her into action. The early signs include a lethargic manner, inconsistent appetite, diarrhea, blood in the stool (a serious symptom). The signs of heavy infestation are loss of weight, bloated stomach, loss of fluid, dry and thinning coat, constant drowsiness, and, in some cases, anemia. The most common symptom of parasitic infestation is loss of energy. The dog does not seem like himself.

When you suspect that your puppy or adult dog is infected with some form of worms, take a stool sample to your veterinarian for specific diagnosis and treatment. In some instances, worms do not appear in one stool, but may in others. For this reason, it is more accurate to collect small specimens from one to five stools (collected every other day) and bring the material to a veterinarian for microscopic examination. The irregular appearance in some stool samples can be attributed to the various life cycles of worm eggs. Once the veterinarian has wormed the dog, which takes one day and possibly a repeat ten days later, a stool sample should be examined four weeks later in the case of hookworms and whipworms. Every dog owner should become acquainted with the various forms of internal parasites that sooner or later plague all dogs.

Hookworms. This common intestinal parasite is passed through skin contact with worm eggs or by ingesting worm eggs from contaminated material. Adult hookworms thrive in the dog's small intestine, and it is there that the female worm deposits thousands of eggs daily, many of which are then passed through the stool. Puppies are commonly infected with hookworms shortly after they are born if their mother is infected. The infection is transmitted through the mother's milk. The name "hookworm" is derived from the parasite's ability to hook onto the wall of the host dog's intestine and suck blood.

One result of hookworm disease is anemia because of the daily blood loss. Anemia from hookworms exists in young dogs before they can produce a local immunity to them in the bowel. Only fifty hookworms can cause the loss of one ounce of blood daily. In puppies, poorly fed dogs, or sick dogs, hookworms can cause sudden collapse and even death. Healthy dogs will resist better, but will suffer a slow but steady loss of weight, diarrhea, and bloody stool. Severe infestation sometimes requires hospitalization.

Roundworm (Ascarids).   There is no parasite more common to dogs than roundworms. They are white, cylindrical in shape, and from one to four inches in length. They are often seen in the dog's stool or vomitus. The adult worm embeds in the intestinal tract and there deposits its eggs, which are then passed out of the body through the stool. If the eggs are then ingested by a host, the life cycle is completed and starts again. By eating the eggs of infested soil or fecal matter, the dog becomes infested. Ingestion of infested rodents, birds, and insects also allows entry to a host animal. Ascarids are very commonly found in newborn puppies because of the mother's infection during pregnancy, although the mother need not be infected for puppies to be invaded by these parasites. Seldom do adult dogs experience serious illness from ascarids. However, it can be fatal for heavily infested puppies. All roundworm infestations must be treated quickly.

Whipworms.   These are serious parasites and somewhat difficult to detect. They are very small worms that settle in the dog's colon and cecum. (The cecum is a structure along the intestinal tract. In humans the appendix is attached to the end of the cecum.) Once whipworm eggs are ingested, they develop into larvae and then grow into adult worms in the large intestine. This takes about ten weeks, and they remain there up to sixteen months. During that period, the host animal slowly loses blood with accompanying loss of weight. Diarrhea becomes frequent, with evidence of blood in the stool of heavily infested dogs. Poor health becomes evident.
    Diagnosis is made by microscopic examination of the stool. Sometimes several stool examinations are necessary before the eggs can be detected. There are various forms of medication for whipworms, including oral tablets and intravenous injections.

Tapeworm.   This parasite is known for its tenacity and indiscriminate infiltration of young and old alike. In rare cases it can be passed on to humans and requires a conscientious approach to diagnosis and treatment.
    The tapeworm is comprised of a head equipped with hooks and suckers which enable it to affix to the intestinal wall as it progressively grows into a long chain of segments. Occasionally several

segments pass into the stool, but the head always remains to form new links.

Infection by tapeworm can sometimes take a long time to detect. It can begin as digestive upsets, irregular appetite, weight loss, stomach discomfort, and poor coat condition.

The diagnosis is made through examination of fecal matter, although this is sometimes ineffective. Detection is more commonly made through discovery of segments in the dog's stool, bed, or anal area. At first the segments are light-colored and about one-fourth inch in length. When dry, they shrivel and turn brownish in color and granular in shape, like grains of rice.

Perhaps the most common source of tapeworm is fleas. Your dog also gets tapeworms by eating infected, uncooked meat, either in the wild or from the kitchen, or from raw fish. Lice can also carry the infection. Treatment involves destroying the head within the host's body. Contact with intermediate hosts such as mice, rats, squirrels, and rabbits must be avoided.

Tapeworms are of different types:

(1) Taenids are tapeworms which void segments from a dog or cat's bowel, which are then ingested by an intermediate host (rabbit, pig, hare, goat, sheep, deer, cow, etc.). Meat or the body of the intermediate host animal is then eaten by your dog and infects your pet with tapeworms.

(2) Dipylidiinae are tapeworms which void segments from a dog or cat and these are ingested by flea larvae or adult biting lice. Another dog or cat ingests the flea or louse and is then infected with tapeworms.

(3) Other tapeworms are obtained by dogs and cats when they eat reptiles and birds.

By far the most common tapeworm problem is from infection with dipylidiinae via fleas. You cannot rid your pet of these parasites without ridding its environment of fleas.

Tapeworms are not as rapidly debilitating as the other internal parasites, but will cause problems for your pet if you allow it to be infected for a long period of time. They often require more than one treatment for cure. The services of a veterinarian are crucial for a successful cure. (Only the Echinococcus type of tapeworm is potentially contagious to humans, and it is very uncommon.)

Heartworms.   Heartworm disease is a very serious illness for dogs and can be fatal if not treated promptly and properly. Heartworms are large worms that lodge in the right side of the heart and in the pulmonary vessels of the lung. Because of this, the heart has to work much harder to pump blood to the lungs, and as such a process takes place continually, the heart must work harder and harder to accomplish its task. The hearts of dogs with heartworm therefore become old before their time. As the heart becomes weak, almost every other organ in the body becomes affected because of insufficient blood flow to these organs.

In this disease the enemy is really the mosquito, as it is the transmitter of the heartworm during its larval stage. The female heartworm, while in the host dog's body, produces great quantities of moving embryos called microfilaria. Mosquitoes living on the blood of a host dog ingest the microfilaria. They remain in the mosquitoes' bodies for fourteen to twenty-one days and are then transmitted to the body of the next dog they bite. Now in their larval stage the heartworms enter the body through the new victim's skin by the mosquito's injection and then take five to six months to develop into mature worms.

The symptoms of an infected dog are exhaustion, coughing, loss of weight despite good diet and appetite, and breathing difficulties. Chronic cough brought about by strenuous exercise is the first symptom of a classic case. Death, in the advanced stage, may be brought about by collapse during severe exercise.

Heartworms can now be prevented by using the drug *diethylcarbamazine,* which must be gotten from a veterinarian. CAUTION: DO NOT ADMINISTER HEARTWORM PREVENTIVE MEDICATION UNLESS YOUR DOG HAS BEEN TESTED AND SHOWN TO BE FREE OF ADULT HEARTWORMS. This drug can be extremely harmful to a dog that is already infested. All dogs can be injected with microfilaria from the bite of a mosquito, but only those who are on preventive medication will kill these microfilaria two to six weeks after infection. It is necessary, therefore, to administer medication from the first of April until the first of December, or until six weeks after leaving an area of the country where heartworm is prevalent. Test dogs each April through a blood sample and laboratory analysis before the new preventive medicine administration season. If all uninfected dogs can be kept on heartworm prevention and those that are carriers treated for the disease, there may soon be a day when heartworm disease will all but disappear.

External Parasites

These are the true enemy of dogs and humans alike. Fleas, flies, ticks, and lice are the carriers of disease, allergies, and, in some cases, internal parasites. When a dog's body is invaded by external parasites, a veterinarian can best determine what the pests are and how to treat them. In addition, most veterinarians have staff and facilities for bathing dogs and administering flea and tick dips. Removing embedded ticks may be too harrowing for some dog owners, who would rather pay to have that chore taken care of.

The best treatment for internal and external parasites is a good prevention-control attitude. If a dog becomes infested with parasites, it is not enough to provide medical attention. All areas that the dog inhabits must be cleaned thoroughly with soap and water and attacked with a proper pesticide. Nontoxic sprays are good, and so are concentrated solutions mixed in water. Disinfect all locales where the dog might have acquired fleas, ticks, lice, etc., and use the strongest solution possible for his kennel or doghouse. Clean out the corners of the house where the dog lies around, and disinfect his sheets, blankets, and other equipment. Spraying the house furniture, carpet, baseboards, floorboards, crevices, and cracks is necessary to prevent reinfestation. Fleas and ticks and their eggs are tenacious and very difficult to eliminate. Preventive spraying is an even better method of dealing with the problem. You may require the services of an exterminator. Fleas can live in a house for a long time, even after the dog moves out, and months later can infect humans.

Fleas.   Watching a dog attempt to rid himself of a flea is not as amusing as some have made it out to be over the years. Fleas live off the blood of the host animal. They not only annoy the host, they also cause anemia and often spread tapeworms.

They are small insects, brown or black in color, wingless, and rapid-moving. They live in the coat of the animal they have infested. Fleas can be found in nearly all parts of your dog's body, but they prefer the neck, tail, head, and chest. One variety prefers the ears and their rims.

The life span of this difficult pest is one year. Its eggs hatch into larval stages remaining in the environment up to 200 days. The cycle begins anew when the larvae become adults. Treatment involves interfering with the life cycle and killing off those fleas which have already hatched.

Symptoms of fleas involves frenetic scratching and nipping with the front teeth deep into the coat. A flea-ridden dog often chases his tail, rubs his back on the ground, and even whimpers as he scratches. At these moments the fleas are biting into the skin, drinking blood, and moving to another location.

There are several ways to rid the dog of fleas. A bath and a shampoo containing a flea-killing insecticide are foremost in importance. Immediately following the last rinse, a flea and tick dip may be applied. Flea dip can be purchased in a pet-supply outlet and comes complete with instructions. This is a concentrated insecticide that must be diluted with water and then sponged or brushed into the dog's wet body. The dip leaves a residue on the body and must be allowed to dry in so that stubborn fleas and eggs eventually are killed and fall off.

Sprays and powders are available along with the very popular flea collars. They are all effective up to a point, but nothing works like a bath and a dip. Flea collars and flea tags have a good preventive effect when there is no infestation in the dog's living quarters. If your dog has fleas, he must be checked for self-inflicted skin irritations and possible secondary infections. This may involve a topically applied medication prescribed by a veterinarian. Quite often, ridding the dog of his fleas does not end his itching. Consult your veterinarian.

Lice. When a dog begins scratching, biting, and rubbing, it is quite possible that he has lice. The principal difference between lice and fleas is that lice remain in one spot and dig in. They are the smallest part of an inch and extremely difficult to see. When a dog bites and scratches, the louse will react by burrowing in deeper.

Some lice live on the animal's blood while others eat loose particles of the skin. If infestation is great, the bloodsucking lice can cause a considerable blood loss, hence an anemic dog. Eggs laid by the female are attached to the hairs of the dog by a sticky substance. These are eliminated by a bath and an insecticidal shampoo obtained from a veterinarian. Check with a veterinarian for any secondary skin infection caused by the dog's scratching and biting.

Ticks. The most common tick is the brown dog tick, sometimes called the American dog tick. Another variety is the wood tick. The brown dog tick lives in the house (in cracks, bedding, carpeting, and walls) and kennels. They infect dogs at all times of the year. Wood ticks infect dogs only in their adult stage and do not infect houses or kennels. Ticks exist in three stages after eggs are laid on the dog: (1) larval, (2) nymphal, and (3) adult. Both types of ticks can jump onto the dog when outdoors in the summer. Ticks may live up to a year in each stage. Wood ticks infect animals other than dogs in larval and nymph stages and attack pets in the adult stage. Wood ticks can survive for many months without feeding. If a tick (brown dog tick) infestation exists in your house, an exterminator will be needed to remove them. Care of the dog involves removal by pulling the tick off with a tweezers (usually a small male tick exists alongside an engorged female); do not use matches or kerosene.

Some ticks may be removed by hand, using your thumb and forefinger. However, this is not a recommended method considering the rise of Rocky Mountain spotted fever. This disease, which is carried by some ticks, is an acute, infectious illness that ranges from mild fever to death. When handling a tick that is infected with Rocky Mountain spotted fever, it is possible to introduce that disease into the body by rubbing the infected fingers into the eyes or worn areas of the skin which of course includes slight cuts and openings. It is safer to remove ticks with tweezers, forceps, gloves, or a sheet of Saran Wrap to avoid contamination of the fingers. A good flea and tick dip is an effective means of killing and removing ticks from the body of a dog.

The favorite hiding places for ticks on the dog's body are on the abdominal region, the neck, the armpits, between the toes, in the anal region, and on the face and neck of some breeds. A dog living in a tick-infested area must be checked by hand every day. Long-coated dogs are much more susceptible than short-coated dogs because it is easier for the ticks to hide.

Ticks attach themselves to the skin of the dog and feed on its blood. Dogs become injured by the irritation of their bites and the loss of blood. When a tick is pulled away from the dog's skin after it has become attached, a small amount of tissue will also be pulled away. This causes a blood smear and sometimes a swelling. An antiseptic or antibacterial medication applied topically is important to prevent infection. Iodine, Mercurochrome, Merthiolate, or Bacitracin may be used. The effects from some ticks can produce fever, paralysis, and even death. Although dogs seldom develop fatal disease from ticks, tick diseases can be transmitted to humans.

Mites There are many varieties of mites, and they attack the dog's body in different ways. The demodectic mange mite is present at the base of the hair follicles of most dogs from birth. It is as yet unknown why they cause disease in some dogs and not at all in most. Other mites are the sarcoptic mange mite and the ear mange mite.

Demodectic mange is a serious parasitic skin disease. It involves

Above: The most common tick is the Brown Dog Tick. As pictured above, it often imbeds in the skin of long-coated dogs, hidden by the fur. Here you see a small male imbedded next to the much larger female. *Below:* Removing a tick is best accomplished by getting under its body with a tweezers or forceps and slowly but firmly pulling it away from the dog's skin. It is inevitable that a small amount of tissue will come away with the tenacious tick, causing slight bleeding.

several areas of hair loss, usually around the head and front legs. The exposed skin is reddened and scaly. It is completely curable except for some advanced cases.

Sarcoptic mange is the cause of irritating itching, loss of hair, and crusting of the skin. The most affected area are the ears, front legs, chest, and abdomen. It often leads to a bacterial skin infection involving scabs over large portions of the body.

Ear mites cause the formation of a dark, crusty material in the ear canals of infected dogs. They produce vigorous ear scratching and head shaking.

Demodectic and sarcoptic mange mites must be identified under a microscope. A scraping of skin is taken from the dog for this purpose. Ear mites are just barely visible to the naked eye. They are miniscule white objects moving through a mixture of ear wax and dried blood. Treatment of all mites requires a veterinarian, whose instructions must be carried out faithfully.

MEDICAL SYMPTOMS

It is not always easy to know when to take your dog to a veterinarian. In addition to annual checkups and vaccinations, your dog may need medical diagnosis and treatment for any one of dozens of ailments that befall the average pet and range from important to gravely serious. To help you decide when to call and ask for help or information, here is a list of symptoms. If your dog has one or more of these symptoms, call your veterinarian and ask for an opinion.

excessive coughing, sneezing, or snorting
frequent wheezing, running nose, gagging
hoarseness
moaning, crying, or whimpering
repeated vomiting
excessive and sudden appetite
excessive and sudden thirst
unusual lack of appetite
unusual lack of thirst
inability to ingest food or water
unusual slobbering
abnormally pale gums
foul breath
difficulty breathing
constant shaking of the head

dizziness
convulsions
paralysis
limping
trembling and shivering
sudden weight loss
excessive shedding as an abnormal condition
swellings, lumps, sore spots, especially on the abdomen
rampant diarrhea
cloudy urine
inability to urinate
uncontrollable urination
odorous urine
gritty or sandy urine
dark yellow or orange urine

First Aid and Emergency Care

Ernest Hemingway defined courage as grace under pressure. When a beloved dog is injured, it is hard to keep your head and do what is necessary to keep the dog alive until professional assistance is available. If you value your dog, you must not give in to hysteria. You must move coolly, competently, and quickly, if you are going to keep faith with your dog's confidence in you. First aid is your first line of defense when your dog's life is threatened.

There are several medical supplies necessary for successful first aid. The thoughtful dog owner will develop a kit for this purpose and keep it available for emergencies. When traveling, the kit must travel, too. The list that follows will cover most emergencies efficiently.

FIRST AID KIT

tincture of Merthiolate or Mercurochrome
Bacitracin
antiseptic powder or spray
aromatic spirits of ammonia
mineral oil
Kaopectate
tongue depressors
sterile gauze bandage—1" and 2"
first-aid cream
ipecac (to induce vomiting)

eye ointment
styptic powder (to stop bleeding)
Vaseline
scissors
tweezers
absorbent cotton balls
cotton applicators
large and small gauze pads
hydrogen peroxide (3% solution)
adhesive tape
rectal thermometer
activated charcoal (for poisoning)

You may prefer to purchase a preassembled kit designed for pet owners and breeders. For one of many assemblies write to: PET AID, Remac Pharmaceutical, P.O. Box 339, Wilmington, MA 01887.

WHEN YOUR DOG IS HURT

There is a protocol for approaching an injured animal: the objective is to help without becoming the second injured victim. A dog in extreme pain, shock, or in a semiconscious state is not responsible for its behavior. The normally loving animal may bite, growl, or scratch and kick when approached even by its owner. Approach with gentle caution, speaking in a quiet, soothing tone. Move slowly. A leash or any makeshift lead must be applied loosely around the dog's neck so that he may be restrained if necessary. A temporary muzzle must be tied around his nose to prevent biting. A dog with a broken bone must not be allowed to walk or run as it may be prone to do when frightened.

See if the dog is breathing and what is the quality of the breathing. This will determine if the dog requires artificial respiration or a mad dash to the veterinarian. Check for blood or signs of bleeding. If the dog is conscious, try to observe any particular area of pain. Apply a muzzle around the animal's mouth so that you will be able to touch him without getting bitten. Check for broken bones with your hand. The dog will let you know when you touch a fracture. He will cry or squirm in pain.

If there is bleeding, follow the procedures outlined in this chapter. Cover the dog with a blanket or one of your garments to help the dog preserve his own body warmth. Get help immediately. Send for a veterinarian, an SPCA rescue truck, or the police. Do not move the dog unless he is lying in the middle of a road or

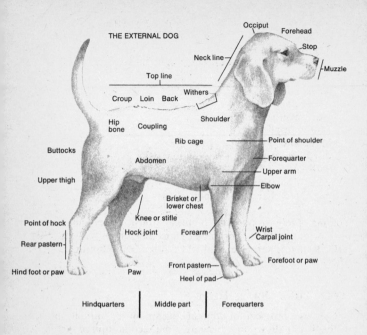

THE EXTERNAL DOG

Occiput
Forehead
Stop
Muzzle
Neck line
Top line
Withers
Croup Loin Back
Shoulder
Hip bone
Coupling
Rib cage
Point of shoulder
Buttocks
Abdomen
Forequarter
Upper arm
Upper thigh
Elbow
Brisket or lower chest
Point of hock
Knee or stifle
Hock joint
Forearm
Wrist
Carpal joint
Rear pastern
Forefoot or paw
Hind foot or paw
Paw
Front pastern
Heel of pad

Hindquarters | Middle part | Forequarters

street, or if help cannot reach you. If you must move the dog, lift him with as little movement to the spine as possible. Place both your arms between the dog's four legs and lift him in a rigid position. Do not allow the middle to sag or the neck and head to fall forward. The dog should be upright with his body resting on your chest. Use a blanket as a stretcher for larger breeds. Two persons must grab the corners and carry the dog to safety. If the dog has a broken bone, it is less painful for him to be moved on something rigid like a wide plank of wood or atop a suitcase. If the dog is seriously hurt, it is best if he doesn't have to be moved until professional assistance arrives. Do not prevent the dog from sitting or standing if he insists. His pain will limit his movement. Do not add to the dog's terror with overpowering restraints if they upset him more than he is already. Always have the animal checked by a veterinarian after an accident. You may avoid blood loss, shock, and death.

THE MUZZLE

An improvised muzzle is one of the most important techniques for successfully rendering help to an injured dog. Without this

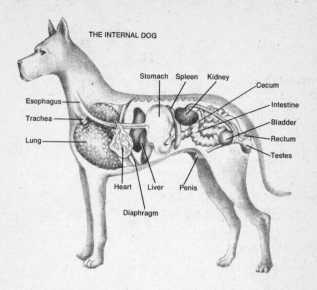

THE INTERNAL DOG

Esophagus
Trachea
Lung

Stomach Spleen Kidney

Cecum
Intestine
Bladder
Rectum
Testes

Heart Liver Penis

Diaphragm

form of restraint, it is almost impossible to examine or aid a dog in distress without getting bitten. All you need is a bit of cord, twine, gauze, or doubled string. A necktie will do, and so will a belt, if nothing else is handy. Do not use adhesive tape because it may be necessary to remove the muzzle quickly if the dog has an urgent need to vomit.

The muzzle is created by making a loop (half-knot) with your cord and slipping it over the dog's nose, halfway up. Make sure the cord is over bone rather than cartilage, which begins at approximately two-thirds up the snout. Pull the cord gently until it tightens, holding the mouth securely shut. Bring the ends of the cord under the jaw forming another half-knot. Secure the ends behind the dog's ears with a bowknot, as you would tie a shoelace. Once the dog cannot bite you, begin first-aid treatment.

BLEEDING

External. Bleeding that is apparent comes from wounds (lacerations or punctures) caused mainly by auto accidents, dog fights, or falls. External bleeding requires control of blood loss and prevention of infection. Dark-colored blood that flows slowly is from a

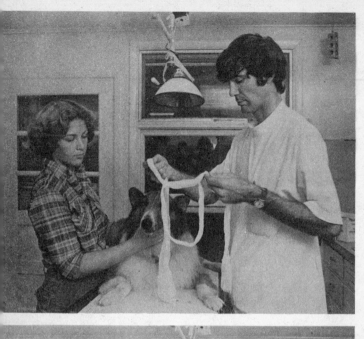

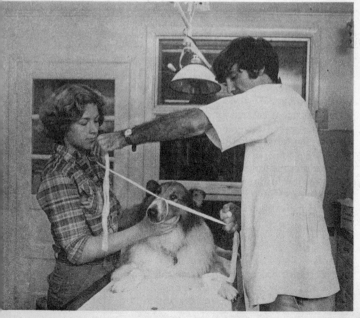

vein. Light-colored blood, rushing quickly from a wound, means an artery is damaged. Slight wounds or breaks in the skin should be washed clean of debris and then covered with a film of Vaseline to keep the tissue moist and viable.

A laceration or puncture will extend beyond the skin and to the tissue beneath. Professional treatment will be necessary and should be taken care of as soon as possible. Superficial wounds will stop bleeding within ten minutes. A wound with light bleeding requires a gauze pad and rolled bandage or other material wrapped several times around the leg or body. This will control the bleeding at the point of injury. If the blood soaks through, then a pressure bandage is necessary. Begin treatment with a pressure bandage for all moderately bleeding wounds.

To make a pressure bandage, use a gauze pad (or something similar) and apply it directly over the cut. Wrap rolled gauze

Creating a temporary muzzle so that first aid can be rendered without getting bitten. Make a loop with cord, leash, or bandage gauze. Slip it over the dog's nose, halfway up, so that it rests on bone. Tighten it and bring it around, behind the dog's ears, and secure it with a bow knot (as in tying a shoelace). (*The Photo Works*)

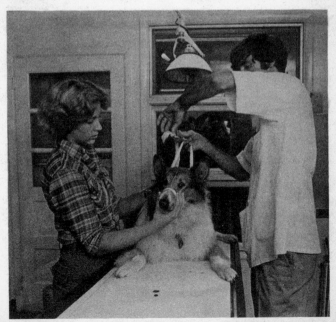

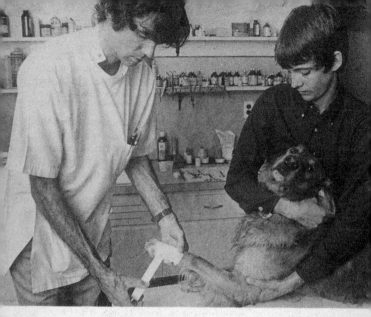

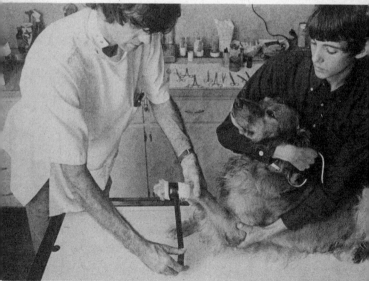

Making a pressure bandage. Apply a gauze pad directly over the wound and secure with rolled gauze strips. Cover the rolled gauze strips tightly with adhesive tape, electrical tape, or even cellophane tape if necessary. (*The Photo Works*)

bandage (or cloth strips) tightly around it several times. Cover the end of the rolled gauze completely with adhesive tape. Black plastic electrical tape will serve the same purpose. If no tape is available, tie the gauze or cloth strip by tearing it down the center and knotting the two ends. If the bandage is going to remain over the wound for more than an hour, it is best to bandage the entire foot or tail, if that is the part that is injured. This will prevent swelling of the area below the wound. If the bleeding persists, apply pressure with your hand directly over the wound until the bleeding stops. It may take a while. If the cut is on the trunk, the wound must be bandaged tightly around the entire girth. Long or deep cuts will require stitching by a veterinarian to promote faster healing. Do not allow a pressure bandage to remain on the dog for more than an hour and a half. See a veterinarian immediately.

When the pressure bandage does not control the blood flow and applied pressure by hand fails, the only alternative is a tourniquet. It is effective on arterial wounds, although a tourniquet applied improperly can be damaging. You may use a cord, rope, rolled gauze bandage, or belt, if necessary. You will also need something rigid, like a stick. Form a loop and apply it around the leg or tail between the main portion of the body and the wound. Place the stick, pencil, or tire jack over the loop and then complete a simple knot. The tourniquet must be tightened to stop the flow of blood to that portion of the body. It must be loosened every ten minutes to permit the tissue to expand with blood. This will prevent the tourniquet from causing gangrene.

Some body, neck, or head wounds are impossible to stop bleeding with a pressure bandage. In that situation, grab a gauze pad or another wad of material and simply hold it over the cut with firm pressure. With luck, the blood will eventually coagulate and stop the bleeding. Caution is required when pressing near the lungs or air passages. Press the pad hard, forcing the blood back into the cut. Never allow a wet bandage to remain on the dog for any great length of time.

Internal. Bleeding from the nose or mouth may indicate internal bleeding, which is very critical. Blood in the urine, shock, abdominal pain, coughing blood, pale gums, and labored breathing could all be signs of internal bleeding. This must be regarded as an extreme emergency. Get to a veterinarian quickly.

SHOCK

The most serious aspect of an accident is the possibility of the patient's going into a state of shock after initial treatment has been rendered. Shock is a frequently misunderstood term largely because of its complicated nature. According to the *Merck Veterinary Manual,* shock is "a state of collapse characterized by an acute and progressive failure of the peripheral circulation."

No one in medicine is fully sure what causes shock in the most specific sense. They do know that it often follows trauma from auto accidents, heart failure, severe bleeding, serious burns, lethal infections, and other forms of extreme stress. During a mild state of shock the body compensates by accelerating the heartbeat so that blood can be delivered throughout the body. If the state of shock worsens, this compensation slows down considerably. During severe shock, circulation becomes poor, and denies the heart and its system of the necessary blood it requires. The heart begins to weaken, the blood flow diminishes even further, and the body becomes unable to maintain its own vital chemistry. If treatment is not given promptly, death ensues.

After a serious accident, look for signs of shock. They are apathy, prostration, rapid then weakening pulse, hyperventilation, thirst, and temperature 100°F. or lower. The dog's extremities will begin to cool to the touch and the pupils of the eyes may dilate. Look for nearly white gums, panting, unconsciousness (which could mean coma), or listlessness.

To prevent shock, bleeding must be arrested, pain relieved, and infection prevented. Place a blanket or clothing over the dog to help him preserve his own body heat, but do not overheat with electrical appliances such as heating pads. Keep the dog quiet and calm. Offer no liquids, as the dog may gag and possibly strangle. Immediate veterinary care is essential, the primary goal being to restore blood volume and pressure to normal.

ARTIFICIAL RESPIRATION

Following drowning, electric shock, obstruction in the throat, or any other accident where the dog's breathing has stopped, artificial respiration will sustain life. The heart must still be beating, no matter how faintly, and the pulse must be present if resuscitation is to take place. If there is no heartbeat and pulse, the dog is dead and emergency treatment is futile. However, a nonprofessional without a stethoscope and unfamiliar with the unique heartbeat patterns of a dog may not be able to make a proper determination. Artificial respiration should be attempted until a veterinarian is consulted.

When breathing stops but the heart continues, the dog can survive for approximately five minutes until air begins to flow back into the body. Every precious second counts. During this time artificial respiration substitutes for normal breathing and keeps the animal alive until his independent breathing is restored and self-sustaining.

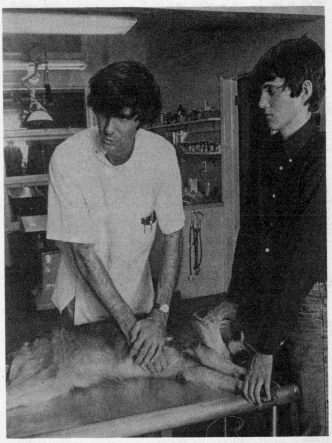

Artificial respiration. Place both hands over the dog's heart, which is just behind the front legs, under the rib cage. Gently press inward, forcing the lungs to exhale. Then relax pressure to allow lungs to inhale. Sometimes a larger dog will require more pressure. Apply one hand, folded into a fist, over the other. This will help the dog to breathe on his own faster. *(The Photo Works)*

How to Apply Artificial Respiration.   Open the dog's mouth and pull out the tongue so that it does not interfere with breathing. With your fingers, probe the dog's throat and clear it of accumulated solids or saliva that may block air from entering the body. With the dog lying on his side, place both hands, one atop the other, over the dog's heart and gently press inward, forcing the lungs to inhale and exhale. The dog's heart is located in the rib cage just past the front legs. Your pushes should be timed approximately fifteen to the minute for the average-sized dog. Large dogs require ten and toy breeds require approximately thirty per minute. Each push should take about four seconds. As you press, be sure to force the air out of the lungs (about two seconds), relax the pressure, wait two more seconds for air to be sucked in, then press again. Counting the seconds aloud will help you keep track of the timing. Repeat this procedure until the dog begins to breathe on his own. It may take as long as an hour or more. Have someone call for professional assistance.

DROWNING

There are two steps to reviving a drowning victim. First, try to get the water out of the lungs. Second, artificial respiration is applied to start automatic breathing again (see preceding section). Speed is important and artificial respiration must begin quickly. Pull the dog's tongue from his throat and let it hang outside his mouth. This prevents it from rolling back and causing suffocation. Lift the dog either by the hind legs or, if the dog is small enough, hold him by the rear of his trunk. Hold him upside-down so that as much water as possible will empty from his body. Ten or fifteen seconds is about all you have to devote to this. Artificial respiration must then begin if the dog's life is to be saved. Place the dog on his side and begin pushing air in and out.

FRACTURES (BROKEN BONES)

There are three types of fractures. A simple fracture is a bone that has been broken in one place with no open wound near the bone. A compound fracture is a bone that is broken and has punctured its surrounding tissue and may possibly protrude from the wound. A comminuted fracture indicates a bone or bones broken in more than one location and may be accompanied by an injury to an important component in the body such as the lungs, blood vessels, etc.

It is usually not very difficult to determine if your dog has broken a bone. If a leg is broken, your dog will not be able to bear his own weight on that limb. A deformity of the affected limb will be apparent by swelling, abnormal angulation, or other deviation. Compound fractures may show bleeding. It is sometimes difficult to tell if a leg is swollen or broken. If swelling occurs use cold towels. If the swelling worsens or fails to stabilize, see a veterinarian.

First Aid Treatment for a Broken Bone.   A simple or compound fracture may cause injury to another part of the body if the animal is not restrained and immobilized. For example, a broken rib may puncture a lung if the dog flails about. Similarly, a simple fracture can become a compound fracture. The first step in giving aid to the dog is to tie a gauze muzzle over his mouth so that you may help without getting bitten. Once you have determined that a bone has been broken, immobilize the injured area with a splint. Use any firm object such as a small plank of wood, a tree branch, heavy cardboard—even a wrench, hammer, or screwdriver—so long as it is long enough to brace above and below the break. Use gauze or cloth strips to wrap the limb or other broken area in a layer of absorbent cotton or newspaper so that the splint will be padded evenly. Place the splint against the broken bone and fix it in place with gauze bandage, rope, twine, or what-have-you. Do not tie it so tight that the circulation is cut off. *Under no circumstances should you attempt to set the bone in place yourself.* Incorrect procedures can destroy the surrounding tissue's ability to convey and absorb vital fluids.

Assume that a degree of shock has taken place, and treat the dog for that. Keep the animal still and wrap him in a blanket or clothing to help retain his own body heat. Watch for breathing difficulties, bleeding, and other aspects of shock and seek professional care immediately.

BURNS

Burns destroy the skin, its mechanism, and the underlying tissue. Direct flame, scalding liquid, electricity, corrosive chemicals, or friction are the causes of all burns. Friction burns are sometimes caused by a rope's being rubbed against the skin during restraint. Electrical burns come from exposure to live wires or lightning. Burns from corrosive chemicals involve acids, some disinfectants, alkaline cleaning preparations, and car battery acid. The most common burns come from scalding water or other cooking preparations, such as soup or stews.

For a burned dog, first saturate the burned area with cold water to wash away the hot material. This also prevents the heat from burning deeper into the tissue.

Next, douse the area in a solution of baking soda and water. Four tablespoons of soda to one quart of water is sufficient. Do not rub or scrub the area with the solution—just sponge gently.

You can gently apply an antibacterial ointment such as Bacitracin to the area. A & D ointment is also good for this. If none is available, soak a gauze pad or other cloth in the solution of baking soda and water, place it over the burn, and secure it with a bandage taped or tied lightly in place. All burns, no matter how slight, should be examined by a veterinarian as soon as possible. This is especially true of puppies who are burned by chewing into an electrical cord. Look for signs of shock, breathing difficulties, or coughing.

Dogs burned by chemicals require a thorough dousing with liquid. The use of a hose is preferred to wash away the acid or base. If the chemical was an acid, wash the burn with water and then apply a paste consisting of water and sodium bicarbonate. Give the dog a tablespoon of liquid antacid such as Maalox or Mylanta, egg white, or baking soda (sodium bicarbonate) mixed with a little water. If the chemical was an alkali, apply water mixed with vinegar to the burned area. Then give the dog a tablespoon or more of vinegar to be taken internally. See a veterinarian immediately.

INSECT BITES AND BEE STINGS

The only real danger is an allergic reaction to a bee sting or insect bite. The signs of serious reaction are restlessness, diarrhea, vomiting, circulatory problems, seizures, coma, and suffocation leading to death. If a dog is having breathing difficulties, it will keep its mouth closed. The first signs of an allergic reaction should signal the owner to seek professional help immediately and treat the situation as a genuine emergency. Time is of the essence because breathing difficulties develop rapidly.

Normal reaction to an insect bite or bee sting is a swelling accompanied by localized pain. Relief is accomplished with the application of cold water to the stung area. A common reaction is a very swollen face due to unknown allergic situations. Cold water will keep the swelling down. Often the eyes will close if the swelling is severe enough. This type of swelling is common in puppies up to twelve months old. If there are no breathing difficulties, there is no need for alarm. If the sting can be located, carefully pull it out so that no particle of it remains. Most insect bites and bee stings are located on the legs, face, or other areas where the coat is thinnest. The bites from black widow spiders and scorpions are rare but lethal. Apply ice packs to the site of the wound until a veterinarian takes over.

SUNSTROKE, HEATSTROKE, HEAT PROSTRATION

Although there are differences between these three conditions, the symptoms are similar and the first-aid treatment is the same. Fat dogs, old dogs, heart or lung patients, and dogs with short noses (such as bulldogs and pugs) are most susceptible. Next to traffic deaths more dogs die from heatstroke than any other type of accident. It is too common an occurrence to see a dog locked in a car parked in a supermarket lot on a warm day. So many owners are fooled into believing that if the windows are open two inches and if the outside temperature is only 75° or 80°, there is no danger to the dog. This is absolutely incorrect, and many dogs pay with their lives because their owners did not know better.

When the temperature is 80°F. outside the car, it will quickly climb beyond 100° inside if it is poorly ventilated and if the parking lot surface is covered with a heat-absorbing material such as asphalt or crushed pebbles. The car itself literally becomes an oven as the sun shines directly on the roof and absorbs enough heat to fry eggs. The roof quickly radiates the intense heat inside. Leaving a dog locked inside a car in such a situation is to condemn him to death.

Dogs allowed to play or exercise too strenuously on a hot and humid day where there is little shade and very little breeze will develop heat prostration, heat cramps, heatstroke, or sunstroke. Either way, the dog's life will be endangered. The conditions for these various forms of heat stress are high environmental temperature, high humidity, and inadequate ventilation. Exposure to direct rays of the sun may also bring about the symptoms of heat stress.

The signs of heat-connected illness are weakness, muscular tremors, collapse, muscle spasms, a staring expression of the eyes, vomiting, and abnormally rapid breathing. During the episode, there may be any combination of these symptoms. Immediate help is necessary to save the dog's life.

First you must reduce the temperature of the dog's body. The most effective way to do this is to immerse the dog in ice-cold water up to his head. Somehow, cool water must be applied to the body. Throw buckets of cold water on him. An air-conditioned room is an efficient way to lower the temperature. Ice packs applied to the head and cold-water enemas are useful. During heatstroke, a gallant dash to the veterinarian's office with the breeze blowing on the dog from the open car windows may be the only chance the dog has. Prevention is easy, and the best way of avoiding this deadly situation. Keep your dog out of locked cars. Keep your dog out of the direct sun on hot and humid days. If the temperature is high, take the dog inside where it's cooler, and if you have air conditioning, so much the better.

POISONING

MY LOCAL POISON CONTROL CENTER PHONE NUMBER IS:_____

Before you read another word, please call your information operator and ask for the telephone number of your nearest Poison Control Center and write it in the space above. Check it once a year and keep the number current. It may someday save your dog's life (not to mention any member of your family). When an emergency involving poison strikes, you may have only minutes to do the correct thing.

Unless one is writing a book on the subject of poison, its effects and cures, it is impossible to do the subject justice in a limited work. Though far from adequate, generalized information can be useful. Calling your local Poison Control Center is the best chance you have next to living with a veterinarian. If you know or even suspect that the dog has ingested a specific poison, call the control center and give them the name of the poison by brand name if it is a manufactured product. These centers maintain huge files of close to one million products by brand name and list their ingredients and proper antidotes. If you do not know what your dog has ingested, call your veterinarian and describe the dog's symptoms and ask for help.

The usual symptoms of poisoning are some manifestation of pain in the stomach, howling, whimpering or yelping, vomiting, convulsions, muscle tremors, and labored breathing. First, if the dog has not swallowed corrosive materials such as kerosene, strong acids, or alkalis (lye, cleanser, etc.), make the dog vomit up the toxic material. If the dog has swallowed corrosive materials, vomiting will further harm the throat and mouth. In this situation, first neutralize the poison while it is still in the stomach. For alkali poisoning, force the dog to swallow one or two tablespoons of vinegar or lemon juice. For acid poisoning, neutralize with one teaspoon of bicarbonate of soda mixed with a small amount of water. An emetic (for induced vomiting) often used for poisoning is 3 percent solution of hydrogen peroxide. Use with equal parts water or straight from the bottle if time is short. Give one tablespoon for every ten pounds of body weight. One-half teaspoon of mustard powder mixed with one cup of warm water will also produce the desired effect. Because emetics are essentially unpleasant to take, you will have to force them down the dog's mouth. (Antifreeze is one of the most common poisons; dogs love it. If the dog has swallowed it, induce vomiting and rush the dog to the veterinarian.)

The next step in emergency treatment is giving the proper antidote for the specific poison ingested. If this is not feasible, the next best step is to administer five heaping teaspoons of activated charcoal mixed in one cup of water. This will absorb some of the poison, thus weakening its effect until you can get the dog to a veterinarian. It will buy you some time. No poisoning incident should be concluded without a proper examination and consultation with a veterinarian.

Home Nursing Procedures

Once your sick dog has visited the veterinarian and is safely home again, he will need some amount of nursing care to return to his old self. Obviously the medical instructions given by the veterinarian must be followed faithfully. Among those tasks often required of the loving dog owner are the taking of the dog's temperature, feeding special diets, and administering pills and/or liquid medication. As a handy reference for those who forgot the techniques given by the veterinarian, here is a refresher.

Temperature. By necessity, all dog temperatures must be taken rectally. Rectal thermometers manufactured for humans are used for dogs also. Shake the thermometer down below 99°F. Allow the dog to stand or place him on his side and lift his tail. Smear the tip of the thermometer with Vaseline. Insert the thermometer into the dog's anus. If the dog is large, the thermometer should be inserted to half its length. Smaller dogs require less. Leave the thermometer inside for two minutes. Do not allow the dog to move while the thermometer is in. Very few dogs find this objectionable and will hold still if petted and spoken to soothingly. Do not allow him to sit. Remove the thermometer and take the reading. The average reading for a normal dog is 102°F. This indicates no fever. Large dogs will run a slightly lower normal temperature at around

99.5°F. Many veterinarians consider fever to start at a reading of 102.6°F. Record the dog's temperature every time it is taken so that it can be given to the veterinarian upon request. If the dog is recovering from a serious illness, a complete record of the daily temperature is invaluable for the veterinarian.

ADMINISTERING PILLS, CAPSULES, AND TABLETS

A sick dog or one that is on the road to recovery will probably have to be given some form of dry medication. If you are lucky, your dog will simply lick the pill out of your open hand. He may even be the kind of a dog that will accept it mixed in with the food in his bowl. But do not be surprised if the dog refuses your hand gesture and leaves the medicine lying at the bottom of the dish after he has devoured everything else. We do not smell these pills and capsules, but dogs do, and sometimes they don't like what they've smelled. Your only alternative is to force the pill down the dog's throat. It's not as difficult as it sounds. If your dog is used to

Administering a pill to an uncooperative dog. Grasping the dog's muzzle, press inward on the upper lip. As the dog's mouth opens, slide the pill to the back of the tongue and hold mouth closed until he swallows. This procedure is best accomplished by two persons; however, it can be done by one person. Coating the pill with vegetable oil can help. *(The Photo Works)*

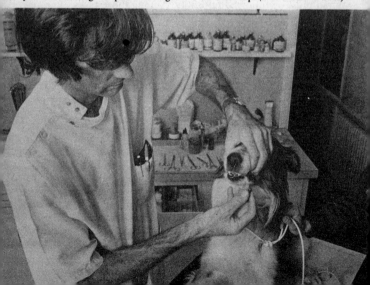

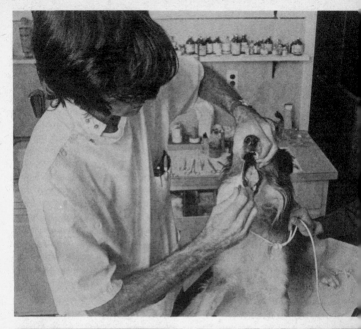

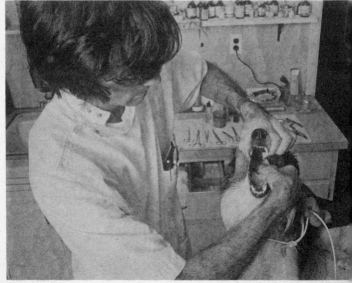

being handled by you for other procedures such as bathing, grooming, training, etc., and you've always been gentle and loving, then you'll easily get the dog used to taking his medicine by hand. Grasp the dog's muzzle with your left hand and raise it upward. Press gently on his upper lips so they push against his teeth. The dog should open his mouth to ease the discomfort. When he opens his mouth, take the pill with your right hand (holding it with your finger and thumb) and quickly slide it to the rear of his mouth. Deposit the pill directly on the back portion of the tongue and remove your hand. The dog will probably close his mouth. When he does, the pill should go down. Hold his mouth closed with one hand, raise his head upward, and gently stroke his throat. This will force him to swallow. If you have a very small dog with a tiny mouth, you will have to drop the pill in once you open his mouth. Take care to drop the medicine onto the back of the tongue rather than get it caught in the windpipe. Sometimes smearing the pill with oil, margarine, or butter helps. Another technique is to pulverize the medicine and mix it into a favorite food snack.

LIQUID MEDICINE

The most commonly used technique for administering liquid medicine to a dog is the "lip pouch" method. Pour the medicine into a spoon (a small bottle is easier), grasp his lower lip near the corner of his mouth, and pull it out. This will form a pouch or cup between the inner wall of the lip and the rear molars. Pour the liquid in the pouch in small quantities, close the pouch, lift the dog's head upward, and stroke his throat. The dog has no choice but to swallow the medicine. Keep repeating this procedure until the dog has taken the full dose. Do not simply pour the liquid down the dog's throat because it may enter his lungs and that could be the beginning of pneumonia or a congestion difficulty.

For an especially difficult dog, use a dropper or syringe. This will allow small amounts to be introduced steadily on the middle of the tongue. A used syringe can be obtained from your veterinarian. After the dog swallows the liquid, it will lick its nose. Then you will know if it went down.

FORCE-FEEDING

A recuperating dog must eat even if he doesn't want to. The veterinarian will outline the necessary diet for a sick or recovering animal and will take into consideration that the dog is finicky or

Creating a lip pouch for liquid medicine.

not hungry. There are those times when feeding must take place with or without the dog's consent. This will require force-feeding.

Liquid food such as lukewarm broth or milk can be fed in the same manner as liquid medicine (see above section). Solid food is somewhat more difficult. The ideal situation is to stimulate the dog's interest so that he will take it himself. This is done by rubbing some of the food on your fingers and offering them for him to lick. Once the dog licks your fingers and likes it, he may then take small bits of food from your hand.

If none of this works and the dog must take in specified solid foods, there is no choice but to force-feed. If the food is too solid for forming into small sausage shapes, a blender and a little moisture will solve the problem. Once the food is formed into small, soft shapes, force-feed them as you would a pill or capsule. If the food is too soft, work it into the mouth with a spoon as you would liquid medicine.

Force-feeding a dog can have emotional consequences for the dog if the experience is too upsetting. If the animal is young enough, it can distort his behavior toward food for the rest of his life. One must be gentle, loving, and patient for this procedure. Do not lose your head or get hysterical. Do not be surprised or revolted if the dog chooses to vomit the food and then eat it in that form. In the wild and in domestic puppy litters, that is exactly what the dog's mother does for the puppies in order to make the transition from breast milk to semisolid food. Do not judge your dog's behavior by human standards. It is unfair and inhumane.

There is more than luck involved in living with a healthy dog. The proper care and concern on the part of the dog's "family" are absolutely essential for a long life that is blessed with a minimum of sickness and a maximum of unfettered joy and pleasure. The dog is yours *in sickness and in health*. Health is better.

9. Dog Disasters

Have you and your dog ever been trapped in a small bathroom together because the knob slid off on the other side of the door as the clogged commode began to spill over onto the floor? How about sitting atop the roof of your house during a flood as your dog decides to take a swim? What do you do when your dog leaps from your car window while on vacation at Craters of the Moon National Monument and then disappears in the vapor and rocky terrain? These are dog disasters, and they range from eating mistletoe (a poisonous plant) to being the extorted victim of a dog abduction, complete with ransom.

Dogs are like children in almost every way including the trouble they can get into; sometimes quaint, sometimes quite tragic. During such crises, remaining calm and performing like a pro can make the difference between a favorable outcome and a sad event of grim consequence. In the throes of dog disasters, you are the cavalry coming to the rescue, the Batman and Robin of canine calamity. It is not impossible to be the one who rescues your dog or resolves a horrible situation. Knowing what to do in the event of emergencies saves precious time and thus the day. Dog disasters are common enough to make it necessary to keep helpful information and suggestions within fingertip reach for as long as you live with your dog. I sincerely wish that this section is never needed beyond the initial reading.

In almost every situation covered in this chapter, there is offered an obvious set of preventive measures. They will be described along with the not-so-obvious preventives. Because of the totally unreliable nature of all dogs to rush blindly into situations, plus their mischievous impulses, it is not a bad idea for every dog owner to be a little distrustful and a bit paranoid when it comes to dog safety. When you love a dog, his safety seriously involves your emotions. Protecting your dog from disaster is really another way of protecting yourself from emotional pain.

The Lost Dog

It is more than grammatically correct to say, "I lost my dog." The sentence implies that the person speaking did something wrong to allow the dog to be lost. This is almost always the case. Our dogs fool us all the time. For six years a dog may ride in the family car with the window open and always behave. Then, unexplainably, one day he darts out the open window and disappears. It is common. The same applies to dogs that suddenly run out of the house when the door is opened. All the stunned owner can say is, "He never did that before." A haunting refrain, often heard. One must never be lulled into taking a dog's reliability for granted. The best-trained, most loyal and obedient animal may possibly sense a female in heat a mile away, out of your sight, and take off in pursuit of a call of nature. From then on anything can happen. Dogs do get lost and travel in the wrong direction thinking they are heading home. The animal could end up in another part of the state. Any dog can decide to roam, but this is especially common in males.

PREVENTION

The preventive measures are worth mentioning even though they are quite common. Obey all leash and confinement laws in your community. Set your own strict leash laws for your family. Even the best-trained dogs may someday forget their off-leash training and take a powder. Make it a household rule for children and adults that the dog must not be allowed outdoors without being restrained by a leash. It is against the law in most cities to allow a dog to wander around off-leash.

Be certain that fencing around yards and kennel runs cannot be tunneled under. Dogs are very clever with their paws. When the dog is caught in the act of digging, reprimand him vigorously. Although it is a common practice for suburban and rural dogs to be allowed to roam around, do not be deceived by that accepted practice. More country dogs are killed by automobiles than any other. The same applies for lost dogs. It is a very poor policy to give a dog that much freedom. They cannot handle it. Tying a dog with rope or chain is undesirable due to its negative effect on your dog's personality. Besides, you cannot rely on rope or even chain to restrain a dog that truly wants to go. A restrained dog should be hooked up to an overhead clothesline (or trolley) and allowed a degree of free movement. Even then, observe your dog from time to time to be sure he doesn't get into trouble.

Be cautious of family get-togethers, backyard barbecues, or other at-home functions where the dog is not under careful scrutiny. That is the most likely time the dog may pick to sneak off.

Never let your guard down. Owners must understand that a dog who runs off is not one that really wants to leave home for good. It is an impulsive response to canine curiosity and the genetic instinct to mate, hunt, and mark off new territory. Dogs live a cause-and-effect existence. They do not realize the consequences of their actions, nor can they perceive what will happen beyond the next moment. The door is open, they hear sounds, scent distant aromas, or sight moving objects several hundred feet away and follow the call of the wild. It may be too late once they decide to return home. Hence, more lost dogs.

Among the less obvious preventive measures is a good leather collar that cannot easily be pulled off the neck. If there is a flat metal plate riveted to the collar, have it engraved with the family name, address, and telephone number. Do not rely on rabies vaccination tags as effective ID or any other tag that dangles. The friction wears the inscription off in a short time. The same applies to license tags although they are extremely useful to dog pounds when they are legible. A legible dog license can save your dog's life if he is rounded up as a stray.

There is no ID more reliable than an ID tattoo inside his right hind thigh. This can easily be accomplished for a nominal fee by most veterinarians once the dog has been sedated. The next step is to register the animal's tattoo with either of the two leading nationwide dog registries. Write to: National Dog Registry, 227 Stebbins Road, Carmel, New York 10512, or Ident-a-Pet, 401 Broadhollow Road, Melville, New York 11746. Some local animal shelters throughout the country are starting their own tattoo programs. A low fee is paid one time, and your dog is registered for life. If your dog is found and the registry is contacted, they will contact you and bring you and the dog together. The tattoo system is most useful if the dog has been stolen and sold to a laboratory for research purposes. It is now against the law to harbor or sell a tattooed animal. Consequently, the research laboratories, the pet-store chains, and most of the large commercial breeders will not purchase tattooed animals. The penalty can be costly. Tattooed dogs have become less profitable for dognappers or those cashing in on lost dogs. In addition, animal shelters, dog pounds, and police departments are becoming more aware of the registry operations and know to look for the tattoo.

The next preventive measure is fairly easy and very important for helping to retrieve a lost dog. The thoughtful dog owner must develop an identification file and keep it handy for that awful day when it becomes necessary to write out a complete description of

Most dog disasters can be prevented by not allowing the dog to roam free. For greater freedom without losing control, hook the dog to an overhead trolley made of clothesline or metal cable.

your dog. If you can accurately and specifically describe your dog and provide photographs, your chances for recovery are considerably enhanced. Almost every pet-food manufacturer offers a blank form ID chart for your records, and you can send for it. For your convenience, here is such a blank form. Fill in the blank spaces and attach one or two photographs of your dog. In this way you will always know where to look for your dog's description and vital statistics. Take the time to fill it in immediately. You will never regret it.

MY DOG'S DESCRIPTION

Dog's full name (AKC Registration) _____
Name to which dog responds _____
American Kennel Club Registration Number _____
Tattoo Identification Number _____
Dog License Number _____
Rabies Tag Number _____
Date of Birth _____
Date Obtained _____
Where Obtained _____
Veterinarian's name, address, telephone number _____
_____
_____

Breed or Breed Combination _____
Sex _____
Weight _____
Height (from top of shoulders) _____
Dog's Coat: Colors. Markings. Texture (Rough, Silky, Curly).
Short or Long-coated. _____
_____
_____

What to Do When Your Dog Is Lost. Like all good police work, retrieving a lost dog involves a great deal of legwork and telephone work. By developing an emergency telephone list of the various people and agencies to be notified, you will save considerable effort at a time when energy and emotions must be conserved. Fill in the blank lines below and always refer to *The Good Dog Book* for The Lost Dog Telephone List.

Police (Local Precinct) _____
City Dog Pound or Shelter _____

SPCA-Type Organization _____

Other Shelters and Humane Groups _____
_____
_____

Local and Neighborhood Newspapers _____
_____
_____

Radio and TV Stations _____
_____
_____

Neighborhood Veterinarians _____
_____
_____

Local Merchants and Supermarket Managers _____
_____
_____
_____

Neighborhood Letter Carrier _____

Neighbors With Children _____
_____
_____
_____

First, telephone everyone on your list and tell them that your
dog is missing. Ask them to watch for the dog if they haven't already seen him. In the matter of dog pounds and city shelters (in
some cities this means the SPCA-type society), go in person at
least once a day until the dog is found or given up for good. These
organizations are, for the most part, bound by law to destroy stray
dogs shortly after they have been captured. Some organizations
hold the dog up to ten days, others for only forty-eight hours.
Checking with them by telephone after your initial call is ineffective because of their overload of work and understaffing. Your
dog may be sitting in a cage unnoticed and unprocessed. Do *not*
rely on ID attached to the dog to save him from euthanasia. It may
have fallen off, gone unnoticed, or not made any impression on an
overworked or inefficient shelter worker. Sometimes red tape and
inefficiency allows an identified dog to be led to the euthanasia
room and destroyed despite the fact that the animal's owners have
been identified. Go once a day to look the dogs over for yourself.
Take your description list and photographs.

Next, create a Lost Dog Notice. Type or block-print a notice in-
forming the neighborhood that your dog is lost and that a reward

is being offered. Describe the animal completely. Have the notice duplicated by Xerox machine or mimeograph. Here is a sample to follow:

LOST DOG

On or about _____(fill in date)_____ our beloved dog disappeared from the vicinity of _____(fill in location)_____.
(He or She) answers to the name _____.
The dog is a (male or female), is _____(fill in age)_____
years old, and is a _____(give breed or breed mix)_____.
The following is a brief description: _____
_____
_____

A REWARD IS BEING OFFERED FOR THE DOG'S RETURN, NO QUESTIONS ASKED.

Please contact: (fill in your name, address, and telephone number)
_____
_____

(Xerox your dog's photograph at the bottom if possible.)

INDICATE DOG'S COAT MARKINGS

Type Ears: Prick [ ] Hanging [ ] Other   [ ] _____
Type Tail: Long [ ] Short   [ ] Ring   [ ] Plume [ ] Other _____
Muzzle: Long [ ] Medium [ ] Short   [ ] Pushed In [ ]

PHOTOGRAPHS

FRONT   SIDE

Circulate your notice in as many public locations as you can. Supermarkets, local merchants, school bulletin boards, all the veterinarians' offices in your neighborhood, every conceivable location in your neighborhood, and then some. The offer of a reward may inspire someone who stole your dog to come forward. Because it is impossible to prove that someone stole your dog, be grateful to get the animal back and pay the reward.

Once your notices are up, talk to the children in the area. They may have valuable information because of their heightened awareness of neighborhood pets. Talk to the local merchants, the cop on the beat, your letter carrier, or anybody else that spends time on the street. Try to pick up a trail, even if it's only a general direction that the dog headed. Once you know the direction the dog headed, you can start localizing your efforts. It is amazing how one piece can fit into another. Always carry your notices and photographs with you while on the trail. Show them frequently, even to strangers.

Check the lost-and-found section of your local and neighborhood newspapers. You might even consider placing an ad. Many local radio and TV stations offer a free lost-pet service on the air, and you may be able to take advantage of it.

A little-known service of the American Humane Association is the Pet Patrol. Through the efforts of the AHA, close to 700 radio stations throughout the United States and Canada cooperate in public-service programs listing lost-and-found pets in their respective localities. A complete list of all participating radio stations is available by writing to: The American Humane Association, P.O. Box 1266, Denver, Colorado 80201. You may call all the radio stations in your own area and ask if they will run your Lost Dog Notice. It is amazing and quite touching how many broadcasters cooperate and sympathize.

There is every good reason to believe that your dog is simply lost and will turn up at your door or will be seen by someone who read your notice. Try to be of good cheer and keep going to the city pound or shelter every day. Efforts to return lost dogs at these pounds are slight, but a persistent taxpayer can get results. Many dogs are recovered long after they have been listed as missing. Keep trying.

Dognapping

There are several ways for dognappers to profit from their cruel and sadistic crime. They may unload the dog to a middleman who then sells it to a research institution or to a puppy-mill operator as breeding stock. Others will forge American Kennel Club papers and sell the animal retail to someone who wants a pet. Another source of profit may be a ransom payment that is disguised as a "reward" for returning the stolen animal. Payments in the thousands of dollars have been made to these thieves by emotionally distraught dog owners overpowered by their own despair and grief.

How It Happens

It is very difficult for a dog to be stolen if he is leashed and restrained. Dogs that are allowed to roam free or run about off-leash are the most likely victims of dognapping. Dogs that are left alone in their own back yards are also potential victims. Watchdogs and even attack dogs can be easily subdued and stolen with the help of food that has been laced with a tranquilizer. Dangerous dogs can be shot with a tranquilizing dartgun similar to the ones used by zookeepers. A bold and surprising technique is used in some cities and works like a purse snatching. Any frail-looking man, woman, or child walking a leashed dog is selected by the thief. He will approach the dog and throw a blanket or jacket over the animal to avoid getting bitten. In one swooping action, the thief scoops the dog up in his arms and yanks the leash out of the hands of the owner and runs away.

There is a trickier, even more devious way that dognappers obtain victims. They answer ads in the newspapers placed by persons seeking new homes for their loved but unwanted pets. Unsuspecting pet owners literally hand away their dogs to these criminals who promise to give the dogs good homes. It is safe to assume that if the pet owners knew the fate awaiting their dogs, they would not permit this horror to occur. Those who answer the ads are what is known in the humane movement as "bunchers" because they collect as many stray and stolen animals as possible and sell them to various subdealers who in turn sell them to state or federally licensed dealers. The licensed dealer is legally entitled to sell the animals directly to medical centers, universities, and industrial laboratories where the dogs are systematically mutilated in the name of scientific experimentation.

All that the licensed dealer needs is a bill of sale from his source, and these are very often forged by the original buncher. Bunchers may round up stray dogs in their spare time in order to earn supplemental income. The problem is that stray dogs are not consistently available and so other, more devious and illegal means are used. Unless the buncher is caught red-handed, he can claim he found the dog wandering from home. Quite often the dogs are overtly stolen from back yards, taken off the streets (despite the fact that they might have worn ample ID), and lured into the trucks by female dogs in heat. Bunchers have also been known to post false "Humane Society" signs on their trucks as they cruise neighborhoods for dogs. It is cruel and vicious, and the dog owner seeking "a new home in the country" for an unwanted dog must be very careful. The buncher is part of a network or secret pipeline leading to the USDA licensed dealers, who then make legal sales to the labs.

Other funnels leading to the laboratories are the "dog and cat auctions" that take place all over the United States. Here licensed dealers purchase dogs of every description and then resell them to the research institutes for a handsome profit. Bills of sale (many of them phonied) are presented by the bunchers and other private individuals out to make a bloody dollar. The dogs are bartered, haggled over, and sometimes auctioned off to the highest bidder, who usually buys in quantity. During the auctions, before and after, the animals are often treated cruelly and transported in unbelievably crowded cages, exposed to the heat and cold, unfed, unwatered. At the auctions the dogs are frequently found tied to the bumpers of trucks and cars and allowed to fry in the sun or freeze in the cold. This all takes place in a country fair setting along with the put-up beets and blue ribbon bake-offs. These auctions are capable of attracting criminals from five and ten states away with lost, stolen, and abducted dogs from the heartbroken pet owners of this country.

The most common dognappings take place because the owner tied the dog to a parking meter while shopping at the supermarket. Leaving a dog in a parked car is risky, and so is tying the animal to a street pole or fire hydrant while dining in a restaurant. Dog thieves know exactly where to look for this convenient behavior that makes their business easy and profitable. A dognapper will watch the newspapers for your ad or look for your reward notice around the neighborhood. He will hold the dog just long enough to give you a sense of hopeless despair and then make contact when you're desperate enough to pay a good amount. The negotiation is delicate, and the word "reward" is used instead of ransom. By this time the owner is so emotional that he will pay almost any amount asked. Carelessness, neglect, the failure to restrain or leash the dog are among the greatest reasons for the success of dognappers. Dog owners beware!

Prevention

Because of the legislation regarding the harboring and selling of stolen dogs, it is difficult for thieves to sell dogs that have been tattooed. A veterinarian can tattoo your Social Security Number or other form of ID on the inner thigh of your dog's right hind leg. Tattoos must be registered with a nationwide dog registry for identification purposes if and when needed (see *The Lost Dog* section). It has always been easy for dognappers because there has been no way to prove in a court of law that any given dog belongs to the person pressing charges. Once a dog has been tattooed, the stolen dog becomes legal evidence and tangible proof of ownership. The thieves are very aware of this and tend to release dogs that have been tattooed. No other form of identification can accomplish as much as the tattoo.

Preventing dognapping involves leashing, good fencing, and careful observation of your dog if he is allowed outdoors. Do not allow him to roam free. Do not leave him tied outside a supermarket. Do not leave him unattended in an automobile. Have the animal tattooed and registered.

The Automobile

In the twentieth century automobiles and pet dogs have both proliferated at a rate surpassed only by human population. It is interesting that both of these fixtures in modern society tend to be in opposition to each other. It is quite clear that most dogs do not like automobiles from the inside or the outside.

Like a primitive society that refuses to accept technology and modern culture, dogs find it difficult to make their peace with the four-wheeled enemy. If the locomotive was the *iron horse* to the American Plains Indians, then the automobile is the *steel wolf* to domestic dogs. Given their choice, dogs would rather walk. But dogs are not given their choice, nor should they be. It is the responsibility of the dog owner to prevent dog disasters caused by automobiles. Viewing the problem inside and out will help the owner prevent accidents, emergencies, and fatalities.

Inside the Auto

Dogs become quite unhappy inside moving cars because they have lost control of their immediate environment, feel somewhat trapped, are disoriented, confused over territory, and cannot keep a consistent footing. Sometimes these factors bring about motion sickness, which is characterized by nausea, vomiting, and excessive salivation. This condition involves the inner chambers of the ears and is induced by constant motion. Probably the greatest factor here is the animal's fear of the automobile. This ailment can be corrected primarily by conditioning the dog to car travel.

One or two very short rides a day for a week will do the job if the rides are happy experiences. Open the door to the parked car and invite the dog in with a snack treat. Allowing the doors to remain open, sit in the car, and praise the dog with a constant patter of good-natured remarks and compliments. Once the dog is comfortable, close the doors and drive away slowly. Continue to relate to the dog in the happy manner you started with. After two or three blocks, drive home, open the doors, invite the dog out, and give him a great deal of praise. Repeat this until entering the car is a pleasant idea for the dog. It is important that you do not allow the dog to take a dominant position in the situation. Praising and speaking to your dog in a friendly tone does not mean relinquishing your position as leader of his pack. As a matter of fact, the dog will become more easily adapted to car riding if you are able to command him. For severe cases of motion sickness, see your veterinarian. There are now drugs available that effectively combat the symptoms of motion sickness and can even help to prevent them. Many of these drugs are administered orally, and several are injected.

When traveling in a car with your dog, there are several rules that must be followed if the human and canine occupants are to arrive at their destination safely. (1) Always lead the dog inside the car from the sidewalk side. A dog that bolts from this side cannot be hit by an oncoming automobile. (2) Be certain that the dog is nowhere near the door when it is closed. To prevent pinching a paw, close the door in a slow, deliberate manner. Do not slam it shut. (3) Avoid placing the dog near the driver, if possible. An excited dog may interfere with the operation of the vehicle. (4) Do not allow the dog to lie on the shelf behind the back seat. If the car comes to a sudden stop, the dog will fly like a missile. (5) Lock all doors before the car is set in motion. (6) If possible, use a restraint for your dog. A dog harness can be effectively used with a seat belt to prevent falling about. (7) Always travel with your dog's first-aid kit. (8) Do not allow paws, muzzle, or tail to hang out of the car windows. It is unhealthy and unsafe. Foreign objects can blow into the dog's eyes, ears, or nose, causing injury or illness. A dog hanging out the window can lose his footing, fall out, and become severely injured or killed. When riding in a car with a dog, do not allow the windows to remain fully opened. Any dog—no matter how old or how obedient—is capable of jumping out of the window of a moving vehicle on an impulse. (9) When leaving the car, do not let the dog out on the street side and do not allow the dog out first. Someone must remain in the car, restraining the dog with a leash until other passengers are out. The dog should be the last to exit so that proper control is maintained at all times. An obedience-trained dog adjusts best to car travel.

OUTSIDE THE AUTO

An estimated 1,000,000 animals a year are savaged by moving vehicles. Many of these fatalities are hit-and-run accidents. It is a crime in some states to leave the scene of an animal death if your car was the cause, but this does little to keep the fatality figures down. Contrary to common belief, most of these animal deaths occur in the country or rural areas. It is there that dogs are more likely to be allowed to roam free without leash or tether restraints. City dogs have more than their share of auto accidents, but fewer dogs are allowed to run free in the city because of enforced leash laws. Dogs that are leash-controlled have less opportunity to become traffic statistics than those that roam free. The choice is quite clear.

CAR CHASERS

More dogs are killed chasing cars running at slow speeds than in any other circumstance. This problem is common in all communities, but especially in the suburban and rural communities. Prevent this dangerous behavior from developing in a puppy rather than wait for the problem to emerge unexpectedly.

To prevent car chasing, one must first understand what it really means to the dog. The breeds most likely to chase cars are the sight hounds. Such breeds as the greyhound, whippet, Afghan hound, Russian wolfhound, and basenji are hunting dogs with fine vision. They are especially adept at following game spotted from long distances and then chasing it down. It is for this reason that greyhounds and whippets chase mechanical rabbits at dog tracks. It is rare, however, to have one's car chased by a sumptuous-looking Russian wolfhound or delicate whippet. These are valuable dogs, and few of their owners would dream of allowing them to run loose.

Every dog has the instinct to hunt for a living and to protect territory, mating rights, and social position in almost the exact terms of the wolf. Much like a wolf, a dog in the wild seeks his prey rather than waiting for it to come to him. Wolves (and ancient dogs) are the predators of large game such as moose, deer, caribou, and cattle of all description. When something as large as an automobile moves across the territory of a dog it does not seem as formidable to the dog as it does to any human. When the car enters the dog's field of vision, a reflex is set off and the uncontrollable desire to give chase takes over. The dog cannot help himself.

A dog's need to chase cars is probably genetic in origin, but it is behavior that can be taught directly by other dogs or by imitating the attitude of the dog's owner. Another way a dog develops this tendency is in an attempt to cope with passing cars while tied up or restrained behind a chain fence. These barriers frustrate the animal and intensify the desire to attack the intruding vehicle.

A young puppy can be conditioned at an early age to "permit" strange cars to enter his territory without making a fuss. If the dog is walked on a leash frequently and exposed to approaching automobiles, chances are it will not develop this behavior. Take the puppy to the perimeter of his territory and quickly turn for home every time a car passes. The best you can hope for is a conditioned reflex that induces the dog to head for home when he sees a car.

Adult dogs chase cars because they cannot help themselves. They must be regarded as eccentric. It is extremely difficult to break them of the habit without the use of an abusive and sometimes dangerous technique. Many dog experts recommend some caustic solution in the eyes of the dog when he misbehaves. Although this may be effective, it can damage the dog's eyes or at the very least inflict pain. Sometimes these punishment methods work in reverse and provoke an unalterable antagonism toward the car and its occupants. Incurable car chasers must not be allowed to roam free on the streets and roads because sooner or later they will get caught up in the wheels of the steel wolf and will be lost to the great dog-killer.

Poisonous Plants

Stalking the wild this-and-that has become a popular pastime for many because of recent literary encouragement. Munching on wild onions and dandelions may be a pleasant respite after an afternoon's hike, but God help you if your children or your dog bite into the handsome jimson weed. All parts of this plant are poisonous. Cattle, horses, and sheep have been poisoned by feeding on the tops. Children have been poisoned by eating the unripe seed pods. Contact with the leaves or flowers produces dermatitis in some individuals. Victims of the jimson weed experience headache, nausea, vertigo, extreme thirst, dry burning sensation in the skin, dilated pupils, loss of sight and voluntary motion, and, in extreme cases, mania, convulsions, and death. All this from one of nature's more attractive bits of flora. It can be found in many areas where the soil is well irrigated, including farms, gardens, and wild woods. One just never knows about plants.

As a rule, dogs are not terribly interested in plant material as a source of food. Wolves obtain plant protein from the stomach contents of herbivorous prey that have been captured and eaten. Sometimes wild canids eat berries and some grasses. The domestic dog—the best-fed animal in the kingdom—is not really after nutrition when he chews on house plants, shrubbery, or ornamental growths found in and around the home. Boredom, the need to chew, visual and scent curiosity are more likely what make some dogs take a bite out of your favorite tomato plant. Some plants have been scent-posted by other animals, and that would inspire the family dog to sniff them, lick them, and finally take a chomp. If the poor dog has gotten into the boxwood shrubs around the house, a few clippings can kill him. Most plants are bitter tasting and cause animals to avoid them as food. Domestic dogs, not having experienced life in the wild, will go after an innocent-looking (but poisonous) house plant if bored enough.

Because of the highly popular hobby of apartment and house-plant cultivation, it becomes enormously important for all dog owners to know something about poisonous vegetation that is all around us. There is no need for alarm but . . . there are over 700 species of poisonous flora growing in the Western Hemisphere. We are ahead of the game because our well-fed dogs do not try to satisfy their hunger with any of them. Having a reference table of the most common poisonous plants will help the dog owner and parents of small children avoid an unnecessary health hazard in the home. Do not take into your home nor plant outside of it those flora that are listed in the following table:

COMMON POISONOUS PLANTS

HOUSE PLANTS

Name	Poisonous Parts
Alocasia	All
Avocado	Leaves and stems
Bird of Paradise	All
Caladium	All

Name	Poisonous Parts
Dumb cane	All
Elephant ear	All
Holly	Berries
Ivy	All
Mistletoe	Berries
Philodendron	All
Poinsettia	All
Skunk cabbage	All
Snow-on-the-mountain	All
Wild call	All

GARDEN PLANTS AND SHRUBBERY

Name	Poisonous Parts
Amaryllis	Bulb
Azalea	All
Bayonet	Root
Black-eyed Susan	All
Bleeding heart	All
Boxwood	All
Burning bush	Leaves and fruit
Buttercup	All
Cactus, Candelabra	All
Castor bean	All parts, beans most toxic
Cherry laurel	All
Chinaberry	All
Christmas rose	All
Cornflower	All
Crocus, autumn	All
Crown-of-thorns	All
Cyclamen	Tuber (a swollen underground stem)
Daffodil	Bulb
Daphne	All
Death camas	Bulb
Delphinium	All
Flax	All
Four o'clock	Root, seeds
Foxglove	leaves, seeds
Golden glow	All
Hyacinth	Bulb
Hydrangea	All
Ivy	Leaves
Iris	Bulb
Jessamine	Flowers

Name	Poisonous Parts
Jerusalem cherry	All
Jonquil	Bulb
Lantana	All
Larkspur	All
Laurel	All
Lily, climbing or glory	All
Lily, spider	Bulb
Lily-of-the-valley	All
Lupine	All
Mock orange	Fruit
Monkshood	All
Mountain laurel	All
Narcissus	Bulb
Oleander	All
Oleander, yellow tree	Nuts
Peony	Roots
Pimpernel	All
Poinciana	All
Poppy	All
Privet, common	All
Rhododendron	All
Rosary pea	All
Scotch broom	Seeds
Snowdrops	All
Star of Bethlehem	Bulb
Sweetpea	Stem
Tobacco	All
Tulip	Bulb
Tung tree	Nuts
Virginia creeper	All
Wisteria	Seeds
Yew	All

GARDEN FRUITS AND VEGETABLES

Name	Poisonous Parts
Apricot	Pits
Cherry	Leaves, bark of tree
Cherry, ground	Foliage, sprouts
Eggplant	Foliage, sprouts
Elderberry	Leaves, bark of shrub, opening buds, young shoots
Peach	Leaves, pits, bark of tree
Potato	Foliage, sprouts
Rhubarb	Leaves

Name	Poisonous Parts
Tomato	Leaves, sprouts
WILD GROWING	
Arrowgrass	All
Baneberry	Root, stem, berries
Beargrass	All
Bittersweet	Leaves, unripe fruit
Bloodroot	Roots, stem, juice of stem
Bluebonnet	All
Buckeyes (horse chestnuts)	All
Buttercup	All
Cherries, most wild varieties	Berry
Corydalis	All
Dicentra (bleeding heart)	All
Hellebore	All
Hemlock, poison	All
Hemlock, water	All
Horsebeans	All
Horsebrush	All
Horse chestnut (buckeyes)	All
Iris, wild	All
Java beans	All
Jimson weed	All
Laurel	All
Locoweed	All
Mushrooms (toadstools)	All
Nightshade	All
Pokeweed	All
Staggerweeds	All
Tansy mustard	Flower

Every plant listed in this table can make a human adult or child, large or small animal, painfully ill or cause death. The size of the animal, the toxicity of the plant, and the quantity ingested determine the seriousness of the poisoning. All poisonous plants must be regarded as highly dangerous and approached with caution and care.

According to the booklet *Typical Poisonous Plants*, published by the U.S. Public Health Service: "Encourage the emptying of the stomach of a [poisonous plant] victim by vomiting as a general measure in preventing serious injury. Vomiting should not be induced if the victim is unconscious or convulsing." (See Chapter 8, *Poisoning* section.) If your dog has eaten a poisonous plant, contact your veterinarian immediately. Without touching the plant directly, remove a specimen for the doctor's examination and identification. Although the seriousness of each accident must be judged individually, it is necessary that the plant be accurately identified and that sufficient information on its toxicity be readily available. Either you or the veterinarian can telephone your local Poison Control Center for specific information regarding the toxic principles and their effects in the case of the plant eaten by your dog.

Of course, prevention is the safest measure for protecting your dog from plant poisoning. Do not buy poisonous plants that are listed in the table. Check the grounds around the house and remove those growths that are dangerous. Check your house plants and remove those that can kill you or your dog. Do not allow your dog to roam free. This is one dog disaster that can be easily avoided with a little effort and a willingness to trade off aesthetics for safety. Besides, for every poisonous plant, there are hundreds that are not.

10. Life Begins at Eight

Old boys have their playthings as well as young
ones; the difference is only in the price.
—BENJAMIN FRANKLIN

When you look down at your dog and notice the gray in his fur,
here and there a chipped or missing tooth, bear in mind that unlike a septuagenarian, your old dog is more like an aging puppy.
The children may have sprouted and gone off to college to create
new worlds, but Queenie and Duke still want to retrieve a rolled
ball and walk the same old sidewalk with you. As long as you have
your dog, there is still a child in the house. Dogs never retire, never
ask for a gold watch or count their fringe benefits. You and your
families have always been their social security since the first night
everyone was kept awake with the yipping. The aging puppy simply wants to go on enjoying the best life he can possibly have without interruption, without too much change. The port-of-entry sep-
arating youth from old age is a state of mind. The body is all
too willing to cross that frontier, but a clear mind resists the
temptation.

Dogs that grow older experience some physical changes and become more vulnerable to illness. But in many, many ways, they
also become more valuable, more important than they ever were.
They are living connections to those portions of our lives that feed
our spirit and sense of well-being. Years spent with a dog are filled
with milestone experiences that give shape and meaning to where
we've been and where we are. Emotions run high for our old dogs.

Still, dogs are more than four-legged scrapbooks and should not
be viewed as clocks that have stopped. The biggest problem with
an older dog is finding that sensitive distinction between moderation and termination. It is quite true that older dogs require more
physical supportive care, but by no means should they be expected
to hang up their tails and lie around dreaming about the bones
that got away. Active dogs kept in a state of good health do not
physically deteriorate into prolonged states of debilitation leading
to slow, painful ends. The average healthy dog lives approximately one-fifth the lifetime of the average healthy human. But the

Another aging puppy up to his old tricks. Older dogs are not clocks that have stopped.

concern here is the quality of that lifespan rather than the length of it. A healthy, enjoyable dog, living out a dignified and pleasant old age, honors his home and loving family. He is a good dog living the good life. He makes us proud of him and proud of ourselves.

The typical dog enters middle age between six and seven years of age, when his metabolism begins to change. After nine years, begin to treat the dog as an elder statesman. During this period, his life can be extended and his enjoyment of that life can be enhanced when you provide a somewhat altered and more cautious regimen. The routine is no more difficult than the one the healthy dog was already living with; it is simply modified.

Food

In our culture, the tendency to express our emotions with food is greater than ever—especially when it comes to our dogs. An older dog usually evokes greater emotions, mostly sympathy, and finds himself being overfed to a dangerous degree. This is dangerous because his body now needs fewer calories than before. Overfeeding will result in added weight, and this places too much strain on all his vital organs which are already losing some of their reserve capacity for functioning during stress.

The eight-year-old lessens his physical activity and begins to lead a more sedentary existence than before. Because the animal is underfoot more, the tendency is to pamper him with food and indulge his every eating whim. Sudden and radical feeding changes are definitely *not* recommended. Any major change in your dog's life can be disturbing, and that has its physical consequences. A slight adjustment in your older dog's diet is beneficial. Feed him only enough to maintain his weight and condition. Do not allow him to gain weight. A sharp increase or decrease of weight in a healthy senior dog may likely indicate illness. When a dog loses weight but still eats the same quantity of food, something is wrong and he must be seen by a veterinarian. A dramatic increase of weight can imply fluid buildup, glandular malfunction, or some major disease.

The quantity of food your dog should be fed daily can best be determined by your veterinarian. It is safe to say that after the metabolic slowdown of your dog (seven years old) it is best to feed him 25 to 35 calories per pound of body weight per day. A can of the average dog food contains approximately 500 calories. An equivalent number of calories is contained in six ounces of soft-moist dog food. Quality commercial dry foods contain between 1,600 and 1,700 calories per pound depending on the fat content. See Chapter 6, "Chow Time," for preparing your dog's food at home. The diet of older dogs should contain 0.5 percent or more calcium and the properly balanced percentage of phosphorus (normal ratio: 1.2 percent calcium to 1.0 percent phosphorus). When the ratio of calcium to phosphorus is imbalanced, proper metabolism of these essential minerals is interfered with; this is detrimental to the healthy maintenance of bone tissue and other important functions.

When preparing a diet at home for your dog, fat intake should be somewhat reduced. Digestion is greatly aided when carbohydrates are cooked to help break down the starch. The protein offered must be of high quality such as eggs, meat, milk, and soybeans. Do not feed more protein than necessary. Excessive protein can be too much for an old dog's kidneys. Full vitamin and mineral requirements must be satisfied and can be found in high-quality commercial dog food. Therapeutic supplementation is sometimes desirable, but should be determined by a veterinarian.

Nutritional management is critical for the supportive care of the aging dog. Two meals a day are better than one, and self-feeding is best if the dog has been on that program most of his life. A balanced diet is absolutely necessary, which means the proper quantities of protein, carbohydrates, fat, vitamins, and minerals. Cycle 4, the last category of the Cycle Dog Food series, is formulated for the nutritional demands of older dogs. It contains fewer calories, less protein and fat. The product offers high-quality protein and other nutrients, bulk for digestive tract regulation, and mineral and vitamin additives in the proper ratio. As a feeding option for aging dogs, the manufacturer states that it will maintain the animal at optimum nutritional health.

Assuming the dog has been fed properly all of his life, there is no real reason to change his diet unless he becomes ill or is overweight. A slight reduction of food intake may be necessary to maintain proper weight, but no dietary change should be initiated quickly. Changes in diet must be effected through a slow and gradual process.

The Body

Like all mammals, the dog's body experiences an aging process in the latter part of life. Through the course of his lifetime, his body is subjected to many forms of stress both physical and emotional. General stress during a typical dog life produces a gradual aging process that leads to the conclusion of a normal lifespan. Serious illness—especially that which damages a major organ—tends to shorten the lifespan.

Conformation is the first component of the mammalian body to indicate the aging process. Muscles lose their tone and the skin loses some of its elasticity. There is also evidence that the body's cells mutate, causing them to perform poorly. The replacement of mutated cells is considerably slower in old age with the result being that the older body continues to function with less recuperative power. In a young body, mutated cells wither away and are replaced by new, efficient cells.

This in part explains why an older dog's metabolism slows down. Because there are fewer cells in his tissue, and those that remain are anatomically smaller, there is less enzyme activity in those cells. With a slowdown in metabolism, less food is converted to energy and more is converted to fat stored in the body. Arthritis and rheumatism are common canine old-age ailments, and surplus weight places an added burden on aching joints and muscles. The heart also has to work harder if the dog is allowed to gain excessive weight.

The heart's abilities can be reduced by as much as 30 percent in the older dog and the kidneys may reduce their capacity by as much as 50 percent. Old age will reduce the metabolic rate by 20 percent in some dogs. The aging process in dogs causes all of the vital organs to lose some of their ability to function during periods of stress and can cause health problems. This loss of reserve power in the organs, inability to replace old tissue cells efficiently, combined with the animal's difficulty in adapting to change are the key factors when considering the health of the older dog. The aging dog is more likely to have physical problems that require medical attention, so a regular physical checkup by a veterinarian every six months is desirable. All illnesses should be attended by a veterinarian. A slight illness in a young dog can fast become a serious problem in an older one. Do not hesitate taking your aging dog to the veterinarian at the early stages of sickness.

Dogs appear to age at such a gradual rate that you hardly realize it's happening. Far too many owners wait for a major medical crisis before regarding the dog as an older gentleman or lady. This is a disservice to the animal and can shorten the animal's life. Watch for ear infections, eye difficulties, and kidney problems. Older dogs have a very high rate of kidney problems and should be allowed all the water they desire. Constipation, flatulence, discolored urine, too much or too little urine may indicate a serious illness. Consult a veterinarian about these symptoms. Do not subject the dog to extreme changes of temperature. If your aging dog experiences a dramatic weight loss, becomes apathetic or depressed, vomits, or has difficulty in walking, see your veterinarian.

Parasite control is extremely important at this time in the dog's life. Protect him from internal and external parasites. Keep him indoors or in a screened area during fly and mosquito seasons. An older dog has more difficulty protecting himself from flies and other insects. Excessive scratching is more likely to cause infection than ever before. Keep your home and the dog's area parasite-free.

Do not treat your dog like an invalid simply because he is getting older. Aging dogs, especially arthritic dogs, must be encouraged to remain active. Preventive medicine, good hygiene, and physical checkups are all meaningful. An older dog's longevity and relatively healthy existence are greatly influenced by all these factors. The knowledge and skill of veterinary medicine has progressed to a remarkable degree, and as a result, a dog can live longer and enjoy a healthier old age than ever before.

Dentistry

Very few young dogs have real dental problems because they are seldom plagued by cavities. Over the years, however, dogs experience broken teeth, teeth falling out, and a general wearing down of the biting surfaces. Pyorrhea develops in dogs as it does in humans from a buildup of tartar. When the teeth are not cleaned regularly, tartar develops from the exposed surface of the tooth to that which is under the gum. Inflammation, infection, and bleeding are the result. When visiting the veterinarian, have him check the dog's teeth.

You can clean your dog's teeth with a washcloth or gauze pad. A saltwater solution rubbed over the surfaces is effective. Water and baking soda (bicarbonate of soda) also clean teeth. Some veterinarians even recommend using a toothbrush and toothpaste. If the tartar buildup is great, have the veterinarian remove it. Loose or broken teeth should be removed. The symptoms of gum disease are loose teeth, red or spongy gums, receding or bleeding gums.

Grooming

Nail care is very important. Your old dog will have stiff hindquarters, which will affect his gait. Long nails make it more difficult to keep a steady footing on the ground and will add to the dog's straining muscles. This will tire him quicker and make him less secure. Because he is getting less exercise, is not gripping the ground as well as he used to, his nails do not wear down naturally. Therefore they must be checked for length and clipped as often as necessary (see Chapter 8).

A daily brushing and /or combing will help retain some of the luster in the coat, although all dogs lose a degree of aesthetic coat quality in old age. Older dogs shed more often, and it is healthier to remove the dead hair. One of the major benefits of daily grooming is maintaining close control over parasitic infestation. The older dog's skin is more susceptible to infection and must be spared the irritation of constant scratching. When brushing the dog, watch for fleas, lice, ticks, and mites. You may bathe an older dog when necessary, but keep him out of drafts and dry him well. Grooming also provides the dog owner the opportunity to check the animal for abnormal growths and lumps. The older dog's body requires more frequent inspection than ever before.

Exercise

Although a dog is considered aging at eight, there is a considerable difference in his physical capabilities between eight and fifteen. A healthy vigorous eight-year-old that has led an active life should not be assigned the status of a shut-in. Conversely, a dog that has moped around the apartment most of his life mustn't suddenly be taken to a health spa for workouts. Consistency tempered by moderation is the best policy.

One of the best exercises for the eight-year-old dog is swimming if he likes it and has engaged in that activity before. This is, of course, especially true for all water dogs such as Labrador retrievers and other famous swimmers. Most dogs enjoy a ball toss or a stick throw, and these are good exercises for an eight- or nine-year-old dog, providing he is in good shape. Do not overtax the dog with prolonged physical activity.

As your dog gets older, he will give you signals for reducing his physical activity. When this happens, the ideal exercise is several short walks a day. If you've been good to your dog, he will enjoy your company on these walks whether you've done it before or not. Gentle exercise is important for the dog's appearance, his circulation, his appetite, and his digestion. Take care not to overexert the dog and watch for signs of fatigue, such as panting, slowing down, irregular gait, saliva gathering in the corners of the mouth, low growling, and difficulty keeping up with your pace. When walking, take smaller, slower steps and stop for a rest several times along the way.

Allow the dog to sleep when he wants to and make his bed nice and soft. Keep him away from indoor drafts and do not walk him in the rain or freezing snow. The dog is exceptionally sensitive to temperature extremes at this time in his life. Do not expose an old dog to the hot summer sun, especially on humid days. Keep him in a shady, cool place. A dog's physical condition, breed, size, and

Senior dogs live longer, healthier lives when allowed to spend their retiring years in an anxiety-free atmosphere. Real social security means a life without emotional stress.

past medical history determine his capacity for exercise. Many German shepherds working for police and military guard units stay on their demanding jobs past ten years of age. Most toy breeds are still yipping and running back and forth at the doorbell well into their second decade of life. Common sense, indications from the dog, and advice from the veterinarian all help to shape exercise activity for senior dogs.

Stairs

Old dogs and young dogs alike ascend stairs like a tossed can of Tinkertoys. In an effort to achieve momentum and rhythm, they lope into a clobbering gallop. It is usually a desperate, clawing, clumsy affair until they land at the head of the stairs, wagging their tails in triumph. The older a dog gets, the more difficult it is for him to achieve the scaling of Mount Stairway. The only answers for older dogs are a slower pace (near impossible), fewer trips up the staircase, or being physically carried. One could line the bottom of a shopping cart with cardboard and tote the old dog up, providing you don't feel ridiculous.

Very old dogs and dogs with heart problems simply cannot make it up or down the stairs on their own. It is a physical activity that offers too much exertion for the heart. If you are very lucky, your dog will climb stairs slowly and gently, but it is a rare dog that can. Small to medium dogs can be carried but owners with large old dogs must teach their old guys and gals to use newspapers for toileting. Pride goeth before a fall.

Emotions

Emotional stress can shorten a dog's life as surely as any disease. In human medicine, as well as small-animal medicine, it is recognized that anxiety can bring about various forms of physical collapse including heart problems. However, it is not very difficult to maintain a dog in an anxiety-free state.

As your dog gets older, his routine, habits, and established behavior patterns become increasingly more important to him than ever before. It is the only security the dog has now that his capacity for self-defense and other survival mechanisms have diminished. Even though your old dog may become a grump and a grouch, he will need your love, devotion, and reassurance. In the wild, an old wolf that becomes a burden to the entire pack is usually torn to pieces in an effort to maintain pack security. Your dog may instinctively fear this once he becomes infirm. By allowing no interruption of services, no change in his routine, no change in his diet (unless indicated by the veterinarian), no change in his living conditions, you will automatically reassure the dog and avoid emotional stress.

At this time in the dog's life, it would be a mistake to place him in a kennel or separate him from his family for any great length of time. If the dog is taken away from home for any reason, including a long stay in a hospital, he may not eat or rest. He may pace back and forth and tax his body beyond endurance. If you have no choice but to hospitalize an old dog, ask the veterinarian about tranquilization and special attention from a gentle and loving member of his staff. Emotional support from a dog's family can make all the difference between life and death, sickness and health. Do not underestimate the importance of affection, attention, and a rigid compliance with the dog's established routine. Your old dog may become as testy as a gout-ridden baron, but deep in his eyes, behind the moisture, is a tender look. Perhaps it's gratitude.

CM·

At no other time in a dog's life is it more important to overcome fear and anxiety than in old age. Hypertension, insecurity, fatigue, and all manner of emotional stress tear a dog's health apart even if he is holding his own and is well looked after. The ordinary rigors of everyday family life may place an emotional strain on an animal once capable of jumping into the children's games or diving into the surf after an important stick. Noise, everyday family activity, or even pollution can send an old and distinguished pet into a state of depression or anxiety. There is a technique to abate this form of stress that may work for some dogs (and their owners).

Eastern religions have for centuries encouraged various techniques of meditation as a means of cleansing the spirit and coming to terms with oneself and one's relationship with the rest of the world. Although meditation is far from new, it has swept into Western culture recently with the force of a benevolent hurricane. Millions practice meditation with great success and many, many members of our society swear that their lives are better for it.

CM or Canine Meditation is a unique possibility as a technique for lessening the emotional stress of old age in dogs. We will now pause to allow the laughter and snickering to subside. . . .

Okay. Some may equate Canine Meditation with shaggy dog stories and canine sunglasses, but that is to pass up an opportunity, a long shot, for easing terror and emotional pain suffered by many aged dogs. Dogs cannot pop tranquilizers when they feel bad; they can't even tell you about it. Analysis won't work. Five martinis

CM for the older dog makes him more secure, more confident and less frightened. Small dogs can be held in the lap, while larger dogs can be touched while sprawled out on the floor. Canine Meditation means simply giving your older dog fifteen or twenty loving minutes a day.

and a hot bath is out of the question, and so is tennis. So what can you do for an emotionally stressed dog besides see the veterinarian five times a week (try and get a fifty-minute hour of a vet's time)? Canine Meditation is worth a try if you have a serious emotional problem with your dog.

If you haven't thrown this book across the room by now and are seriously interested, I suggest that you do not mention this to anyone. Unless the love of your dog is stronger than the fear of criticism, experiment with CM and keep your mouth shut about it. Don't tell anyone what you are up to—not even your dog.

THE TECHNIQUE

First, take the dog into a quiet part of the house where you're certain you will not be disturbed for at least fifteen minutes to a half hour. Take the phone off the hook if necessary. Resolve not to answer the doorbell or a call from another member of the household. Close the door behind you and insist on privacy. Next, get into a sitting or lying position on the floor with the dog. You may lean against a wall with your legs tucked up under or lie on your side facing the dog who, we hope, is also prone.

If your dog is small enough, place him in your lap. Place the flat of both hands as near the dog's heart as possible as you would if administering artificial respiration (see Chapter 8). Allow your hands to gently rise and fall on the dog's rib cage, moved only by the expansion and contraction caused by each breath he takes. Relate to the dog visually, but not with an intense stare. Do not look him square in the eyes. Say nothing. Keep track of the time.

As the dog breathes try to match your rhythm to his so that eventually you are breathing together. Once you and the dog are breathing at a relatively close pace, together, stroke his fur with one hand while the other remains over his heart. Close your eyes and whisper the dog's name so that he just barely hears it. You may vary this technique by using a brush to stroke his fur instead of your hand. If your whispering distracts the dog in any way, discontinue it. Say his name silently to yourself.

Bear in mind that this meditation is for the benefit of the dog. The objective is *his* relaxation. Try to make yourself as comfortable as possible, but do not be concerned it the technique does nothing for you personally. What is being sought is fifteen to thirty minutes of pure relaxation, communication between you and the dog, and a soothing expression of love and personal contact. You may find that you can combine your own meditation with the dog's by emptying your mind of disturbing and distracting thoughts. Do this once or twice a day, in the morning and before the dog retires for the evening. He may just drift into sleep and get a full night's rest, and that's good.

If Canine Meditation sounds absurd, do not do it. But if you are the least bit curious, try it and see what happens. It could become one of the most meaningful experiences of your life. It depends on how close you can afford to be with your dog. The point is to express your feelings and concern to the dog. Whether you accomplish this in the prescribed manner or simply hold the dog's paw for ten minutes is not really the important part. Your dog craves a sense of emotional well-being, and CM is one of many ways to accomplish that. When his end comes, you will have the quiet knowledge that you did all that was humanly possible to give him the best life he could have had. A *good dog* bears that distinguished title because someone loved him and took care of him.

With loving care, almost any dog can look as good as Frosty, who is in her tenth year. She is one of the millions of good dogs.

Afterword

Some evening you may receive a late call from a panic-stricken friend who regards you as a dog expert. It may be that your friend's dog is in the process of whelping puppies and your assistance is desperately needed. If you answer the call, you already know that the best thing you can do for the new mother is not to interfere with the natural whelping process unless there are delivery complications. A veterinarian is required for them.

The newborn puppy will be delivered in an amniotic sac attached to a mass (placenta) by an umbilical cord. The sac must be broken and licked away by the mother to allow the pup to take its first breath. If the mother neglects to open the sac, someone has to do it if the baby is to live. It may be up to you. Tear it with your hands. Start removing the sac from the puppy's head first, and then peel it off the rest of the body. Clean the mucus from the puppy's face with your finger once you have removed the placenta from his head. Rub the puppy's chest, abdomen, and sides in a towel to facilitate breathing. Rub the right side forward, the left side backward—and then reverse the action.

Breathing must begin immediately. There will be a slight squeal if the puppy has started functioning on his own. If he isn't breathing, hold the puppy in your hands, supporting its head so that it doesn't jog about. Starting from your chest, move the little guy in a downward direction toward your knees. The puppy's face must be pointing downward in the direction of the floor, so that the excess fluids run out its nose and mouth. It is essential to remove these fluids from the breathing passages. You may use a small syringe or suck the fluid out with your mouth if the situation is desperate.

Once you hear breathing and whimpering, the miraculous life cycle has started once again. If the puppy's mother is too busy delivering other puppies, it is then up to you to separate the little dog from its umbilical cord. This is usually accomplished when the mother snips it off with her teeth and then begins licking the puppy clean. Grab the cord tightly with your right hand one inch from the puppy's body. With your left hand, grab it one-and-a-half inches from the body and tear off the excess umbilical cord.

Leave it on the floor with the placenta for the mother to clean up.

Wipe the newborn with a towel and shake him just a bit (without tossing his head about) to be sure that he's still breathing. Hold him tightly for a minute and give him back to his mother. Help him find a teat. As you watch the infant dog take milk for the first time, remember your old dog and then weep for joy. A new life has begun.

SUGGESTED READING

Behavior

Bergman, Goran. *Why Does Your Dog Do That?* New York: Howell Book House, 1971.

Burton, Maurice. *The Sixth Sense of Animals.* New York: Ballantine Books, 1974.

Darwin, Charles. *The Expression of the Emotions in Man and Animals.* Chicago: The University of Chicago Press, 1965.

Ewer, R.F. *The Carnivores.* Ithaca, New York: Cornell University Press, 1973.

Fox, Michael W. *Behavior of Wolves, Dogs and Related Canids.* New York: Harper & Row, 1971.

Kikkawa, Jiro and Thorne, Malcolm J. *The Behavior of Animals.* New York: Plume Books, 1971.

Lorenz, Konrad. *King Solomon's Ring.* New York: Signet Books, 1972.

——. *Man Meets Dog.* Middlesex, England: Penguin Books, 1964.

Maier, N. R. F. and Schneirla, T. C. *Principles of Animal Psychology.* New York: Dover Publications, 1964.

Pfaffenberger, Clarence. *The New Knowledge of Dog Behavior.* New York: Howell Book House, 1963.

Scott, John Paul. *Animal Behavior.* 2d ed., rev. Chicago: The University of Chicago Press, 1974.

—— and Fuller, John L. *Dog Behavior: The Genetic Basis.* Chicago: The University of Chicago Press, 1974.

Trumler, Eberhard. *Your Dog and You.* New York: Seabury Press, 1973.

Dog Training, Care, and Health

American Kennel Club. *The Complete Dog Book.* 15th ed., rev. New York: Howell Book House, 1975.

Campbell, William E. *Behavior Problems in Dogs.* Santa Barbara, California: American Veterinary Publications, 1975.

Caras, Roger. *The Roger Caras Pet Book.* New York: Holt, Rinehart & Winston, 1976.

Howe, John. *Choosing the Right Dog.* New York: Harper & Row, 1976.

Kenworthy, Jack. *Pet Library's Dog Training Guide.* London: The Pet Library, 1969.

McGinnis, Terri. *The Well Dog Book: The Dog Lover's Illustrated Medical Companion.* New York: Random House and The Bookworks, 1974.

The Merck Veterinary Manual. 4th ed. Rahway, New Jersey: Merck & Co., 1973.

Miller, Dare. *Dog Master System.* Santa Monica, California: The Canine Behavior Institute Library, 1975.

Siegal, Mordecai and Margolis, Matthew. *Good Dog, Bad Dog: Training Your Dog at Home.* New York: Holt, Rinehart & Winston/Signet Books, 1973.

——. *Underdog: Training the Mutt, Mongrel, and Mixed Breed at Home.* New York: Stein & Day, 1974.

USAF Military Working Dog Program. Training. Air Force Manual 125-5, Volume 1. Department of the Air Force, 1973.

Children

Dodson, Fitzhugh. *How to Parent.* New York: Signet Books, 1970.

——. *How to Father.* New York: Signet Books, 1974.

Ferretti, Fred. *The Great American Book of Sidewalk, Stoop, Dirt, Curb, and Alley Games.* New York: Workman Publishing, 1975.

Gesell, A. and Ilg, F. L. *Infant and Child in the Culture of Today.* New York: Harper & Brothers, 1943.

Kelly, Marguerite and Parsons, Elia. *The Mother's Almanac.* New York: Doubleday & Company, 1975.

Salk, Lee and Kramer, Rita. *How to Raise a Human Being.* New York: Warner Paperback Library, 1973.

U.S. Government Report. *Your Child from 1 to 12.* Foreword by Lee Salk. New York: Signet Books, 1970.

Index

About the Author

Mordecai Siegal writes a monthly column for *House Beautiful*. He is a contributing editor to *Pure-Bred Dogs—American Kennel Gazette* (AKC) and *Dogs Magazine*. He is the co-author of the best-selling book GOOD DOG, BAD DOG, which is available in a Signet edition.

Author-journalist Siegal lives in New York with his wife Victoria, their son Thomas Jesse, their Siberian husky Pete, and their "half-Manx" cat, Max.